THE QUEST FOR BEAUTY

James L. Jarrett •

Western Regional Director
The Great Books Foundation

Englewood Cliffs, N. J.

• *The*
Quest
for
Beauty

Prentice-Hall, Inc.

PRENTICE-HALL PHILOSOPHY SERIES
DR. ARTHUR E. MURPHY, EDITOR

LIBRARY OF CONGRESS
CATALOG CARD NUMBER: 57–7846

First printing .... *May, 1957*
Second printing ..... *March, 1958*
Third printing .... *April, 1962*

PRINTED IN THE UNITED STATES OF AMERICA
74822–C

PREFACE

There are at least two popular reasons for neither writing nor reading a book on aesthetics. In the first place, it is widely believed that beauty in and out of art is simply to be enjoyed, not analyzed and discussed, such intellectual activities being profanations and in any case doomed to failure. The second reason takes the opposite tack, saying that art is not too lofty but too lowly to justify serious efforts toward understanding: why should time be wasted worrying about what is, after all, merely a way of "pleasuring an idle moment"? The first objection has as its sandy base a cluster of misconceptions. Although beauty doubtless calls for enjoyment, that enjoyment itself is by no means always or necessarily a simple reaction to a simple stimulus; indeed, if it threatens to defeat philosophic explanation it does so not by virtue of any ethereal simplicity but by virtue of its complexity—ethereal, earthly, and subterranean. The curious notion that some things are above human inquiry seems to be founded on an attitude of disparagement toward man's mind, as if to say that it taints whatever it glances at. But surely our whole history shows an opposite conclusion: intellectual activity, in any field, is both good in itself and productive of other goods that flow from increase in understanding.

There is the other supposition, that art is a trifling amusement, perhaps a casual and superfluous adornment of useful objects, perhaps a sweetened surface for pills of propaganda—and in any case an easily dispensable detail in the serious business of making a living and living. Part of the answer to this objection to aesthetics is given by anthropology; here, for instance, is a statement by Ruth Bunzel:

> Before man learned to ensure his food supply by the cultivation of
> plants, or to lighten his labors by domesticating animals to his use,
> long before he had stumbled upon simple inventions like the
> wheel, or primitive industries like pottery, he had developed a
> pictorial art so perfect in style that the modern painter stands in
> wonder before his creations. . . . Just as the antiquity of art
> proves it to be a basic form of human behavior, so also does its
> universality among the living races of man. Among all existing
> groups there is none, however rude its culture, that does not have
> some characteristic form of art.*

Art is not only ubiquitous, but to many persons it is exceedingly
important, constituting one kind of satisfaction that justifies the
effort of making a living; and therefore justifying whatever effort
goes into trying to understand it.

Yet, even among professional philosophers, aesthetics has long
suffered a certain disrepute, partly because so many works on art
and beauty have substituted purple prose for analysis, partly from
the fact that alongside metaphysics, epistemology, logic, and ethics,
aesthetics has had a limited history, at least before the nineteenth
century. Even Kant, Schelling, Hegel, and Schopenhauer, with
metaphysics that seem insupportably heavy to many thinkers of our
day, are now largely neglected as aestheticians.

Still, the condition of the subject is not so bad as it appears to
some. Although there is not a large historical literature, yet some
of it is very enlightening. Nor is it to be found purely in the writings of professional philosophers: much of it usually passes as
"literary criticism" and some of it is by painters or composers. But
even more important is the fact that aesthetics has flourished in recent decades. Certainly I owe much to the writings of DeWitt
Parker, Stephen Pepper, C. J. Ducasse, R. G. Collingwood, and
John Dewey—who of course hardly constitute a single school of
philosophic thought; to psychologists as diverse as Freud, Jung,
Bullough, and Rudolph Arnheim; to critics from A. C. Bradley to
I. A. Richards, John Crowe Ransom, and Cleanth Brooks; to art
historians such as Erwin Panofsky, Meyer Schapiro, and Bernard
Berenson—and so on; but there is a bibliography at the end of
the book.

* "Art," in *General Anthropology*, ed. Franz Boas (New York: Heath, 1938), p.
535.

An aesthetics presents special structural problems. On no subject is there such a temptation—and almost a need—to say everything at once, to refuse to divide the problems and the topics. For how can one discuss representation without discussing emotion? How can form be analyzed without the simultaneous analysis of ideational content? How can beauty be defined without first discussing criticism—and vice versa? These puzzles spring from the very organic unity of the thing of beauty and of the aesthetic experience.

Still, division and succession are necessary if one is to avoid a hodgepodge; just as, if one is to avoid a sterile neatness, repetition is required. Consequently, the reader will find that most of the subjects introduced first are not at that point heard from for the last time, even though they may for a moment yield the stage to others.

After introductory chapters on aesthetics, art, and beauty, there are three chapters having to do with the "creative" aspects of art. Then the emphasis shifts to the experiencer of beauty and to the beautiful object, its content and its form. Next the moral and then the aesthetic evaluation of works of art come under consideration. A final chapter deals with the relation of art and religion, and the place of aesthetic values in a well-ordered life. A relatively brief note on some theories of comedy and tragedy is appended.

This book is intended to be elementary, at least in the sense that sophistication in the arts and in art history and theory is not presupposed. A constant attempt has been made to make the text at least recurrently concrete by the use of illustrations and references to actual works of art and other instances of putative beauty. The several principal arts have not been divided up for separate treatment, except insofar as painting and sculpture lend themselves especially well to a treatment of the problem of representation, as literature does to the problem of ideational content, and as music does to the problem of form.

Apart from artists, aestheticians, critics, and historians, whose public work has helped me, many others have, of course, played a part, but it is not easy to acknowledge one's debt. There is always the danger of incriminating others in one's own intellectual misdemeanors, or the risk of forgetting a donor. Perhaps the grossest thefts sink into one's unconscious, and it is easy to mistake a friendly feeling for a reliable sign of influence. In any case, my wife Marjorie has been so close an associate in this enterprise that she must be held partly to blame for its faults.

CONTENTS

*Photographs of the following works of art appear in an insert
after page 182:*

*A selective bibliography of books pertaining to aesthetics
may be found at page 309.*

The index for this book may be found at page 313.

• *Chapter 1*

AESTHETICS:
NATURE
and
JUSTIFICATION

• *Aesthetics,*" Paul Valéry somewhere says, "is an irresistible temptation." It is irresistible, we might suppose, in that to most
of us an experience of beauty is somehow incomplete until it has
been verbally shared. However rapt our attention be to the
sounds of the orchestra or to the colors and moving lines of the
ocean breakers, however awesomely quiet the moment after,
sooner or later—lest we burst!—must come the telling, the comparing, the wondering, perhaps the arguing. And if those activities
are not quite aesthetics, they are the very *stuff*, the indispensable
material, of aesthetics.

Most of us have a vague idea of what aesthetics is, but it is hard
to make an exact and otherwise satisfactory definition. A few starts
may be made:

(1) *Aesthetics is the science of* . . . Wait right there! Is aesthet-

ics a *science?* Surely that is claiming too much, if the word "science" means a highly precise, systematic, quantitative type of investigation, with exacting techniques of experimentation and controlled observation. Although there are perfectly respectable scientific aspects of aesthetics—for instance, psychological measurements of human reactions to colors, tones, shapes—these do not bulk large enough in importance, at least not yet, to constitute a separate science. Consequently, the more modest word "study" may be preferable: Aesthetics is the *study* of . . .

(2) *Aesthetics is the study of beauty.* Yes, but of more than beauty. We do not want to limit our study to the successful cases. Economics is concerned not merely with sound investments and profitable enterprise, but with bankruptcy as well. Aesthetics must deal with beauty,[1] but also with ugliness and drabness, and perhaps with sublimity too, often distinguished from beauty.

(3) *Aesthetics is the study of art.* This is both too broad and too narrow. There are other studies of art than aesthetics; for instance, art history. Furthermore, aesthetics need not be confined to art. What about the beauty of nature? What about the creative activity which precedes the accomplished work of art? No one will deny that art-works and artists figure very prominently in aesthetics, but they do not quite constitute its subject matter.

(4) *Aesthetics is the study of the aesthetic.* This sounds like a trick. Yet it would be no bad definition of "economics" to speak of it as the study of the economic—that is, of economic processes and values and institutions and whatever else the adjective "economic" can modify. Aesthetics is the study of aesthetic experience, aesthetic attitude, aesthetic quality, aesthetic value, and derivatively of closely related topics such as artistic creativity, artistic standards, beauty and its opposites. This, it will be noticed, shifts the whole burden off the word "aesthetics" and promptly onto its slightly abbreviated cousin "aesthetic." What, now, about the word "aesthetic"? But everyone knows what *that* means, if only he thinks a moment. Consider your most noteworthy occasions of listening

---

[1] For the time it must be assumed that one knows, at least in a general way, what "beauty," "art," and certain other key terms mean. They will receive their own definitional attention in due time.

to music, of gazing over a scene in nature, of standing before a
great cathedral or monument. Remember the times when you have
been impressed with the sheer perfection of a painting or a dance
or a poem; and the times, too, when you have felt that something
must have gone wrong. Do not forget, either, those moments when
we ourselves—though we may not pretend to be artists—have
"brought something off," fashioned some material (cloth, wood,
pencil and paper, words, dance movements) so that it was "right,"
so that it held us and perhaps others in rapt and respectful attention. In such experiences, known to everyone—though in different
degree and frequency—the meaning of "aesthetic" lies.

(5) *Aesthetics is the* philosophical *study of the aesthetic.* The
ancient counsel of Aristotle on the task of defining is summarized
in the formula: genus and differentia. Tell what sort of thing the
troublesome object is, and then determine how it differs from others
of the same sort. Aesthetics is a study which belongs to the field of
philosophy.[2] But what is philosophy? And then, what are the differentiating marks of aesthetics among the several fields within the
philosophical discipline?

Philosophy, its advocates like to say, is the love of wisdom—such
is the very meaning of the word. Yes, but as with most etymology,
this does not carry us very far. Then, there are the humorous
characterizations, the best ones by philosophers themselves: Philosophy is the systematic abuse of terms especially invented for
the purpose—Bertrand Russell. Philosophy . . . is the search in a
dark room for a black cat that isn't there—William James.

More seriously but hardly more satisfactorily, philosophy has
been called the Queen of the Sciences, the capping stone of all
knowledge, the synthesizer of all human search into the ways of
man and his world. But today's philosophers are likely to be embarrassed by such pretentious claims. They recognize no royal
philosophic road to truth, no special philosophic pipeline to ultimate
reality; they are but little inclined to set up their own field as a
rival to, or in any sense to discount the discoveries and methods of,

---

[2] This need not be thought unduly restrictive, for philosophy is here conceived
very broadly. The work of the psychologist, the art critic, and the historian are
not excluded or ignored but importantly used.

physics and biology and psychology and the other empirical sciences.[3]

Judging not only by their different characterizations but even
more by their different practices, contemporary philosophers disagree as to the nature of their vocation. There are some who emphasize the clarifying function of philosophy; for instance, Ludwig
Wittgenstein wrote that "The object of philosophy is the logical
clarification of thoughts. Philosophy is not a theory but an activity.
. . . The result of philosophy is not a number of 'philosophical
propositions,' but to make propositions clear."[4] Others have opposed this description as a trivialization of philosophy and have
insisted that philosophy's highest aim is the presentation of new
visions, new insights into the nature of reality. Alfred North
Whitehead was one who believed this, adding: "The use of philosophy is to maintain an active novelty of fundamental ideas
illuminating the social system. It reverses the slow descent of
accepted thought toward the inactive commonplace."[5]

Still, there seems no reason to set these views over against each
other, except as indicating differences in emphasis. Philosophy *is*
primarily a clarifying activity—philosophy is philosophizing about
the meanings of words, concepts, categories, ideals—but clarification both is and results in new insight, clearer visions, novel ap-
prehensions. But what is philosophy *about?* A modern dictionary,
after noting that the "distinction of philosophy from the natural
and humanistic sciences is relatively recent," goes on to say:
"Philosophers themselves differ concerning the ground of this
distinction, some finding it in the greater generality of philosophy,
others in philosophy's concern with evaluation rather than description and still others in the combination of the two."[6] Again, we may
go with the more liberal account. Typically, the philosopher directs

---

[3] This will surprise those who are accustomed to regard philosophers as hard-
bitten in their anti-scientific prejudices. Yet in point of fact, for many centuries
not only have there been men distinguished for their contributions to both philosophy and science, but most thinkers counted great in philosophy have been respectful of the sciences, and even distinctly pro-scientific in their attitudes. Today more
than ever before, philosophers tend to count themselves allies and fellow-workers
with scientists in every field.

[4] *Tractatus Logico-Philosophicus* (London: Kegan Paul, Trench, Trubner & Co.,
1922), 4.112.

[5] *Modes of Thought* (New York: Macmillan, 1938), p. 237.

[6] *Webster's New International Dictionary*, 2nd ed. (Springfield: Merriam, 1947).

his clarifying lights on appraisals: consider the centrality in philosophical literature of such concepts as Truth, Beauty, Goodness, Justice, Wisdom, and the like. But *as philosopher* he is not primarily concerned with the actual evaluation of this or that concrete thing, the tastiness of Aunt Suzie's latest plum pudding, the truth of a new account of light polarization, the beauty of Picasso's "Guernica." What he is concerned with are the standards themselves, the norms which may be employed in evaluation. Thus his interests are typically evaluative *and* general. He attempts to clarify the nature of generalized norms for the sake of fresh insight into man and his world.

Originally philosophy was vaguely synonymous with all intellectuality, but today can no longer count mathematics and astronomy and biology and political science as branches of its own trunk. Still, it does have branches, particularly these: metaphysics, epistemology, logic, ethics, and aesthetics. Each of these studies may be characterized by displaying its most central concepts. For metaphysics, reality, being, existence, cause; for epistemology, truth, error, knowledge; for logic, validity and invalidity; for ethics, good, evil, right, wrong, duty; for aesthetics, beauty, ugliness, the aesthetic.

— Now if aesthetics is a branch of philosophy and philosophy aims at the clarification of the general norms we employ in our judgment and appraisal of various aspects of the universe, we may say that aesthetics concerns the norms applicable to art and to nature as aesthetically regarded. Beauty is the most characteristic such norm. The aesthetician asks not whether such and such an actual work is beautiful—that is the job of the art critic[7]—but rather what it is like to be beautiful or at least what it has been thought to be like to be beautiful. This latter distinction is of some interest. The aesthetician may be primarily an advocate, a proponent of some standard, whether someone else's or his own; or he may be primarily a scholar, one who displays for comparison and contrast the theories advanced by others.[8]

It may be granted that the aesthetician, amateur or professional,

[7] This is an ideal description. In practice, art criticism and aesthetics are not always so sharply separated.
[8] Again the functions are often mixed.

is the philosopher probing beauty and the lack of beauty in art and nature, and still be asked: Why? That is, what justification can be offered for such an activity? What good is aesthetics?

The temptation is to answer with a rhetorical question: What good is poetry or music or a redolent summer's breeze? But there are other answers. Three may be especially urged.

(1) *A sound aesthetics may make for better artistic creation.* Suppose, for instance, a painter, an especially gifted craftsman, but one who had gone along with a naive conception that his art had to be slavishly imitative of nature until in the course of reflections about aesthetic topics it came home to him that nothing about the very nature of art required him to act like a camera. It is easy to imagine that his own artistic achievement might gain immeasurably from the freedom his new theoretical insight afforded.

No one would be so foolish as to argue that all that is needed for the creation of good art is a good conception of what art is, but it is certain that an inadequate conception may block or cramp creativity. Artists themselves may or may not be *especially* interested in aesthetic theory, and some who are may be relatively weak on the theoretical side, though the names of Coleridge, Joshua Reynolds, Tolstoy, and Schumann indicate the possibility of combining a talent for artistic creation with a flair for aesthetics. Some practicing artists are afraid of heavy indulgence in aesthetics, lest their work become too intellectualized and too little fresh and spontaneous, and lest they siphon off energy which might be utilized in the making of new art-works. Perhaps there is ground for this fear, but in any case it is never required that the artist be a professional aesthetician in the sense that he spend a major portion of his time philosophizing, but only that he be sufficiently conscious of the principal achievements of the aestheticians not to be restricted in his own output. Put another way: there is a reasonable division of labor between artist and aesthetician but perhaps neither does his best work in ignorance of the best work of the other.

(2) *A sound aesthetics may make for better art criticism.* In one sense the art critic stands halfway between artist and aesthetician. Like the artist, the critic usually concentrates his attention concretely on a single work of art at a time; like the aesthetician, his interest is analytic and discursive. If his judgment of art-works is to

be defensible and valuable he must possess not only a keen sensitivity to the type of art in which he specializes, but a grasp of the norms applicable to such art and an understanding of the place that that art occupies among the arts. The subject of norms and the subject of the interrelations of the arts are right at the center of aesthetics.

Competence in aesthetics no more guarantees good criticism than it guarantees good artistic production, but almost without exception the really great critics in the several different arts have been men distinguished by their broad philosophical orientation instead of by a narrow technical facility: consider, for instance, Ste. Beuve in literary criticism, Eduard Hanslick in music criticism, and Bernard Berenson in painting criticism—to mention only three.

(3) *A sound aesthetics may make for better appreciation of the arts.* Bertrand Russell, in order to suggest the highly abstract, mathematical nature of physics, has said that a blind man could conceivably know the whole of the subject. But no one could seriously argue that a blind man might know the whole of painting, though he might be perfectly well acquainted with all of the theories of painting; nor could a man deaf from birth be said to know all of music, though he might know all about music, intellectually. There is a serious difference between immediate sensuous acquaintanceship with any of the arts and an exclusively conceptual grasp of artistic principles and theories, so that it is *conceivable* that a person should be a lover of music or architecture, say, and yet be ignorant of philosophy; and conceivable, too, that a learned and canny philosopher of the arts should at the same time have little if anything to do with actual arts, or even be a despiser of art experience.

Yes, the separation is conceivable, but unlikely and unfortunate. To look for expertness in the one field without help from the other is doing it the needlessly hard way. The threadbare figure of thinking with the head and feeling with the heart might be refurbished and made to serve if only we will recall the elementary physiological fact that heart and brain are utterly interdependent. But even then, such an image may be mischievously misleading: there is no quite separate appreciative faculty or organ any more than there is a quite separate intellectual or philosophic faculty or organ. Gen-

erally speaking, the more an aesthetician gains in acquaintanceship
with beauty, the deeper becomes his philosophic penetration; and,
conversely, he who aspires to a fuller converse with art does well
to sharpen his philosophic tools, not in order to erect philosophy
as a substitute for aesthetic experience, but in order to improve
the very quality of that experience.

This claim, that aesthetics helps appreciation, is a dangerous one
to make in a book on aesthetics, precisely because the means for
verification are so readily available to the reader. The book, perhaps, should end with the question: Reader, has it helped?

Still, let us take the case at its worst and suppose that the study
of aesthetics should *not* help creation or criticism or appreciation of
art, that it should *not* facilitate the quest for beauty. Even so, aesthetics would not be worthless; perhaps even its chief value would
not be forfeit. For, whatever be the usefulness or uselessness of
philosophizing about art and beauty, the activity is, at least for a
great many persons, worth while in and of itself.

To understand this assertion it may help to think for a moment
about man. Man is the animal who knows he must die; the animal,
too, with a sense of humor. He is the symbolizing animal, the rational animal, the animal who shares with the gods some knowledge
of good and evil. Could we not say with equal adequacy that man is
the animal who is seldom or never content simply to *do* things but
must think about and talk about what he does or might do? In all
times and places, wherever men have gathered, they have talked and
discussed and traded opinions on the weather and the ways of the
gods, on pushpin and poetry, on sleep and sex—and everything else
under sun and stars.

It is no less noble or interesting to discuss than to read or listen
to a sonnet or a song. Fortunately the two kinds of activity need
not often conflict or compete with each other.

In short, aesthetics does not require justification by its practical
results any more than art itself does: the one and the other are intrinsically good in their very doing. Yet if in addition such a study
fructifies aesthetic creation, criticism, and appreciation—as very
often it seems to do—so much the better.

Aesthetics is an "irresistible temptation." Why should one try
to resist?

Chapter 2

WHAT

is

ART?

Auscultation
Bee-raising
Courtly love
Cosmetics
Quarterbacking
Falconry
Fly-tying
Automobile lubrication
Canoeing
Zebra-breeding

• *This* is a selected list of—Arts! Yes, each of these activities is, or can be, an art. Indeed, libraries contain books describing The Art of practically everything from A to Z. Anything that can be done can be done well, and that which is done well is done artfully or artistically, and its doer is, in his way, an artist. In its broadest signification, the word "art" means skilled performance or distinctive ability in any activity whatsoever.

Yet when a college student announces that he has signed up for an art course, he is understood to mean no other art than graphic art: he is receiving instruction in drawing or painting. The conception of the "fine arts" is slightly broader. And what are they? Schools and Colleges of Fine Arts include, at the very least, painting and sculpture and such related arts as ceramics. Probably architecture too. Music often gets in. Sometimes the dance and theater. Sometimes literature.

CLASSIFICATIONS OF THE ARTS

But is it not well known that there are *five* fine arts, namely Architecture, Painting, Sculpture, Music, and Poetry? Certainly this is a tradition among us, but contrary to some supposition, it is neither a very old tradition nor a very current one.[1] We think of the ancient Greeks as pre-eminent in architecture and sculpture and drama, but they seem to have known nothing about such a conception as "the fine arts." Indeed, their word which we translate as "art" applied as much to sciences and crafts as to what we think of as fine arts. Not only were music and dance and drama intertwined, but poetry is scarcely to be distinguished from grammar, or music from mathematics and astronomy. The visual arts seem not even to have been assigned a muse.

Somewhat later there grew up a conception of "seven liberal arts," including grammar, rhetoric, dialectic, arithmetic, geometry, astronomy, and music, which in the Middle Ages comprised the Trivium and Quadrivium of the famous curriculum. For Thomas Aquinas, whose perceptive remarks on beauty are still deeply influential, "art" is exemplified not only by painting and music, but by shoemaking and cooking and juggling. Only with the seventeenth-century rise of science were astronomy and physics clearly separated off from what we think of as arts, and by the eighteenth century there arose the expressions "*beaux arts*" and "fine arts" and even "aesthetics," though it was not until the time of Hegel, in the nineteenth century, that the word "aesthetics" acquired its present meaning. In 1746 a treatise was published which separated

[1] For the following historical material we are much indebted to Paul Oskar Kristeller's "The Modern System of the Arts," *Journal of the History of Ideas*, XII, No. 4 and XIII, No. 1.

the fine arts from the mechanical arts, the former distinguished in having pleasure for their end and being five in number: poetry, music, painting, sculpture, and the dance. Thomas Jefferson, however, included landscape gardening as an important member of his list of fine arts. And in the nineteenth century prose fiction and drama became increasingly serious candidates for inclusion, as did the "mixed art" of opera. In our own day, the art of the film demands increasing attention, as well as still photography; and we are no longer sure of our ground in excluding the designing of glass and silverware, rugs, window coverings, furniture, and other aspects of "interior decoration." And of course there is automobile design, and so on and so on. If this is going too far, then where exactly is the line to be drawn? Is it a matter of *usefulness?*

The distinction between the liberal and the servile arts and between practical or applied arts and fine arts is frequently an invidious one going back to the ancient Greek prejudice against those who work with their hands and who serve utilitarian interests. Aristotle wrote that it was a mark of a true gentleman that he surrounded himself with beautiful and useless things; presumably only a man of wealth, leisure, and good breeding would be sufficiently spiritual to cultivate uselessness whereas the philistine, the base mechanic, and the slave would be tied to the menial and the merely practical. A horror of subordinating aesthetic value to utilitarian ends has occasionally begotten art-for-art's-sake reactions, which in turn lead to excesses branded as decadent and sterile. For all of Thorstein Veblen's labors to expose the economic and "status" motives behind such snobbery, there lingers today—even in our ultra-practical society—some antipathy to the "applied" as distinct from the "pure."

Yet this is not to say that there are no sounder grounds for emphasizing the aesthetic efficacy of nonuseful arts. So long as we are taken up with what an object does, what it is good *for*, how it functions, it is hard for us to concentrate our attention upon the way it looks or sounds. Aesthetic interest seems to require, in Kant's famous phrase, a certain disinterestedness.

Even so, that we must sternly *refuse* to draw any such line is indicated by the case of architecture, so clearly both a useful, practical, "mechanical" art *and* a fine, aesthetic art. It is not merely the fact that its products, at their best, have utilitarian value as well as value in the very perception, but that the two kinds of value are here inseparable. A great cathedral's beauty is in very large measure a matter of its being so *visibly* a house for the worshipper.

Still, because no defensible line can be drawn, it does not follow that we must fail to distinguish fine art from—now to use the most neutral term—nonfine art. To nearly all of us there seems something wrong with a list which puts bee-keeping and juggling and even cobbling alongside sculpture and music, not because the first three are low or in any way disreputable activities, and not, either, because they do not afford pleasure, for there is simply no question but that some persons take keen and enduring delight in, say, tending bees. But the fact is that such arts as music and sculpture admit of greatness of achievement in individual products—masterpieces, one might best say—which serve their creators' needs for expression and afford to qualified appreciators rare and intense satisfaction of an aesthetic kind. Any art is a fine art which demonstrates its potentiality for such accomplishment. Such a criterion leaves open the possibility of developing entirely new fine arts in the future, as the fine art of the film, for instance, has come into being in our own time.

Employing the stated criterion, we offer the following list of fine arts, or of the *principal* fine arts, in mid-twentieth century.

Architecture
Sculpture
Graphic arts
  Drawing and Engraving
  Painting
Music
Literature
  Poetry (including Poetic Drama, as written to be read)
  Prose Fiction (including Prose Drama, as written to be read)
Theater[2]
  Staged drama
  Films
  The Dance
  Opera

[2] All forms of theater here mentioned are, of course, mixed or combined arts. It is unusual to subordinate the dance and opera to theater, but this seems a convenient classification.

Nonfine arts will then include those which are chiefly practical, such as cobbling and airplane mechanics; those which are engaged in for their own sake but which are insignificantly creative, like skiing and falconry; and those which, though they issue in created products, are generally thought to be relatively restricted in their potentiality for beauty and expressiveness, such as basket-weaving and typography. The latter group might with equal appropriateness be referred to as *minor fine arts.*

Sometimes a distinction is made between *decorative* arts and *expressive* arts. Some aestheticians have taken the expressive aspect to be *the* most important distinguishing feature of the fine arts. Consider, for instance, such a definition as the following: "Art is expression, not of mere things or ideas, but of concrete experience with its values, and for its own sake."[3] Another approach is to define art very broadly and then to distinguish the decorative and the expressive as subdivisions. For instance:

> *There are two distinct kinds of art. The one, decorative art, we understand to be that whose main object is the gratification of the eye and ear. . . . Such art rests upon the desire for beauty, by the sight of beautiful objects.*
> *The chief characteristic of modern art—of art, that is, left to follow its own inspiration free from academic patronage—is power of expression. Through form this, the second kind of art, traces the moral life, and endeavors to occupy man, body and soul, but with no thought of sacrificing the one to the other.*[4]

For our purposes we will let "expressive arts" be considered equivalent to "fine arts." The decorative arts are those concerned to adorn or "beautify" anything which has its own independent function. Wallpaper design is a good example: here is a blank wall which serves as a support and a partition; now we add to it a gay pattern which relieves the monotony, provides a pleasing if momentary resting place for the eye, and even makes a contribution to the prevailing *mood* of the room. The designing of fabrics, silverware and steelware, furniture, automobiles, pottery and china, among other objects, will come to mind as other examples of decorative art,

---

[3] DeWitt Parker, *The Principles of Aesthetics*, 2nd ed. (New York: Appleton-Century-Crofts, 1946), p. 42.
[4] Eugene Véron, *Aesthetics* (London: Chapman & Hall, 1879), p. 126.

though in many cases the decoration is not by any means so distinct
from the function as is the case with wallpaper. Perhaps a more
important essential characteristic—though also a more subtle one—
of decorative art, is that it aims at pleasing, at gratifying, at affording delight, even though, typically, in an incidental fashion. If it be
objected that this is true of the fine arts in general, it will suffice
by way of answer to indicate the vast amount of tragic, pathetic,
tortured, agonized art-work that is to be encountered in literature,
music, sculpture, painting, and theater. Decorative art offends if
it does not please, and please in a narrow sense of the word. It is
generally not meant to be long and seriously contemplated; rather
it offers a bonus pleasure, something in addition to the usefulness
of the object decorated.

The expressive arts, on the other hand, may or may not be "de-
lightsome"—perhaps this word suggests the restricted sense of
"please" that is needed here. Rather do they express, in ways we
will presently have ample occasion to explore, whatever feelings,
moods, insights, and qualities of experience imaginative creators or
appreciators can manage. Their aesthetic character is not intended
to be just surface, not something added on to objects functionally
complete or virtually complete, but means rather to be absolutely
permeative.

Now, the fine arts listed admit of several kinds of grouping
among themselves.[5] For instance, they may be arranged under
the headings *static* and *dynamic*, with architecture, sculpture, and
the graphic arts arranged together as static, while music, literature,
and theater would be called dynamic. A related distinction is that
between the arts of space and the arts of time. Or the several arts
may be classified in terms of their media or materials: thus one
might speak of *plastic arts*, where stone or wood or metal or pigments (among other possibilities) are shaped; of *tonal arts*, in
which musical tones are arranged; of *bodily* arts, where the human
body is itself the medium; and of *verbal* arts, in which words are
the stuff with which the creator works.

Still another grouping can be made according to which bodily
senses are primarily appealed to. Thus, there are the *visual* arts and

---

[5] On the subject of classification of the arts see Thomas Munro's large-scale
treatise, *The Arts and Their Interrelations* (New York: Liberal Arts Press, 1949).

the *auditory* arts; and in order to take care of theater one would have to speak of a combined *visual-auditory* division.

This latter classification raises the question about the "higher" and "lower" senses. That is, it has often been remarked that the principal fine arts make their primary, direct appeal either to the eye or the ear or both; that is, *not* to the nose or palate or to senses of touch, hot-and-cold, or movement. Indirectly, however, or derivatively, there may be a strong imagistic appeal to these other senses: in seeing the peach of the still life, we "almost taste it"; in T. S. Eliot's lines

> *The winter evening settles down*
> *With smells of steaks in passageways*

we too may, as it were, sniff, and detect an appetizing fragrance. Surely in watching the incomparable lightness of the ballerina, we may feel carried along in the swiftness and the whirl. But in all such cases, we do not literally taste and smell and move, as we do literally see the painting's colors and hear the sounds of the poem as it is read. Why are there not gustatory and olfactory arts too? Or are there? Perfumery is without doubt a serious and intricate vocation. Nor is anyone likely to underestimate the degree to which knowledge and sensitiveness are important to cooking, at least if cooking is conceived as something less routine than boiling an egg or frying a pork chop. In his novel *Against the Grain*, Huysman has portrayed the life of a jaded decadent, who, tired of all the ordinary pleasures and arts, has invented a device which presumes to do for the sense of taste what a musical instrument does for the auditory sense. He calls his gadget a "mouth organ."

> *He went to the dining room where, built in one of the panels,*
> *was a closet containing a number of tiny casks. . . . A stem could*
> *connect all the spigots and control them by a single movement,*
> *so that once attached, he had only to press a button concealed in*
> *the woodwork to turn on all the taps at the same time and fill the*
> *mugs placed underneath.*
>
> *The organ was now open. The stops labelled flute, horn, celes-*
> *tial voice, were pulled out, ready to be placed. Des Esseintes sipped*
> *here and there, enjoying the inner symphonies, succeeded in pro-*
> *curing sensations in his throat analogous to those which music*
> *gives to the ear.*

Moreover, each liquor corresponded, according to his thinking to the sound of some instrument. . . . He also thought that the comparison could be continued, that quartets of string instruments could play under the palate, with the violin simulated by old brandy, fumous and fine, piercing and frail; the tenor violin by rum, louder and more sonorous; the cello by the lacerating and lingering ratafia, melancholy and caressing; with the double-bass, full-bodied, solid and dark as the old bitters. . . .

The comparison was further prolonged. Tone relationships existed in the music of liquors; to cite but one note, benedictine represents, so to speak, the minor key of that major key of alcohols which are designated in commercial scores, under the name of green Chartreuse.

These principles once admitted, he succeeded, after numerous experiments, in enjoying silent melodies on his tongue, mute funeral marches, in hearing, in his mouth, solos of mint, duos of ratafia and rum.

He was even able to transfer to his palate real pieces of music, following the composer step by step, rendering his thought, his effects, his nuances, by combinations or contrasts of liquors, by approximative and skilled mixtures.[6]

In a less "refined" way we all know what it is to combine tastes to form more or less pleasing wholes, not only by adding horse-radish to the sauce, but by planning a meal to include both a salad and a meat, both soup and dessert. Can we say that this is the kind of combining exemplified in music, by the forming of tones into a chord, by the distribution of themes and the development of themes within a sonata form, by the arrangement of the movements of a symphony?

Most persons want to answer that there is, somehow, a difference; that there is something incongruous about calling a soup beautiful, or an experience of sniffing fully aesthetic, in the way that listening to the Beethoven *Violin Concerto* is. Some have alleged that sight and hearing are simply "higher" senses and the others are "lower," but it may be asked, what does this mean? Is it that smells and tastes, for instance, are peculiarly transitory? Yet

[6] J. K. Huysmans, *Against the Grain*, trans. John Howard (New York: Lieber & Lewis, 1922), pp. 82-84. The ingenious M. Des Esseintes also invented a machine for combining odors into complex works of art. And indeed a "perfume concert" was actually performed—if that is the word—in New York in the year 1902.

how does that distinguish them from musical tones? And if the answer is returned that music can be notated on a score, the analogy can be made with a recipe book. Is it because food is eaten—that is, eaten up, consumed—that it cannot afford the highest degree of aesthetic pleasure and that its preparation cannot quite be called a fine art? Yet it is not the actual eating and digesting of food, but the tasting and savoring of food which constitutes the ground of its appeal to be included along with dancing and architecture. Again, someone has said that the organs of taste and smell are too internal to function aesthetically, but how is this so in a way that the organ of hearing is not internal? Two other reasons have been advanced by DeWitt Parker for the primacy of sight and hearing: first, that these are involved in human communication as the other senses are not; second, that "The chief significance of all the so-called lower senses is practical—sweet invites to eating, cold impels to the seeking of a warm shelter, touch is a preliminary to grasping; they are bound up with instincts and actions."[7] Still, these seem not altogether satisfactory reasons because all senses can be employed for communicative purposes and because sights and sounds seem no less connected with instinct and action than do smells and tastes: the smell of the rose does not normally recommend to us any action other than that of continuing to sniff, whereas the roar of a lion jerks our hand back from the cage without any intermediary reasoning.

David Prall has argued that the *relative* inadequacy of the lower senses for artistic purposes springs from the fact that

> *smells and odors do not in themselves fall into any known or felt natural order or arrangement, nor are their variations defined in and by such an intrinsic natural structure, as the variations in color and sound and shape give rise to in our minds. Hence our grasp of them, while it is aesthetic very clearly, since they may be felt as delightful, is the grasp in each case upon just the specific presented non-structural quality, which is as absolutely different, unique, simple, and unrelatable to further elements intrinsically through its own being, as anything could be. One smell does not suggest another related smell close to it in some objective and necessary order of quality or occurrence or procedure, nor does*

[7] *The Principles of Aesthetics*, p. 45.

one taste so follow another. There are apparently more or less
compatible and incompatible smells and tastes, but there is no
clearly defined order of smells and tastes, or any structure of
smells and tastes in which each has its place fixed by its own quali-
tative being.[8]

This argument is persuasive. It does not say, of course, that there
is an absolute gulf between cookery and sculpture or between
perfumery and music, for there are most certainly strong aesthetic
appeals in well-prepared foods and scents, but it suggests the reason
why most of us feel uncomfortable in calling these arts "fine arts."

So far the discussion has concerned the arts as *activities* or processes, but they may be thought of too as products and collections
of products. That is, for instance, the art of painting is not only
the act of painting but also paintings or pictures. For the sake
of convenience, art products, whether paintings or musical compositions or poems or statues or buildings or the like, may be called
works of art. But this immediately raises a new question: in calling
some artist's product a work of art is one not complimenting it
more than describing it? Certainly you hear people say, talking
perhaps about a statue: "Well, it's very interesting, but is it art?"
That is, is it a work of art? Or you hear: "To my way of thinking,
that new-fangled composition for 'prepared' piano isn't music at
all; certainly it's no work of art."

Neutral and *honorific* uses of the terms "art" and "work of art"
may be distinguished. The honorific sense is being employed when
only that is called a work of art which is a distinguished and excellent example of the kind of thing it is. Thus, among paintings, only
those that are especially admirable or strikingly beautiful will be
called real works of art; others, though they are certainly paintings,
will be thought not to deserve such praise. On the other hand, we
use "work of art" in a neutral sense when we use it to designate all
paintings, all sonatas, all poems, regardless of merit, in order to distinguish such sorts of objects from natural objects, say, or from
tools. Thus, on the neutral use it would be permissible to speak of a
poor, even a disgracefully poor work of art; whereas in the honorific sense, "poor work of art" would be a contradiction in terms.

[8] *Aesthetic Judgment* (New York: Crowell, 1929), pp. 62-63.

ARTISTIC ROLES

We have looked at art as an activity and works of art as products of such activity. What now of the persons who carry on such activity and have to do with such products? What are the several art roles that may be assumed?

In painting and sculpture, the answer is simple. I go to the painter's studio and look on while he shows me his latest watercolor. He is the artist, the creator, and I am the appreciator, the beholder—there seems no perfectly adequate name which will apply to our relations with the different media. But some arts require middlemen. Most of us do not get a very rich experience from just looking at a musical score: we need somebody to play it for us. If it is orchestral or choral, not only performers but a conductor is required. It is similar in the case of stage plays, where actors and a director are needed, but also, usually, a scene designer, a costumer, someone to handle lights, and so on. For movies, we must add cameramen and dozens of technicians of various sorts. In the case of literature, there is the scribe or the typesetter to be considered as one whose services stand between creator and appreciator. And of course, if we bring in economic considerations, publishers and producers and patrons and many other roles must be added. Then, of course, there are important critical and scholarly roles: the journalist, reviewer, the historian of the arts, the evaluative essayist, and so on. Perhaps it will be helpful to arrange some of these in a simplified chart (as shown on the next page).[9]

Of course, any person may assume more than one of the important artistic roles. We are all appreciators and, in our own way, we are all critics. In a very broad sense, we are all at one time or another creators, though perhaps only in the minor arts. And nearly everyone has been a performer of some kind, if in nothing more than a group sing or some amateur theatrical. Perhaps there is reason, today, for fearing that the creative and performing roles are being more and more professionalized with the resultant effect that the vast majority of people are content to assume an exclusively receptive role, solid in the belief that they have "no talent" and

[9] The appreciators and critics, being common to all arts, are not included in the chart.

ART	CREATOR	PERFORMER-INTERPRETER	LEADER-INTERPRETER	TECHNICIANS
Painting	Painter			Framer, glazer, mural helper, etc.
Sculpture	Sculptor			Caster
Music	Composer	Vocalists and instrumentalists	Conductor	Instrument-makers, sound-amplification technicians, etc.
Literature	Writer	Poetry reader, or story reader		Typesetter, book designer, etc.
Theater				
Dance	Choreographer	Dancers	Ballet-master, dance director	Costumers, make-up men, etc.
Staged Drama	Playwright	Actors	Director	Costumers, set-designers, make-up men, lighting technicians, etc.
Film	Scenarist	Actors	Producer and director	Cameramen, set-designers, costumers, make-up men, light and sound technicians, etc.
Opera	Composer and Librettist	Singers and instrumentalists; perhaps dancers	Director and conductor	Costumers, set-designers, make-up men, light and sound technicians, etc.

were not "born to be artists." If there is a tendency today to be wary of art creation, to leave it to the professionals, to suppose that only those with that awesome quality "talent" have any business performing and creating, the tendency is deplorable both because a more active engagement in the arts is frequently a way to better appreciation of their most distinguished products and because of the intrinsic value of such participation. Nearly all children love to paint with watercolors and model with clay and dance and sing, and that kind of sophistication and learning which deprives them, as adults, of these pleasures, is both unfortunate and unnecessary. In point of fact, we exaggerate the difficulty of doing art—of all kinds. As C. J. Ducasse has well pointed out, what is rare is "consummate mastery" of either minor, handicraft, or fine art.

> Moreover, just as among persons who have learned to write, only a few have original or profound thoughts to set forth, so, among those who have developed a degree of capacity to express themselves in some technical art medium, not many have novel or important feelings to express. Most of the paintings, for example, to

be seen at exhibitions are on about the same level of originality or importance as are the themes or term papers handed in by students in college classes. There was a time when only a very few people were able to write; and, because of the rarity of their attainment, they were then regarded—irrespective of what they did write, and much as artists are today—as being especially gifted. Yet the fact, then as now, is that almost everyone else, with a little training and application, could also have learned to write. Likewise, most people today could acquire the similarly modest control of some technical art medium that is all that was needed, for instance, to paint most of the paintings we see.[10]

The present-day "do-it-yourself" movement might be extended to virtually all the fine arts, with a resultant increase in pleasure among the participants, a deepening of critical taste, and eventually, perhaps, even an improvement in the output of professional artists.

THE ARTISTIC VEHICLE

Although there is some justification in speaking of the work of art that may exist in its creator's mind before he has put pencil to paper or chisel to marble, or of the work of art that may linger in people's memory after a great building or statue has been demolished, nevertheless, when one speaks of a work of art, it is most natural to think of an actual physical object, a certain work of bronze or wood or paints on canvas. One could make an inventory of the works of art within some city, and come up with an account of so many statues, so many paintings, so many books of poetry, etc.—that is, of so many *things*. Works of art are physical things. And yet if one brought an orangoutang into the Metropolitan Museum, stood him before "View of Toledo," and made sure that his eyes were pointed in the right direction—would he therefore see a work of art? Would he not rather see just a colored *thing?*

According to Stephen Pepper, the work of art is at least three distinguishable objects. First of all it is the vehicle, the "continuously existing object, generally physical in nature, which carries the aesthetic values, preserves them and controls them for perception."[11]

[10] *Art, the Critics, and You* (New York: Oskar Piest, 1944), p. 67. Reprinted by permission of The Liberal Arts Press, Inc.

[11] Stephen Pepper, *The Work of Art* (Bloomington: Indiana University Press, 1955), p. 16.

Secondly, the work of art is the object of immediate perception by a being of sufficient sensory, emotional, and intellectual acuity to recognize what he sees as at least a putative carrier of aesthetic value. "The third object, the object of criticism . . . is in the nature of a potentiality or dispositional property of the vehicle. It is the full potentiality of aesthetic perception available to the aesthetic vehicle."[12]

On a later occasion, the second and third of these art objects will be examined, but just now it will be well to go a little further with the analysis of the aesthetic vehicle. The importance of the work of art as a physical thing may be illustrated in this way: suppose one hears a beautiful improvisation on the piano; would one not wish this to be set down in musical notation, so as to be preserved for repeated performances? Occasionally it is regretted that a story told by a person now dead had never been actually written down for the enjoyment of many. And there is something very sad about the destruction of a beautiful building, not only because of the deprivation for those who had not seen it, but also for those who had known it ever so well, because the direct stimulus that the physical object provides to perception is almost always richer and fuller than mere memory.

Then too there is the fact of the very stability of the physical object. Our own moods change from day to day, sometimes from hour to hour, and we differ not only from ourselves but of course from others; yet persisting through these changes, almost (you might say) indifferent to them, are Shakespeare's "right words in the right order," and the many other great art objects in all media. It is somehow comforting that they go on, ready to create anew their world for us each time we come to them.

Some there are who take such an ethereal attitude toward art that they neglect to honor the contribution technology has made to the endurance and to the spread of works of art. Today we are able to have not only the score of Beethoven's *Opus 109;* we can also have on record that special playing of it which was Artur Schnabel's. On film it is possible to capture and indefinitely preserve momentous performances of operas and dances. And even a person of modest

[12] *Ibid.,* p. 31.

means can possess a splendid library of literature and his own gallery of reproductions of paintings.

One apparent difference between the arts of painting, sculpture, and architecture on the one hand, and theater, music, and literature on the other, is that the physical vehicle in the first-named group seems always to be singular, there being but one St. Peter's, one "Winged Victory," and so on; whereas one musical score of a certain work is approximately as good as any other, provided only it be a true copy, and so too with literature and a notated dance. However, this difference is neither as clear nor as essential as at first might appear. Painters have sometimes turned out several closely similar versions of a single painting. Some copyists have been so skillful as to be able to pass off their work for originals, even in the company of experts, a fact that testifies not only to the prevalence of dishonesty but also to the insensitive snobbishness of those who disdain copies as necessarily altogether inferior. Furthermore, with the gradual improvement of methods of color reproduction, the time is perhaps not far off when there can be truthfully said to be not one but many physical objects that are, say, Raphael's "School of Athens."

Of course the permanence of a work of art is always relative. There are first of all the physical alterations it undergoes: the fading or darkening of the pigments, eroding or breaking of the metal or stone, the "corruption" of a text or score. Da Vinci's "The Last Supper" is a famous example of a great painting that has unfortunately decayed, and of course many ancient works of literature exist now only fragmentarily or with many inferior substitutions. Sometimes permanence suffers from inadequate notation, as in the case of the dance, and of music before the modern era. But works of art change too because of changes in conventions, traditions, and cultural values. The most devoted modern-day student of Dante can hardly hope to feel the force of a great deal of the personal satire in *The Divine Comedy*, nor can we quite recapture the original meaning of all the words which Chaucer used. The ruins of a Greek temple are inevitably a different object for the tourist than they were for an ancient worshipper.

But in spite of these qualifications, the amazing fact remains that when works of art have come down to us from even thousands of

years ago, though they now be nothing more than a broken torso
of a statue or a few lines from an ode, they can still awaken in us,
despite all the intervening changes in religion, politics, and technology, a delight in their beauty.

THE ARTS—ONE OR MANY?

Some thinkers have insisted that it is nonsense to speak of Science
or Scientific Method since there is this and that science, but no
science in general, and there is the method of Biology and the
method of Physics and the method of Geology, but no scientific
method as such. Analogously, it may be argued that one should
never speak of art in the singular, but only of this art and that art,
there being nothing significant that architecture and music or
poetry and sculpture have in common. Directly contrary to this
position is one which asserts that the differences among the several
arts are only accidental and superficial; as one recent writer has put
it: ". . . Everything one can say of any single art can be said of
any other as well."

Are the arts—the so-called arts—different? The answer is obvious:
of course they are. One may have exquisite talent as a sculptor and
be an ignoramus, musically. One may be a connoisseur of drama
and yet color-blind. The arts differ from each other in the stuff of
their media, in the techniques of their creation, in the manners in
which they are apprehended. No work of art is translatable into
another kind of art; although there may be a tone poem and a lyric
poem on the same subject, still one will be music and the other will
be verbal literature, and that is a big difference. Even one who likes
music and painting equally will know times when he wants to *hear*
and not to *look*, or the other way around.

Then are the arts, being different, therefore *altogether* different,
not being properly classed together as arts? I think the proper
answer to this question is No; there is a legitimate class of arts so
that architecture and music, for instance, have something very important in common. However, it is much easier to show the differences than to show the likenesses. Indeed, almost all that can be said
now is that the several arts *are* arts, are members of a single class, are
importantly similar in this respect: in all of them the single most

significant criterion of the worth of any of their products is its effectiveness as a vehicle of aesthetic value, an assertion which must necessarily at this early point in our exploration be somewhat cryptic.

If the arts do belong together in a class, is there some sort of natural order of greater and lesser among them, even among those we have called the *major* fine arts? Hardly anyone is without his preferences among the arts—even those who pride themselves on being largely unaesthetic find this or that art somewhat less objectionable than the others—and it is of course common here and elsewhere to provide a rationalization for one's preferences. Hegel had an elaborate scheme in which poetry was the crowning glory of the arts. Walter Pater and Arthur Schopenhauer considered music the greatest of the arts. Some have argued that sculpture is superior to painting in having a third dimension; others have voiced the contrary evaluation, perhaps scorning sculpture for its typical neglect of color. Architects—Frank Lloyd Wright, for instance—not infrequently regard both painting and sculpture as properly subordinate to the art of building. And so the arguments go, back and forth. But as has already been said, those arts which are the major arts all possess a rich plenitude of potentiality for expression and for beauty, a fact best evidenced by the existence of many masterpieces in each of the several fields. It has also been asserted that each art is unique in several respects, so that one does not ever quite substitute for another. These two premises strongly suggest the conclusion that there is *not* a universal and natural hierarchy of the arts. The muses are sisters so democratic that not even the eldest, whoever she is, can rightly claim precedence.

It is well known that Richard Wagner defended the ideal of *Gesamtkunstwerk*, the synthesis of the arts; in his own "music dramas" he believed he had created works which in combining musical, visual, literary, and choric arts, surpassed what was possible in any of these singly, or in any lesser combination of them. But Wagner has had his staunch opponents, the staunchest of whom have maintained that the arts admit of no combination, or at least that they always suffer in the attempt. Yet there is good reason to believe that what we regard as separate arts have only gradually become separated from each other. Franz Boas has written:

Primitive rhythmic poetry that is not sung is, as far as I am aware,
unknown. It is therefore more correct to speak of song rather than
of poetry. All song is accompanied by body movements that are
often associated with noise, such as hand-clapping or stamping the
ground; also by swaying of the body. Therefore poetry, music,
and dance form an inextricable unit. Only gradually is poetry dis-
sociated from music and dance, and music from dance, while dance
seems to be almost indissolubly connected with music.[13]

And surely there are in the civilized cultures great songs, great
dances to musical accompaniment, great operas; in short, there are
instances of successful combining of arts. Probably in the majority
of such instances, one art is dominant and the other or others subordinate. Thus, opera plots are notoriously melodramatic and improbable, the words to many fine songs are trite or foolish, the dancing interludes in some dramatic works are too flimsy to stand by
themselves. On the other hand, there are some nonprimitive works
in which the constituent arts are on much the same footing, as in
the cases of Schubert's music to Goethe's words and the operettas
of Gilbert and Sullivan. Yet even in these cases it does not follow
that the two add up to something necessarily bigger and better than
either one separately. There is probably nothing any better than
certain paintings which are just paintings, and certain statues which
are just statues. Nor is a poem by Goethe improved as a work of art
by being set to beautiful music. Schubert's "Death and the Maiden"
is as great as a quartet as it was as a song. Art-works seem not addi-
tive, and sometimes they even interfere with each other as when
music on the radio may distract one from his reading of a novel
(and vice versa); but sometimes too they do combine to make new
wholes for whose existence we can be grateful, such as the opera
Lohengrin or the film *Gate of Hell.*

Thus the fine arts, though several, are nevertheless common members of a class; they are approximately equal in their potentiality for
creative genius; and they admit of a variety of combination in unified works of art, instances of mixed art being neither anomalous
nor naturally superior.

[13] "Literature, Music, and Dance," in *General Anthropology*, ed. Franz Boas
(Boston: Heath, 1938), p. 593.

Chapter 3

BEAUTY

and the

AESTHETIC

*The beauty of things was born before eyes and sufficient
to itself; the heart-breaking beauty
Will remain when there is no heart to break for it.*

• *R*obinson *Jeffers'* lovely lines raise a query.[1] *Is* beauty
self-sufficient? *Is* it a property of things, such that it exists quite ob-
jectively, out there in trees and mountains and clouds and the sea
dashing against Point Sur; or out there in works of art? *Is* it there
to be seen and admired, there to awe and break hearts and inspire
love? *Was* there beauty before there were men to say "How beautiful!"—even before the world contained any sentient life? And if the
earth grows cold and all life dies, will there be beauty still, a beauty
of rocks and ice and thin shadows from the feeble sun—a beauty to
be forever unobserved?

If one is tempted to answer "Well, of course!" the questions need
to be expanded a little. Compare three sentences:

[1] At least they do taken thus outside their proper context. Some would argue
that if they function properly within the poem, the whole will be self-contained
and not question-raising.

(1) That object is square.
(2) That object is yellow.
(3) That object is beautiful.

Grammatically the three sentences are identical. In each case a quality or property is attributed to, or is asserted as belonging to, a certain object. Suppose now we wanted to know, in each instance, whether the attribution is just, whether the assertion is true. Are there dependable ways of finding out if the object really is square? Yes, of course. Indeed, the ways are so dependable, the results so reliable that we would suspect the sanity of anyone who said, "Yes, I see that the sides are of equal length and that each of the internal angles is a right angle, but I still don't think it is square." Is it the same when the question is one of color? Very nearly, except now we would want to admit the fact of color-blindness—the fact, that is, that some persons, because of their eyes, do not have an experience of yellow when they are looking at something we are sure *is* yellow. Here we could always, theoretically, arrive at agreement as to whether the light reflected from the object is or is not within the wave-length range that we designate as yellow, even though not all persons have the same perceptual experience when they are looking at the same object. But now let a question be raised about whether the object really is beautiful, and how is it to be settled? Are there scientific instruments that we can employ to help us decide? Where exactly and what exactly is that beauty, said to belong to the object? The squareness is a matter of the shape of the object and the shape is surely a part, an aspect, a property or quality of the whole. The yellow color is also something definitely about the object, its physical constitution whereby it reflects certain bands of light; the sensation *yellow* occurs of course in the onlooker, but the cause of the sensation and that to which the sensation refers is in the object. If an object's beauty is also thought to be objective, how can it be described? How can it be analyzed? Recognized? It is not hard to say what is similar between the yellowness of a daffodil and the yellowness of a ribbon, but what is similar between the beauty of a sunset and the beauty of the song "Greensleeves"? If I say that the United Nations Building is beautiful and you deny it, is there really some quality that the building has or does not have, so that one of us is right and the other wrong?

One answer is that often labelled Subjectivism. It is a forthright, unillusioned, let's-have-no-nonsense-about-it kind of answer. It says that the *attribution* of beauty is simply a mistake—in every case. Beauty never belongs to an object; it is not a property or quality of things. Rather, if it can be said to exist anywhere, it exists in the experience of individual persons. Beauty is a kind of feeling. As the song says:

> Oh, what a beautiful morning!
> Oh, what a beautiful day!
> I've got a wonderful feeling. . . .

That wonderful feeling *is* the beauty of the morning and the day. "That is beautiful" says nothing about *that* but does say something about the one who utters the sentence, namely that (if he is speaking sincerely) he is having or has had a "beautiful feeling." The feeling of beauty might be likened with the sensation of yellow (or any other color), with this significant difference, that for beauty there is no objective counterpart, no dependable cause; rather is the feeling of beauty associated in an apparently random manner with objects that have no detectable similarity. Again, when you and I disagree about whether a certain object is beautiful, it is more like finding that we are in different moods than finding that we are in disagreement about some object in our common environment.

The Cultural Relativist, though a first cousin to our Subjectivist, differs in emphasis and in the aspects of the problem that interest him. Beauty, he says, may perhaps be a feeling, but the supposition that feelings vary arbitrarily with individuals entirely overlooks the determining power of a Culture. The point will easily emerge if we consider the beauty of women. It is widely known that friends may argue as to whether their acquaintance Venus Jones is or is not *really* beautiful.[2] Or the judges of a Miss So-and-So contest will in all likelihood disagree, somewhat, as to which candidate is most exceptionally beautiful. Yet an anthropologist would be more struck by the similarity of the queenly aspirants than by their difference: they come within a rather narrow range of height and weight; each girl has a slender waist; her bust and hips will be of

2 Here the word "beautiful" is used to name a relatively rare ideal of beauty, so that this one and that will be said to be exceptionally pretty without yet deserving the epithet "truly beautiful."

almost equal measurements; her legs, especially at the ankle, will be slim; her teeth will be shiny and evenly spaced; her nose will be straight and not large—and so on. Are these also the specifications of the reigning beauty of the Ubangis? Of the latest Miss Magnitogorsk? How about Venus de Milo—presumably a feminine ideal of another epoch? What of Rubens' reflections of Renaissance Italian feminine pulchritude, women who to our eyes look like the "before" part of a reducing salon's advertisement?

The beauty is not a quality of the women themselves—quite as the Subjectivist insists—but neither is each individual person free to have just any response to the appearance of a certain woman. His response will already be, as it were, *built in*. His society or his culture will have provided him, whether he knows it or not, with criteria and standards, not merely for judging, but for determining the very way he sees and feels. So too with clothing and houses and eating ware. And even landscapes. In certain times and places, for instance, mountain scenery has been generally thought to be ugly, something to be avoided if possible. In short, if beauty resides in the feelings of individual men, the feelings of individual men are molded by the culture in which those men reside.

From such positions as those taken by Subjectivist and Cultural Relativist, the Objectivist (let us say) is separated by a great gulf. Beauty, he insists, is not a feeling, any more than the clicks of a Geiger counter are uranium. Certain feelings *may* be dependable indications that one is in the presence of beauty—provided, that is, the feelings are those of a sensitive, perceptive, artistically experienced person. But beauty is, given the proper beholder, the *cause* of an aesthetic experience, just as it is the *object* of an aesthetic perception. There is no more obligation to credit every claim to the experiencing of beauty than there is an obligation to credit every claim to the seizing of truth.

Beauty resides in the painting, in the poem, there awaiting the eye and ear and mind capable of appreciating it. If all men should deteriorate into purely practical sorters and soulless automatons, Beethoven's *Emperor Concerto*, the Cathedral at Chartres, Sophocles' *Antigone* would not cease to be beautiful: they *are* beautiful and it is quite a separate question whether there be those capable of enjoying their beauty. Somewhere beneath the earth's outer crust there exists right now, perhaps, the most exquisite piece of jade, the loveliest and most beautiful stone in the whole world. Perhaps, even, it will never be unearthed, never seen. Yet it exists in its beauty, and should somebody find it, its beauty will not suddenly spring into being, but will be simply discovered.

It is nothing to the point if beauty cannot be adequately described or analyzed. Neither can the flavor of curry or the odor of lilacs, but no one would be so foolish as to deny that that flavor and that scent have an external locus. If beauty does not admit of exact quantification, if it does not accommodate to the bore of a machine, is it therefore to be pronounced nonexistent? Because there are passing fads and cultural eccentricities, is beauty to be dethroned? One might as well say that because there are head-hunters, there is nothing essentially good about love and kindness. One might as well say that just because lying propaganda may become the rule of the day in a totalitarian nation, truth has no abiding value. In short, "The beauty of things was born before eyes. . . ."

Each of these three theories, Subjectivism, Cultural Relativism, and Objectivism, is rooted in a fact, and each of these facts is an important part of the whole truth of the matter. It will be well to make a fresh display of these facts in order to determine whether they cannot all be accommodated within a unified, coherent theory.

(1) The fact underlying Subjectivism is that without a gratified, "good-feeling" person present, no event can properly be said to contain actual beauty.

(2) The fact underlying Cultural Relativism is that feeling responses of individuals become conditioned toward uniformity within a given culture.

(3) The fact underlying Objectivism is that beauty is a quality of the things we call "beautiful" and not of the experience that prompts the judgment.

In order to find a way of fitting these facts together, let us go back of the concept "beauty" to find and examine a larger category of which "beauty" is a part. Beauty is a kind of value. (*Comfort* is also a kind of value, and *efficiency* and *truth*—to name only a few.) Now, values may be said to be of three kinds: *instrumental*,

intrinsic, and *inherent*.[3] *Things, objects*, have instrumental or inherent value—if they have any value at all; only *experience* has intrinsic value. Something has instrumental value when it serves as
an instrument or tool for somebody, helping him get what he wants,
whereas "what he wants" is something distinct from the tool that is
employed as a means. An eraser has instrumental value in that there
are times when we want to obliterate a mark and leave a clean
space; there is no special pleasure in erasing, but there may be a
small satisfaction in the end product, the erased space. A filing cabinet may have instrumental value to a white-collar worker, in that
it helps him store papers in such a way that he may find them when
he needs them. A kitchen range has instrumental value to the extent that it plays a part in the preparation of food that satisfies our
hunger.

Intrinsic value is *felt* value. My experience contains value when I
experience gratification or satisfaction, fulfillment or pleasure.
Needs, wants, desires, aspirations may be thought of as the prereq-
uisites of intrinsic value, but the value accrues only when the need
is met, the want is gratified, the desire is fulfilled, the aspiration is
realized. What instrumental value is instrumental *to* is, sooner or
later, intrinsic value; that is, somebody's immediate satisfaction. The
filing cabinet is of no good to the person who never has a need for
readily locating papers; a lawnmower is useless and therefore value-
less to the person who, whether because he has no lawn or for some
more subtle reason, takes no pleasure in having his lawn cut. But let
there be satisfaction for someone—then, whatever serves as a means
or an instrument to that end is said to have instrumental value.

Yet this last statement must be refined, slightly, to make room
for the third class, inherent value. Like instrumental value, inherent
value belongs to things; the difference between the two is a matter
of timing. An object is said to have value inherently if directly, immediately it conduces to felt satisfaction. A cup of coffee has inherent value for you—if you like coffee—in that the very drinking
of it affords satisfaction. The satisfaction itself is the intrinsic value;
that about the coffee which enables this result is its inherent value.
A given object may, of course, have both inherent and instrumental

[3] See C. I. Lewis, *An Analysis of Knowledge and Valuation* (La Salle: Open
Court, 1946). Professor Lewis' scheme is employed here.

value. Your automobile may please you as you drive it or even as you look at it, as well as provide an efficient means of transportation. A piece of cherry pie may both please the palate and nourish the body. A house may provide adequate shelter and be a delight to live in, though at the moment the rain begins to fall, one's satisfaction in the soundness of the roof may make of the sheltering function an inherent value.[4]

Whether a certain object possesses value, either instrumental or inherent, depends upon both itself and—somebody. Value is always ultimately for somebody. Some organism must have a need or a desire, and the object must be such that it answers to that need or satisfies that desire, if value is to be attributed to the object. An object is valuable just exactly insofar as it has the *capacity* to afford intrinsic value.

We are now in a position to return to our central question concerning *beauty*, its subjectivity or objectivity. Our aim, it will be recalled, is to come up with an explanation that will do justice to the Subjectivist's insistence upon individual feelings, to the Cultural Relativist's insistence upon the social conditioning of responses, and to the Objectivist's insistence upon beauty's being a quality of things. If, now, beauty is seen to be an *inherent value*, our problem will have been solved! That is, very concretely: here is a picture on the wall. I insist that the picture is beautiful, and the question is, where is its presumed beauty? The answer is that its beauty belongs to *it*—beauty is a quality of the picture. What? In independence of the observer? No, not at all: in dependence on the observer. How can this be? Roughly, in the way that the nourishing character of milk is dependent upon the digestive system of an organism. Milk is not nourishing all by itself; if after the earth has gone cold, a bottle of milk should be washed up on the shores of Madagascar, it would be perfectly gratuitous to speak of its still having nourishing properties, there being by then nothing to nourish. Yet, would it not be proper to say that the milk still has nourishing properties for any organism who happened to come along with the appropriate type of digestive system—even if one didn't? Yes, surely this would be proper. So, too, with beauty. Beauty be-

---

[4] This last instance indicates that the distinction between inherent and instrumental values, though a useful one, is often delicate and subtle.

longs to this picture for those who can be "nourished" by it. For
me, the picture has beauty; that is, the picture being what it is and
I being what I am, when we are brought into relation my experience (feelings, etc.) is such that I attribute to the picture the power,
the capacity, to do this to me. But it doesn't do anything for you?
You don't find it beautiful? Very well, the picture does not have
the capacity, seemingly, to arouse in you the feelings it arouses in
me. More particularly, the picture leaves quite cold the natives of
the Kamchatka Peninsula? Ah, such a different culture that; doubtless the people there have learned quite different ways of looking at
pictures and have developed quite different feeling reactions to the
colors and lines and symbols that so affect me. In other words, we
are certainly affected by our culture in our perceptions of beauty,
but this does not alter the fact that beauty exists in certain objects
for certain people.

Those objects are beautiful, for me, that have that about them to
which I tend to have a successful aesthetic response. In other words,
for beauty to be present something is required of both object and
subject: the object must be right—right for some person; and the
subject must be ready—ready for engaging this object. Then
beauty emerges in the relation between the two.

Yet this does not, of course, define "beauty." In locating beauty
we have not yet wholly determined its nature, though *partly* we
have done so in describing it as an inherent value, that kind of value
in an object which is realized in direct confrontation with the object. But since not all inherent values are aesthetic, the task remains
of specifying the further marks or differentiating characteristics of
beauty.

One tack that comes to mind is suggested by the question: What
are the rules? What must the artist do and avoid doing in order to
achieve beauty? But the trouble with this approach is that the long
history of art can be read as a series of beautiful achievements that
break and go beyond rules, a fact which suggests that artistic rules
(e.g., Balance the picture on either side of a central axis! Avoid
parallel fifths! Make the action of the play occur within a single
revolution of the sun!), however helpful they may be to the struggling artist, by no means imply absolute criteria for the determina-
tion of beauty.

If beauty is not something attained or measured by the use of rules, may it not be that we must reintroduce into our considerations the other party to the aesthetic transaction, the beholder? If we do this, then we can say that for beauty to *be*, in any given case, a certain kind of interest, a certain kind of attitude, is required on the part of the seeker. Though it will require another chapter to describe the aesthetic attitude, let it be said here, in the simplest possible terms, that this attitude is one of attentive, self-contained regard for the *qualities* of an object or other event. It is often described as contemplative and as savoring, or negatively as nonpractical, nonanalytic. Well, then, *beauty is whatever rewards this kind of attention.* It is whatever there is about an object that satisfies this kind of interest.

Some people are dissatisfied with such an "abstract" characterization of beauty. But what, it is to be wondered, do they really want? Perhaps a recipe?—To get beauty, mix equal parts of . . . . Or a formula? —$B = O \times C$; i.e., Beauty equals Order times Complexity.[5]

As in the case of truth, all that can be done is to specify the general marks by which the value is recognized. It remains always an act of creation to achieve new and significant truth and to achieve new beauty. To say that it is an act of creation is to say that its precise, concrete means cannot be set down in advance.

Now, if the general nature of beauty as an "objective potentiality" or a "dispositional property of an object" has been indicated, there still remains the much larger task of discovering, if possible, the nature of aesthetic judgment or valuation. What has been discussed here is the problem of the locus of beauty; only after this can we take up the relativist-absolutist controversy as it relates to pronouncements of the aesthetic worth of individual art objects.[6]

BEAUTY AND UGLINESS

If sometimes one speaks of a beautiful play, a beautiful ballet, a beautiful building, a beautiful city, a beautiful landscape, it is per-

[5] See G. D. Birckhoff, *Aesthetic Measure* (Cambridge: Harvard University Press, 1933), where a formula *is* worked out. But of course the formula is highly abstract.
[6] See Chapter 13.

haps even commoner to speak of some parts or aspects of any of such things being "perfectly" beautiful, others being less beautiful, still others being not beautiful at all, perhaps ugly. I speak of San Francisco's beauty only to hear the reply that there are certain districts far from beautiful; likely enough I will admit: "Oh, of course I meant *on the whole*." And in nearly everything we feel that over-all beauty is consistent with certain blemishes so long as beauty predominates.

But again, without necessarily finding great beauty in a whole, we may attribute beauty to this or that feature. Thus a man may have beautiful hair; a house may have a beautiful door; a generally unsatisfactory ballet may include a beautiful *pas de deux*, or an indifferent poem may have individual lines of great beauty. A table may be of beautiful wood whether or not its form pleases. A play may be beautifully composed though finally not very significant. Of course a song may be beautifully sung without being especially worth singing. And we may easily recognize that a painter had for his model a beautiful woman without his painting therefore gaining our admiration.

Ugliness, like beauty, is always relative to an aesthetic interest: without such interest there is in objects neither beauty nor ugliness. We call something beautiful which arouses and satisfies our aesthetic interest; we call something ugly, not if it fails to arouse such an interest, but if it arouses and disappoints or frustrates the interest.

Beauty and ugliness are, both of them, more-or-less matters, not only because, as we have already seen, any object that is the least bit complex is very likely to be part one and part the other, but also because we all recognize degrees of beauty and of ugliness. It is easier to see this when we recognize the difference between, for instance, "beautiful," "very beautiful," "supremely beautiful" than when we distinguish between "beautiful," "rather beautiful," and "a little bit beautiful," but this is only because we tend to reserve the word for cases of quite striking and decisive gratification of our aesthetic interest. In the same way, ugliness is ordinarily attributed only to the highly distasteful or hateful; slighter instances of the disappointing may be called "drab" or "dull." Such is usage. Nevertheless, it is accurate and consistent to speak of the "slightly beautiful" and the "slightly ugly."

Bernard Bosanquet has given deserved currency to a distinction between "easy beauty" and "difficult beauty."[7] The beauty of the "Londonderry Air" piped on a recorder, of a sunset over a lake, or of a fresh jonquil is easy—that is, readily available, requiring little of the appreciator, excluding hardly anyone. But the beauty of *Gargantua and Pantagruel*, of Bartok's last quartet, and of Tolstoy's "The Death of Ivan Ilytch" is difficult. Bosanquet lists three predominant causes of the difficulty, width, intricacy, and tension, which are respectively illustrated by the examples just cited. There are some who cannot enjoy the lusty, bawdy, profane humor of a Rabelais. Some are repelled or at least easily discouraged by complex structures such as those of Bartok and much other "modern art." Still others refuse to submit themselves to the pains of tragic and pathetic art, wanting always the happy and pleasant. What for some persons is difficult beauty is, for others, ugliness. Difficult beauty, in short, exacts a price, but the advice of those to whom beauty is a value of highest importance is: pay it.

[7] See *Three Lectures on Aesthetic* (London: Macmillan, 1915), pp. 86-97.

Chapter 4

CREATORS

and

CREATING

• *Of the* thousands of questions about art, there are none which more consistently fascinate both amateur and professional than these so often asked about the creative artist himself: How did he do it? Why? What sort of person is he?

Before attempting to mix some solutions to these not completely soluble problems, let one completely categorical statement be inscribed: *Art creation has many ways and many reasons.* Such an obvious truth would scarcely need to be expressed were it not for the "single principle" theorists around and about; i.e., those who with no apparent uneasiness explain creation with glib formulas. Whenever there is encountered the brave beginning, "All artists create because . . . ," a healthy scepticism will query: Musicians *and* architects? Choreographers *and* poets? The precocious infants like Mozart *as well as* the late starters like Joseph Conrad? Artists working under commission *as well as* the "pure" creators? Romantic and Classical artists *both?* Inspired types like Schubert *no less than* the slow painstakers like da Vinci? The serene spirits such as Trollope and Herrick *no less than* the agonized souls such as

Dostoevsky and Beethoven? In any field it is easy to make and defend a simple theory if one is permitted to leave out all the cases that might give trouble.

THE CREATIVE PERSONALITY

One recent and respectable work in psychology announces in a sober and straightfaced tone that perhaps the chief difference be-tween artist and nonartist is that, on the whole, the artist makes better pictures, writes better poems, and so on. This may even be said to be experimentally demonstrable—except to those who insist that nothing about "better" and "worse" *can* be demonstrated. Is there nothing else that distinguishes the artist as a human type? Is he more introverted? more temperamental? more "bohemian"? more volatile? less practical? less reliable? less stable? According to at least one scientific investigator who made a study of exactly this problem, the answer is that "there are no personality or intellectual traits and no constants in their [i.e., the artists studied] life history which characterize them all and set them off from other persons."[1]

But if we broaden our category and think for a while not so much of artists in particular as of creative or inventive types in general, it may be possible to list something of what is meant by such a type. These seem to be some of the important traits:

(1) *A strong play impulse.* The anthropologist A. L. Kroeber has written:

Generically, all the discoveries and innovations of pure science and fine art—those intellectual and aesthetic pursuits which are carried on without reference to technology or utility—may be credited to functioning of the human play impulses. They are adult sublima-tions, onto a largely supermuscular level, of the sensorily explora-tory and kinaesthetic activities that constitute play in children and mammals. They rest on the play impulse, which is connected with growth but is dissociated from preservation, comfort, or utility, and which in science and art is translated into the realm of imagi-nation, abstraction, relations, and sensuous form.[2]

[1] Ann Roe, "Artists and Their Work," *Journal of Personality*, XV (1946), 2-3.
[2] *Anthropology* (New York: Harcourt, Brace, 1948), p. 357.

Herbert Spencer, and Friedrich Schiller before him, made a similar likening of art to play. Spencer argued that in the higher animals "we find that time and strength are not wholly absorbed in providing for immediate needs. . . . Hence play of all kinds—hence the tendency to superfluous and useless exercise of faculties that have been quiescent."[3]

Play may be divided into the passive or spectator and the active or participating sorts. Active play, in turn, may be divided into that which proceeds according to established rules as in football or checkers and that which is, at least in large measure, made up as it goes along, such as children's games of "house" or the adults' game of charades. Now it seems generally characteristic of the creator that he likes to *play*, in the freest sense of that term, in or with his particular material, whether it be mathematical symbols or clay or musical tones or whatever.

(2) *Imagination.* A creative person is one who is unusually imaginative in the sense of being able to conceive and perceive in novel ways. He can and does suppose things different from the way they are. Sometimes one encounters persons who, when asked to consider a hypothetical situation, reply, "Oh, but things aren't really that way!" and at the renewal of the invitation "just to suppose," can only doggedly insist upon their slavish realism. A creator, at the other extreme, has a habit, as William James said of the philosopher, "of always seeing an alternative, of not taking the usual for granted, of making conventionalities fluid again, of imagining foreign states of mind."[4] The imaginative component of creativity is an ability, as Souriau put it, "to think aside"—that is, to inhibit the customary response in order to permit novelty.

(3) *Alertness.* Closely related to imagination is a certain ability—there is perhaps no adequate name for it—to notice what would normally go unnoticed, to see significance in what others regard as routine or trivial. Henry James, in whom this trait was extraordinarily prominent, spoke often of its importance. His crowning advice to an aspiring writer was: "Be one of those on whom nothing is lost." And elsewhere he described the inception of

[3] *Principles of Psychology*, quoted in E. F. Carritt, *Philosophies of Beauty* (Oxford: Clarendon, 1931), p. 182.

[4] *The Philosophy of William James*, ed. Horace M. Kallen (New York: Modern Library, n.d.), p. 58.

a plot from the smallest detail—the "germ," he called it—in a dinner-table conversation: the creator detects the germ, the start of a new life, even in the most unlikely and apparently unpropitious of circumstances. Writing to a young poet, Rilke said, "If your every-day life seems poor to you, do not accuse it; accuse yourself, tell yourself you are not poet enough to summon up its riches; since for the creator there is no poverty and no poor or unimportant place."[5] To cite a famous example: billions had seen a pendulum swing before Galileo noticed that the time of a complete swing did not vary with the size of the arc.

(4) *Vision.* The great modern composer Paul Hindemith has quoted a scientist to the effect that " 'Everybody can have—and has—scientific ideas, but it takes a scientist to know what to do with them.' " Musical ideas too, adds Hindemith; there is not, perhaps, so much difference as is commonly supposed between the very beginning ideas of the great genius and those which might flit through the head of anybody at all. Beethoven's sketchbooks reveal musical themes which in their very earliest form were most unremarkable. Bach and many another composer would upon occasion even take over a theme from a noble patron, perhaps something quite ordinary, and then "work it up." And if this working up is to be something more than just dexterous manipulation, there is required an ability to envision a large (organically related) whole wherein nothing can be added or subtracted without serious effects upon every other aspect. As Hindemith puts it: "If we cannot, in the flash of a single moment, see a composition in its absolute entirety, with every pertinent detail in its proper place, we are not genuine creators."[6]

(5) *Drive.* The attaining of "visions" is partly, though of course by no means wholly, a matter of interest and industry. Many a person who *gets* ideas, simply lacks the drive required to seek for the vision that will give sufficient context to the germinal beginnings.

When established artists speak to young aspirants, perhaps no advice is commoner than this: Paint (write poetry, compose

5 *Letters to a Young Poet,* quoted in Walter Allen, *The Writer on His Art* (New York: Whittlesey House, 1949), p. 119.

6 *A Composer's World* (Cambridge: Harvard University Press, 1952), p. 61.

music, etc.) only if you have to, only if you can't *not* do it. That
is, unless there is a certain compulsion or urge, a not-to-be-denied
push toward making and inventing, the fashioned product is altogether likely to bear marks of the drudgery which produced it.
Often the creative role is felt as a "mission" to which one is
"called"—the art chooses you rather than your choosing it. George
Bernard Shaw has one of his characters say, "The true artist will
let his wife starve, his children go barefoot, his mother drudge for
his living at seventy, sooner than work at anything but his art."[7]

(6) *Knowledge and technique.* Sometimes the inspirational aspects of creation are so emphasized that one might almost suppose
that the Theory of Relativity might as plausibly have occurred to
Gertrude Stein as to Einstein, or that it is only an accident that
"The Last Supper" was painted by da Vinci rather than by his
cook. Embarrassingly obvious as it is, there is a neglected truth in
just this: mathematical inventions are made by mathematicians,
statues are made by sculptors, ballets are made only by persons
whose lives are saturated with dancing. There may be inglorious
Miltons but there can scarcely be mute ones, for a poet is not a
poet without a certain command of metrical and metaphorical
language. One may be a skillful craftsman—for instance be able
cleverly to copy a great picture—without being importantly creative. But creativity without skill, without knowledge, without
mastery of technique—no, this cannot be; for the creative person is
not just a potentiality, not just a person on fire with an idea, but a
producer, an actual creator, and in order to create one must have
a grasp of his field, his material, his tools.

(7) *Independence.* The creative person seems always to have a
certain characteristic that may be expressed either negatively or
positively. On its negative side, it is a dissatisfaction with the work
of others; however admirable such work may be, it is felt as not
quite adequate, as insufficient, incomplete. Where most persons
would find somewhere in the poetry of John Donne or Sappho or
Mrs. Browning or William Butler Yeats a beautiful and satisfying
expression of his own love feelings, the creative sort insists on his
own, new, completely individualized expression. Nothing else will
quite do. The positive side of this characteristic is a self-reliance, a

[7] *Man and Superman,* Act I.

belief in one's own powers—though perhaps with times of misgivings and even despair. The creator tends to be "inner-directed" (in the helpful phrase of social psychology), by which is meant that he is not just a conformist, not one who takes his directions and readily accepts his directions and goals from others, but sets himself his own tasks, requires of himself performance at a certain level. He may be grateful for praise and distressed at adverse criticism, but more than ordinarily he judges himself. He may be the toast of the public and a failure in his own eyes; he may be neglected or abused, yet remain withal undiscouraged and even perversely buoyant.

(8) *Willingness to venture.* Every creator recognizes that there is something frightening and exhilarating about departing from the safe, ordinary paths into the uncharted seas. But he has, as Conrad put it in *Lord Jim*, to be willing to submit himself to the "destructive element," for only as the old forms are broken up, may new ones be invented. "All poetical impulses," Dylan Thomas has written, "are toward the creation of adventure. And adventure is movement. And the end of each adventure is a new impulse to move again toward creation."[8]

Now two qualifications want to be mentioned. Creators are not to be thought of as standing on the north rim of the Grand Canyon peering across the awful chasm at the benighted noncreators on the south rim. Creativity is a more-or-less matter. Philosophically the name "God" has often been taken to mark the extreme limit of creativity; at the other extreme would be mere Nothing. Human beings are all, no doubt, creative to some degree, though the spread is very great between the peasant depicted in "The Man with the Hoe," an almost completely unimaginative, nearly Simian creature, and, say, Bach or Rubens, that great cornucopia among painters. But there are fine talents among famous artists whose creativity ran only a thin stream: men like Thomas Gray and Vermeer, for instance. And there are genuinely creative persons whose works, for some reason or other, are not famous—perhaps because they devote their energy to household or other unpublicized pursuits.

The second qualification concerns ways in which a person is creative. It is a common-sense observation that a person who is startlingly original and imaginative in one sense may be no more

[8] *Quite Early One Morning* (New York: New Directions, 1954), p. 126.

than a fuddy-duddy in a hundred other matters. The *avant-garde* composer may be living in the feudal ages with respect to economics. The architect who is a veritable beehive of productivity in building design may be exceedingly lethargic in almost every other way. The man of distinctive ideas in the ballet may be uncommonly dull and routine in his literary tastes. History shows us some striking examples of versatile genius—da Vinci, Michelangelo, Blake come to mind—but not many. Very often creativity is specialized, though there is no reason to suppose that it is necessarily so.

MOTIVES FOR CREATING

Right along with the insistence that creators vary widely among themselves, there being a great range of physical, psychological, moral, spiritual, and other types, an attempt has been made to set down some typical characteristics of the person we designate as "creative." If we turn now to the question of reasons or motives for creating, we do well at the outset to observe that these widely variant creators differ in their motivations. Still, once again some general remarks are possible, remarks which in spite of their generality may be helpful.

Roughly, creators create because they want to or because they need to or because they have to. *Wanting to* is no bad reason. If walking along a country road we come upon a painter before his easel and ask "Why are you doing that?" his answer, if civil, might be simply, "Because I like to paint." For those who are comforted by the results of scientific questionnaires, there is this fact: that when a large number of professional inventors were asked for the primary motivation for their inventions, they answered more frequently than anything else: "love of inventing."[9] And the composer Arnold Schoenberg is on record as saying, "I believe that a real composer writes music for no other reason than that it pleases him."[10] To any who might wryly reply that Schoenberg's atonal harmonies pleased no one else, it could be said that such well-loved

9 H. G. Barnett, *Innovation* (New York: McGraw-Hill, 1953), p. 153.
10 "The Musician," in *The Works of the Mind*, ed. Mortimer J. Adler *et al.* (Chicago: University of Chicago Press, 1947), p. 69.

composers as Haydn and Mendelssohn and Stephen Foster would presumably agree with Schoenberg that unless an artist genuinely likes his art, not merely its products but also its process, he can hardly be expected to be other than a drudge and a hack.

But this is not to suggest that the actual process of creation is an altogether jolly, carefree, here-we-go-gathering-nuts-in-May frolic. On the contrary, there is overwhelming testimony from artists and other creators that whatever similarities there may be between art and recreation,[11] art creation is nearly always a deadly serious, sober, intensely agitated, and often even agonized activity—and not necessarily the less so when the work of art itself is a gay tarantella or a drawing-room farce. "Poets speak of the necessity of writing poetry," says Stephen Spender, "rather than of a liking for doing it." And then adds for himself: "I dread writing poetry. . . ."[12]

To some, a *need* for doing anything so seemingly impractical as writing a poem or painting a landscape in watercolor, may sound downright silly, but to the poet or painter there will be times when such other needs as food and drink and sleep and sex must wait their turns after the most urgent demands of art are met.

Now this need to create may be construed in either a primarily social or a primarily individual sense. Any need, of course, must be personal, that is, be the need of some or other person, but it may vary considerably in the degree to which it is related to other persons and their needs.

To the extent that the creator is working at something functional, like dwellings and pottery and textiles, chances are strong that he will conceive of himself as serving his group. And not less so if his work contributes to public occasions; think, for instance, of someone writing a hymn for his church or school or a military march or a work song. Again a frieze or ode or mural commemorating, say, the settling of a new land or a great battle, will surely have important social dimensions. Nor need we think here only of large or sumptuous groups: if the portrait painter or the poet in love serve no more than a single other, the social disposition of the art is not therefore negligible.

---

[11] Play is of course often very serious. Children often wonder why some adults (perhaps themselves addicted to "cutthroat" bridge) do not know this.
[12] "The Making of a Poem," *Partisan Review,* Summer 1946.

Otto Rank, one of the profounder psychoanalytic interpreters of art and artist, has found the artist in the primitive community to be especially social in his motivation.[13] Indeed it is only at a considerably developed stage of civilization that the artist comes to have a recognized individual identity. Before that he is an anonymous expresser—it might almost be said a manifestation—of a collective, religious homogeneity. There seem to be exceptions to this. Some primitive communities have recognized professional artists. Even so, their products are probably more impersonal and unindividualized than is common in our culture. Consider, for instance, the Judao-Christian Bible in which the great poets and historians speak in the name of God and a people, lesser writers being absorbed in the identity of the exalted ones like Moses; and even by the time of the Christian era, the gospel writers can be seen as individuals only by subtle interpretation.

According to Rank, early art serves the primarily religious function of helping the group toward a sense of its own identity and permanence. "Art, then—at least in its beginning—was not the satisfaction of the desire of the individual artist to attain immortality for himself in his work, but the confirmation of the collective immortality-idea in the work itself as a picture of the soul."[14]

It is interesting to note that the appearance of the individual artist, the recognized genius set off from his fellows, differs in time with both place and art. For instance, in Greece it was in the Fifth Century B.C. that the first individual dramatists and sculptors were recognized, though Homer and Hesiod had been honored for centuries. Indeed, the early history of Greek tragedy is a forceful record of this transition from anonymity to individuality. Originally there were just chanting and dancing choruses to enact the tragic tales. Then there emerged from the chorus a single actor to play the part of a highly individualized hero, one who carried on a dialogue with the collective people. The use of the individual actor corresponds with the appearance of the first clearly identifiable dramatist, Aeschylus. A few painters are heard of, some sculptor-

---

[13] This is *not* to imply that all primitive art is functional. Much primitive decoration seems not to have even any magical significance, and there are many instances of purely "aesthetic" art among pre-literate groups.

[14] *Art and Artist* (New York: Tudor, 1932), pp. 14-15.

architects, but not musicians or choreographers. Yet ages later there appear in England the great anonymous epic Beowulf and the "mystery" and "miracle" plays, followed not very long after with the appearance of writers whose names we know; then gradually artists in the plastic and tonal media. And only in very recent times has the identity of choreographers been recognized. In our own day the prominence of big-name actors almost completely obliterates the scenarists of films.

This discussion of the anonymous artist should not be supposed to imply that when artists as named and distinct personages come to be known, social art automatically gives way to individual art. No, even the recognized and honored craftsman and genius may, at the very least in his own intention and belief, serve as spokesman, prophet, clarifier, rebuker, and guide for any group from his own small coterie up to humanity itself. Even the comic artist, who too often is not seriously honored, serves group needs, not merely in being an entertainer and a provider of comic relief, but also as a satirist, a revealer of evil and folly. Neither should the emphasis upon the social function of the primitive artist be supposed to imply that it is necessarily development and progress to pass from social to more purely personal motivations. Indeed, distinguished artists and critics of our own day have urged artists, even in the interest of their own art, to seek a closer identification with their nation, race, church, class, or other groups.

Nevertheless, there does seem to be a real, if gradual, historical emergence of the artist as a self-conscious, self-concerned being. It may be, as Rank has insisted, that the artist is particularly concerned with the assertion of his own particular personality to protect it from submersion in the collective whole, as well as to save it from the obliteration of death. However much he accept "tradition" as a determinant of his subject matter (for instance, in the Middle Ages, it could hardly have occurred to the Italian painter to look outside the Bible and stories of the saints for his subjects) or of his form (the sonnet, the cantata, etc.), the artist tends to leave on his work the stamp of his own very particular personality, to "sign" his work not only with his name but with his style. This saves him, as it were, from being lost in the group. And his work saves him too, in a

sense, from being lost to the ravages of time. The Shortness of Life
vs. the Longness of Art is a favorite theme of artists in many ages.
As an example, take this sonnet of Shakespeare:

> *Since brass, nor stone, nor earth, nor boundless sea,*
> *But sad mortality o'er-sways their power,*
> *How with this rage shall beauty hold a plea,*
> *Whose action is no stronger than a flower?*
> *O, how shall summer's honey breath hold out*
> *Against the wreckful siege of battering days,*
> *When rocks impregnable are not so stout,*
> *Nor gates of steel so strong, but Time decays?*
> *O fearful meditation! where, alack,*
> *Shall Time's best jewel from Time's chest lie hid?*
> *Or what strong hand can hold his swift foot back?*
> *Or who his spoil of beauty can forbid?*
> *O none, unless this miracle have might,*
> *That in black ink my love may still shine bright.*

It is not maintained, of course, that the artist always so explicitly
asserts his hope for his own continuation through his art, but perhaps it is characteristic of him that he has particularly strong drives
to "immortalize himself," so that he "is always seeking to protect
himself against the transient experience, which eats up his ego. The
artist takes refuge, with all *his own* experience only from the life of
actuality, which for him spells mortality and decay, whereas the experience to which he has given shape imposes itself on him as a
creation, which he in fact seeks to turn into a work. . . . In creation the artist tries to immortalize his mortal life."[15] There are a few
examples of artists who became famous almost in spite of themselves
—Gerard Manley Hopkins and Franz Kafka come to mind—but of
course most of them wanted to be recognized and celebrated in their
own lives. But particularly have artists wanted to "live on," and
many have been consoled for the pain of their contemporaries' indifference and disregard by great drafts of hope for the future. For
instance, Stendhal, who died in 1842 (not unappreciated, but far too
little appreciated for his own satisfaction) predicted that he would
get his just deserts from the reading public after 1935.

[15] *Ibid.*, p. 39.

But before continuing this subject of the artist-creator's meeting of his individual needs, a subject that will receive fuller treatment under the separate chapter on Expression, let us have a look at a different sort of motivation for creation. Some will be surprised that so far nothing has been said about a certain very popular answer to the question of motivations for creation—an answer one investigator got from a group of African wood sculptors who when asked why they chose to become sculptors answered simply that though it was hard work, it paid very well. Artists create their works in order to make money!—it would be fatuous and pointless to deny it. Case after case can be cited where an artist settled down to good hard creative work when he got hungry or when the landlord threatened to lock him out—or, as in the case of Samuel Johnson, actually did lock him *in*. However much some aesthetes have supposed that art is too spiritual, lofty, and resplendent to be mentioned in the same breath with money, artists themselves have generally been more sensible, and some artists have been astute business men. Nevertheless, the commercial motivation of artistic creation is not pre-eminent for at least two reasons. Generally speaking, painting pictures, composing music, writing stories and so on, are decidedly *not* good ways of earning a living; in spite of the fact that a few artists have become wealthy by their art works, by far the greatest proportion make in that way only a precarious living, if they make any living at all. Secondly, hardly anything important about art-works seems to be accounted for by the commercial kind of motivation. Doubtless there are artists who have been spurred out of indolence into productivity by the need for money, but probably many an artist would have done more work or better work if he had had no monetary need; and certainly we can wish to have been spared many of the very bad works of art that have been spawned by the desire or need for money. Although most artists need and welcome whatever money their productions bring them, they will not be impelled by the desire for money to do good art unless they have something to say, and if they do have something to say, they are not likely to be motivated to say it better by the promise of monetary reward.

THE PROCESS OF CREATION

In what might be called the "externals" of their procedures, artist-creators differ widely: where one can work only at his desk, another must be out in the open; one likes to have people around, but another requires absolute solitude; one works best in the early morning, another late at night. Schiller liked to have the smell of a rotten apple in his immediate vicinity while he was doing his poetry. Haydn would sometimes jot down musical ideas on a blackboard he carried with him on his walks. And so on.

But about certain features of the act of creation, there seems to be an impressive amount of agreement, an agreement not necessarily destroyed by the fact that some theorists have spoken of three stages, others of as many as six. Somewhat arbitrarily—for as will be seen, the stages or steps are not demarcated with perfect clarity—five stages will be listed here: problem-setting, incubation, idea, development, and critical revision.

(1) *Problem-setting.* This is a period of great uneasiness—something requires doing. Whether or not there is some external impelling cause, such as a commission—for Brahms to compose an Academic Festival Overture for a University convocation, for Frank Lloyd Wright to design a plant for the Johnson Wax Company, for Diego Rivera to make a mural for Radio City, for Molière to write a comedy by next Wednesday at the King's command—the artist will, if he is going to accomplish anything, become aware of a need gnawing from within. But how to manage the task that is gradually presenting itself?

(2) *Incubation.* The problem cannot be solved out of hand. One starts to work and gets stuck. The answer won't come. Or if it comes it seems superficial, merely "intellectual," more on the nature of a pat formula or a habitual response than a genuine solution. Some time is needed, possibly a few hours, but just as possibly years! Other tasks, perhaps altogether unrelated, are taken up, or one sleeps, is apparently passive and lethargic. But all the while something is working, and in the favorable case, there emerges:

(3) *Idea.* "Illumination" it has often been called, though Paul Valéry has spoken of a "gleam of light, not so much illuminating as dazzling." The idea may be only a beginning or it may be the

whole answer, the whole object delivered as it were ready-made, a vision which requires only some seemingly mechanical copying out onto a score sheet or a canvas or a piece of paper; but large or small, a mere germ or the whole plant, its appearance is likely to seem baffling and inexplicable. Thus Beethoven: "From where do I take my ideas? That I cannot say with certainty. They come uncalled, directly and indirectly."[16] Or Mozart: "When I am in particularly good condition, perhaps riding in a carriage, or in a walk after a good meal, and in a sleepless night, then the thoughts come to me in a rush, and best of all. Whence and how—that I do not know and cannot learn."[17]

Probably no account of the creative process has been more widely read, accepted, and endorsed than that of Henri Poincaré, who, though he was of course describing the genesis of some of his important mathematical discoveries, wrote what was recognized by artists as an account of *their* creative acts as well. He in particular made much of the sudden illumination which follows a period of incubation. His notion was that incubation is an *active*, not a passive, phase of the entire process, but that the activity is below the threshold of consciousness. There has to be, of course, something to incubate, hence the indispensability of the problem-setting stage, the more purely intellectual deliberation which, as it were, provides the unconscious with its material. Poincaré used the analogy of molecules whirling in a gas chamber to describe the continuing creative work of the unconscious, certain combinations of these molecules issuing forth suddenly into the consciousness as ideas, as solutions, partial or, occasionally, entire.

Most often the idea is the exciting clue to the mystery rather than the whole answer. Paul Valéry speaks of the one poetic line given by God or Nature—then the poet must "himself" make the rest. What might seem to be the contradictory testimony of Laurence Sterne—"I write the first sentence and trust in God for the rest"—should probably be taken to refer to a different part of the process, the written line being in this case the problem-setting, and

16 Letter, quoted in Frederick Dorian, *The Musical Workshop* (New York: Harper, 1947), p. 8.
17 Letter, quoted in Gardner Murphy, *An Introduction to Psychology* (New York: Harper, 1951), pp. 314-15.

"trust in God" symbolizing the assignment of the problem to the incubator.

(4) *Development*. Mention was made earlier of Paul Hindemith's notion that what really distinguishes the artist of genius from the run-of-the-mill is knowing what to do with the ideas, once they have come. What is here called "development" might in some ways better be called "structuring," except that the former term plays upon the analogy to what the symphony writer does with his themes. Occasionally one hears a work of music in which there are lovely, engaging tunes—but not much more. Just as you get ready for the music to "go somewhere," it goes nowhere but in a circle. Instead of the themes being varied and developed and fitted into a larger whole, they are simply played again.

At this point a certain ambiguity in the word "idea" becomes troublesome. Two sorts of incubated ideas may be distinguished. One is the kind so far suggested, the poetic line, the musical theme or subject, perhaps a drawn line with a unique curve—in any case some actual ingredient of what will become the finished product. The other kind of idea is a plan, a scheme, an organizing principle. It may be a *formal* idea, such as a sculptor's idea of modeling a mother with child in such a way that the child sitting on the mother's knees facing her, completes the curve of the mother's back and inclined head. It may be an *emotional* idea, such as the painter's decision to show in the face of Christ on the Cross a synthesis of physical pain and of compassion. It may be a *narrative* (or *dramatic*) idea, such as the choreographer's notion of exhibiting in a dance the progress of a love affair from initial attraction to satiety and indifference. Or it may be a *philosophical* (or other more definitely intellectual) idea, such as the novelist's choosing to depict the emptiness of that life which is without commitment to a Cause. In these latter four cases, the idea is a means of structuring the whole work of art and of guiding the creative surge throughout.

It is now easier to think of development as that part of the process which works from some beginning—a first line, tune, or the like— toward an ideally envisioned completion. When Hindemith asserts, "If we cannot, in the flash of a single moment, see a composition in its absolute entirety, with every pertinent detail in its proper place, we are not genuine creators," he is going rather far, farther perhaps than we want to follow him, but his pronouncement is valuable precisely in being an extreme statement of the way a vision of the whole (itself growing out of the idea-as-a-principle guides) functions as a guiding light.

(5) *Critical Revision.* This stage follows the achievement of a "draft" of the work of art or at least one of its parts. Tolstoy once said, "In a writer there must always be two people—the writer and the critic."[18] So with any art: there is the making of the brush stroke, or the hit of mallet on chisel, and then there is the stepping back and looking, where "looking" means "assessing." And after the assessment, there is new fashioning, more assessment—and so on. In some artists much of this revision goes on internally before any commitment to the physical medium; many others find they can revise satisfactorily only after they have the colors shining in their eyes or the tones sounding in their ears. Some revise by simply destroying the old and starting over again—but not *all* over since the previous effort will be a strong influence on its replacement. Others prefer to "doctor" the first draft. Dostoevsky would sometimes tear up hundreds of pages and begin again. Keats on the other hand would scratch out words and phrases and insert new ones, which in turn might be rejected. The manner of revision depends partly on the medium. Once one has chipped off a piece of marble—that's that. And watercolor is notoriously hard to touch up or change. Buildings can be altered, but of course only by a difficult and often costly process. Music and literature are comparatively easy to change. Mozart and Flaubert may be contrasted as extremes of the spontaneous and the laborious types: Here is a biographer's account of the writing methods of the author of *Madame Bovary:*

> *He began by jotting down the general idea of a paragraph with perhaps a few metaphors he hoped to work in; and once its contours were clear, he wrote out a preliminary draft, which he then tested for sound and lucidity. He continued to write and rewrite the passage, introducing new images and scrapping old ones, till he was at last sure that it was luminous in conception and unified in mood. In this way he accumulated acres of documents. The final version of* Bovary, *for instance—and it was only a fraction of his labour—was written on 1788 leaves . . . and* L'Education

[18] "Talks with Tolstoy," quoted in Allen, *The Writer on His Art.*

sentimentale of 1869 was represented by 2355 leaves, 72 of which, dealing with Forest of Fontainebleau, were reduced to 4 in the final text. When Flaubert mentioned in his letters that he had spent a week over two or three pages, he meant, of course, two or three pages in their final condition, and he may in fact have covered ten, twenty or even thirty before arriving at a satisfactory version.[19]

Mozart writes of expanding his musical thoughts until a great whole is achieved,

so that afterwards I survey it at a glance, like a goodly picture or handsome man, and in my imagination do not hear it at all in succession, as it afterwards must be heard, but as a simultaneous whole. That is indeed a feast! All the finding and making only goes on in me as in a very vivid dream. . . . When now I afterwards come to write it down, I take out of the sack of my brain what has been previously garnered in the aforesaid manner. Accordingly it gets pretty quickly onto paper; for, as has been said, it is properly speaking already finished. . . .[20]

Frequently a single work of art will in some of its parts come easily and freely from its creator whereas in other parts will be labored over, revision over revision. For instance, A. E. Housman tells of his habit of walking in the country of an afternoon and spontaneously composing poetry as he went. One time, he says, two stanzas came by sheer inspiration, one came after a little coaxing, but a fourth and final stanza was shaped up in its final form by dint of great effort—thirteen rewritings!

This listing of steps—one, two, three, four, five—makes the creative process sound mechanical and pat. It isn't. For one thing, these steps do not by any means always follow each other in perfect order, single file. Sometimes, it seems, an artist will be inspired with an idea before he has ever quite realized what he is doing—i.e., what his problem is. Very often critical revision will be inextricably involved with development. New ideas can come anytime—even after the whole object has seemed done. Occasionally a work may seem to the artist simply dictated to him, he being hardly more than a scribe, with no separate stages of devel-

[19] Philip Spencer, *Flaubert* (New York: Grove Press, 1952), p. 141.
[20] Letter, quoted in Murphy, *An Introduction to Psychology.*

opment or revision. Yet with such cautionary modifications in mind, one may be helped to an understanding of the process of creation by thinking of a period of preparation and preliminary groping, one of continuation in the unconscious, one of bubbling up onto a conscious level of elemental and structural ideas, one of working these up into a formed whole that is subject to scrutiny and revision.

Chapter 5

ART,

DREAM,

and

MYTH

• *Richard Wagner* wrote in his autobiography the follow-ing account of the inception of one of his works:

After a long night spent in fever and sleeplessness, I forced myself to take a long tramp the next day through the hilly country, which was covered with pine woods. It all looked dreary and desolate, and I could not think what I should do there. Returning in the afternoon, I stretched myself, dead tired, on a hard couch, awaiting the long-desired hour of sleep. It did not come; but I fell into a kind of somnolent state, in which I suddenly felt as though I were sink-ing in swiftly flowing water. The rushing sound formed itself in my brain into a musical sound, the chord of E-flat major, which continually re-echoed in broken forms; these broken chords seemed to be melodic passages of increasing motion, yet the pure triad of E-flat major never changed, but seemed by its continu-ance to impart infinite significance to the element in which I was sinking. I awoke in sudden terror from my doze, feeling as though

*the waves were rushing high above my head. I at once recognized
that the orchestral overture to Das Rheingold, which must have
long lain latent within me, though it had been unable to find definite form, had at last been revealed to me. I then quickly realized
my own nature; the stream of life was not to flow to me from
without, but from within.*[1]

It will be found of interest to put alongside this account by a musician of the dream origin of a work the even more famous account
by an author of the writing of a poem. The author is Coleridge;
the poem is "Kubla Khan, or a Vision in a Dream." First the poem:

*In Xanadu did Kubla Khan
A stately pleasure-dome decree:
Where Alph, the sacred river, ran
Through caverns measureless to man
    Down to a sunless sea.
So twice five miles of fertile ground
With walls and towers were girdled round:
And here were gardens bright with sinuous rills,
Where blossomed many an incense-bearing tree;
And here were forests ancient as the hills,
Enfolding sunny spots of greenery.*

*But oh! that deep romantic chasm which slanted
Down the green hill athwart a cedarn cover!
A savage place! as holy and enchanted
As e'er beneath a waning moon was haunted
By woman wailing for her demon-lover!
And from this chasm, with ceaseless turmoil seething,
As if this earth in fast thick pants were breathing,
A mighty fountain momently was forced;
Amid whose swift half-intermitted burst
Huge fragments vaulted like rebounding hail,
Or chaffy grain beneath the thresher's flail:
And 'mid these dancing rocks at once and ever
It flung up momently the sacred river.
Five miles meandering with a mazy motion
Through wood and dale the sacred river ran,
Then reached the caverns measureless to man,*

[1] Quoted in Frederick Dorian, *The Musical Workshop* (New York: Harper,
1947), p. 54.

And sank in tumult to a lifeless ocean:
And 'mid this tumult Kubla heard from far
Ancestral voices prophesying war!
     The shadow of the dome of pleasure
     Floated midway on the waves;
     Where was heard the mingled measure
     From the fountain and the caves.
It was a miracle of rare device,
A sunny pleasure-dome with caves of ice!

     A damsel with a dulcimer
     In a vision once I saw:
     It was an Abyssinian maid,
     And on her dulcimer she played,
     Singing of Mount Abora.
     Could I revive within me
     Her symphony and song,
     To such a deep delight 'twould win me,
     That with music loud and long,
     I would build that dome in air,
     That sunny dome! those caves of ice!
     And all who heard should see them there,
     And all should cry Beware! Beware!
     His flashing eyes, his floating hair!
     Weave a circle round him thrice,
     And close your eyes with holy dread,
     For he on honey-dew hath fed,
     And drunk the milk of Paradise.

When Coleridge published the poem, he included a prefatory explanation which reads in part as follows:

In the summer of the year 1797, the Author, then in ill health, had retired to a lonely farm-house between Porlock and Linton, on the Exmoor confines of Somerset and Devonshire. In consequence of a slight indisposition, an anodyne had been prescribed, from the effects of which he fell asleep in his chair at the moment that he was reading the following sentence, or words of the same substance, in "Purchas's Pilgrimage": "Here the Khan Kubla commanded a palace to be built, and a stately garden thereunto. And thus ten miles of fertile ground were inclosed with a wall." The Author continued for about three hours in a profound sleep, at

*least of the external senses, during which time he has the most
vivid confidence, that he could not have composed less than from
two to three hundred lines; if that indeed can be called composition in which all the images rose up before him as things, with a
parallel production of the correspondent expressions, without any
sensation or consciouness of effort. On awaking he appeared to
himself to have a distinct recollection of the whole, and taking his
pen, ink, and paper, instantly and eagerly wrote down the lines
that are here preserved. At this moment he was unfortunately
called out by a person on business from Porlock, and detained by
him above an hour, and on his return to his room, found, to his no
small surprise and mortification, that though he still retained some
vague and dim recollection of the general purport of the vision,
yet, with the exception of some eight or ten scattered lines and
images, all the rest had passed away like the images on the surface
of a stream into which a stone has been cast, but alas! without the
after restoration of the latter!*[2]

Often enough the practical man has spoken of the artist as a
dreamer. Still oftener perhaps have men and women emerged
blinking from a theater or concert hall or closed the back cover
on a novel with some such comment as "It's like coming out of
a dream." Doubtless from the time that there were great works
of art they have been spoken of as "spellbinders," and what is it
to dream if not to be bound in a spell?

It would seem, then, that both the testimony of creative artists
and of laymen warrants a search into the relationship between
dream and art experience, whether appreciative or productive.
The search must begin with the question, What is a dream?

THE NATURE OF DREAMS

There is an easy answer to the question: a dream is the psychic
activity—the experience of happenings, thoughts, feelings, images
—during sleep. But to go further in our probing is not quite so
easy. Why does one dream? To protect one's sleep, says Freud,
by channeling certain stimuli which might otherwise wake one
up. Not all agree with Freud's answer, but a more important

[2] Quoted in Brewster Ghiselin, *The Creative Process* (New York: Mentor,
1952), pp. 84-85. This is a rich collection of statements by a variety of creators.

question for our purposes is this: Why does one dream what he does dream? And this: Do dreams mean anything, do they signify?

The easy answer—perhaps the most popular one, even today—is that dreams are mere nonsense, just a jumble of images as if the wind caught and scattered the snapshots from an open drawer. There is no reason for dreaming the way we do—except, perhaps, that when our digestive system is having its troubles, we do tend to have troubled dreams; and when our feet get cold, we may have some appropriate dream, such as walking over snow—but nothing more profound than this. So there is no importance or significance to dreams—though occasionally one may be amusing or weird enough to tell at the breakfast table, even if the audience, in such cases, is seldom as interested as the teller. Jonathan Swift in his parody of Petronius has expressed this position:

On Dreams

Those dreams that on the silent night intrude,
And with false flitting shades our minds delude,
Jove never sends us downwards from the skies;
Nor can they from infernal mansions rise;
But are all mere productions of the brain,
And fools consult interpreters in vain.

For when in bed we rest our weary limbs,
The mind unburden'd sports in various whims;
The busy head with mimic art runs o'er
The scenes and actions of the day before.

But not everyone has thought so lightly of dreams—even before the influence of psychoanalysis. Literature of every age expresses people's concern with their dreams; consider Joseph's interpretation of Pharaoh's dream of the fat kine and the lean kine, Chaucer's "Nun's Priest's Tale," or the wife warning her husband in Tolstoy's "God Sees the Truth But Waits" not to undertake a journey because she had dreamed his hair turned suddenly white. Then there are Strindberg's *Dream Play* and Joyce's *Finnegans Wake*, a whole novel expressive of a dream—but the list is virtually endless. Dreams, then, according to some strains of folk opinion, *are* important, at least sometimes. They are ominous, revelatory, prophetic. If they are shadows, they are foreshadows and had better not be lightly dismissed, though their meaning may well be ambiguous and obscure like the pronouncements of the oracles.

Our language employs two other meanings of "dreaming," both so common as to require no more than mention. One is "idle, profitless musing." Thus Wordsworth's "Expostulation and Reply:"

> Why, William, on that old grey stone,
> Thus for the length of half a day,
> Why, William, sit you thus alone,
> And dream your time away?

Another common meaning is: "wishing, hoping, planning." When Jeannie of the light brown hair is dreamed of, there is present, no doubt, something more wishful than a mere phantasmagoria. The "coming true" of dreams is a favorite cliché of song writers and advertising copy writers.

Now, these two latter uses will be noticed to refer especially to daydreams, which differ from sleeping dreams mainly in being somewhat more coherent and certainly under better control from the conscious will of the dreamer; but as the language suggests, the similarity between day and night dreams is more impressive than their differences.

So far, then, mention has been made of four characteristics commonly attributed to dreams; irrationality or silliness, occasional prophetic quality, idleness as contrasted with "up and doing," and wishfulness as contrasted with present reality.

As everyone knows, one of the distinctive and (to many people) outrageous characteristics of depth psychology[3] is its insistence upon taking dreams seriously. Nevertheless, it by no means contradicts the common-sense notions. It too says that dreams are irrational, prophetic, idle, and wishful; and it goes on to say that however ill dreams conform to the outside world, they arise from and therefore potentially reveal the inside world of the dreamer. The primary assumption is that there is some reason for our dreaming everything we do dream. This reason, though usually not perfectly apparent at first, is discoverable; indeed, in some

[3] Not only orthodox Freudian Psychoanalysis, but other forms of therapeutic psychology based upon some conception of an unconscious dimension to the self. In this account it is Freud's ideas that are mainly employed, but an attempt is made to allow room for divergent theories.

sense the dreamer knows the meaning of his own dream though
it may require a therapist to help him realize explicitly what he
knows.

We must distinguish, Freud tells us, between the surface or
manifest plot of the dream and the deeper symbolic latent significance that it almost always has. A child may wish to go on a
picnic and then dream of going on a picnic; but the older the
child gets, the more complex and involved his dreams become. He
begins to employ symbols which are at once richer and more
obscure than the child's direct imagery. At the adult's dreamed
picnic there may be apples and flowers and ants and swings and
lakes, but these things will seem somehow different from their
waking selves—and they *are*, because they are not only themselves
but are also persons and acts in disguise. Above all, the dreams are
the products of our feelings and attitudes, our loves and hates,
wishes and fears, confidences and insecurities. A dream may reveal
to us emotions that we are unaware of, antipathies that we have
never been willing to admit, dreads that we have kept hidden
even without trying to, desires that we consider shameful, beneficial courses of action that for some reason we have regarded as
impossible.

The symbols that dreamers employ are not, according to psychoanalytic theory, entirely understandable without the interpretive
help of the dreamer; yet men for some reason dream more nearly
alike than might be supposed. Consequently, there are a number of
dream symbols which have a nearly constant meaning, however
particularized a significance they have in different occurrences.
Water, for instance, seems always to have to do with birth, as
journeying symbolizes death. And these meanings, it is curious
and interesting to note, apparently do not vary much as to time
and place. However unlikely it might offhand seem, there are
striking similarities in the dreams of a twentieth-century Wall
Street broker; his contemporary, a Zuni warrior; and their ancient
predecessor, a Persian king. Yet perhaps it is not so strange either;
men everywhere and in every time are born, reared, and educated;
they work, marry, raise children, and die. Their bodies are much
alike; they share certain basic needs. All of them must relate in a
variety of ways to their fellows; all of them love and hate, know

fear and hope, have times of joy and times of sorrow. Man, said someone, is the animal who knows he must die. Man, said Aristotle, is the rational animal; but, said Aristotle, he is also vegetative and carnal. And man, as all men know, is a dreamer of dreams.

Dreams are irrational if by that description is meant that their coherence is a coherence of emotional tone and not, necessarily, of orderly sequence of events and of images matching those of waking perception and of thoughts arranged in syllogistic pattern. Their irrationality, however, is not beyond all understanding.

For instance, they may be understood to be prophetic. Not because of their being vehicles of occult omniscience but because they are records of the past and present, which are the seedbed of the future. Take the wonderful case of Pilate's wife. She warned her husband not to deal with Jesus because, she said, "I have suffered many things this day in a dream because of him" (Matthew 27: 19). May it not be that her dream showed her something about her own perception of Jesus that she had not before been quite able to acknowledge? The person who had been dreaming of falling down mountain cliffs might be advised to postpone his ascent of F-6, not because the dreams are a glimpse of fate exactly, but because they perhaps reveal a certain fear of the dreamer, a fear which might during a climb contribute to the actualization of the dreams.

DREAM AND THE ART-WORK

But by now in this discussion of dreams it may be feared that we have entirely lost sight of art, its creation and its enjoyment; so it is time to indicate that besides the cases of actually getting creative ideas within dreams, there are often noted dream-like qualities of art creation carried on during waking states. One such quality is the feeling of being dictated to, of creating almost automatically rather than consciously and deliberately, of being seized and compelled in spite of oneself. T. S. Eliot, for instance, has noted "that some forms of ill health, debility or anaemia, may (if other circumstances are favourable) produce an efflux of poetry in a way approaching the condition of automatic writing—though, in contrast to the claims sometimes made for the latter, the material has obviously been incubating within the poet, and cannot be suspected of being a present from a friendly or impertinent demon."[4]

Then there is the interesting account Friedrich Nietzsche gives of how *Thus Spake Zarathustra* was written—or, as he says, how it "invaded" him:

> *Provided one has the slightest remnant of superstition left, one can hardly reject completely the idea that one is the mere incarnation, or mouthpiece, or medium of some almighty power. The notion of revelation describes the condition quite simply; by which I mean that something profoundly convulsive and disturbing suddenly becomes visible and audible with indescribable definiteness and exactness. One hears—one does not seek; one takes—one does not ask who gives; a thought flashes out like lightning, inevitably without hesitation—I have never had any choice about it. There is an ecstasy whose terrific tension is sometimes released by a flood of tears, during which one's progress varies from involuntary impetuosity to involuntary slowness. There is the feeling that one is utterly out of hand, with the most distinct consciousness of an infinitude of shuddering thrills that pass through one from head to foot;—there is a profound happiness in which the most painful and gloomy feelings are not discordant in effect, but are required as necessary colors in this overflow of light. There is an instinct for rhythmic relations which embraces an entire world of forms (length, the need for a widely extended rhythm, is almost a measure of the force of inspiration, a sort of counterpart to its pressure and tension). Everything occurs quite without volition, as if in an eruption of freedom, independence, power and divinity. The spontaneity of the images and similes is most remarkable; one loses all perception of what is imagery and simile; everything offers itself as the most immediate, exact, and simple means of expression.[5]*

Goethe compares two types of his poetic creation. Of some of them he says, in his *Conversations with Eckermann,*

> *I had carried them in my head for many years; they occupied my mind as pleasant images, beautiful dreams, which came and went, and by playing with which my fancy made me happy. I unwill-*

[4] *The Use of Poetry and the Use of Criticism* (London: Faber and Faber, Ltd., 1933), p. 144.
[5] *Ecce Homo*, trans. Clifton Fadiman, in *The Philosophy of Nietzsche* (New York: Random House, n.d.), pp. 99-100.

ingly resolved to bid farewell to these brilliant visions, which had so long been my solace, by embodying them in poor, inadequate words. When I saw them on paper, I regarded them with some sad-ness. I felt as if I were about to be separated forever from a beloved friend.

At other times, it has been totally different with my poems. They have been preceded by no impressions or forebodings, but have come suddenly upon me, and have insisted on being composed immediately, so that I have felt an instinctive and dreamy impulse to write them down on the spot. In such a somnambulistic condi-tion, it has often happened that I have had a sheet of paper lying before me all aslant, and I have not discovered it till all has been written, or I have found no room to write any more.[6]

Admittedly, these cases of "inspiration," where one has scarcely more control over his creation than he has over the course of his dreams, are not descriptive of *all* art creation. But what *is* common to all art, is imagination. Painting a picture or writing a story is a matter of imagining. To some people it contrasts sharply to "doing"—spading up the garden and selling an insurance policy and putting out a fire are *doing*—and thus to be classed as idling or wool-gathering or dreaming. Without agreeing that imagining is a waste of time, we may agree in finding a certain likeness be-tween the imagining of the artist and the dreaming of Father William. Indeed, William had a reply to him who accused him of fruitless idling just because he was sitting on an old grey stone dreaming his time away:

> *"The eye—it cannot choose but see;*
> *We cannot bid the ear be still;*
> *Our bodies feel, where'er they be,*
> *Against or with our will.*

> *"Nor less I deem that there are Powers*
> *Which of themselves our minds impress;*
> *That we can feed this mind of ours*
> *In a wise passiveness.*

> *"Think you, 'mid all this mighty sum*
> *Of things forever speaking,*
> *That nothing of itself will come,*
> *But we must still be seeking?"*

[6] *Conversations of Goethe with Eckermann* (London: Dent, 1930), p. 355.

In short, idling is sometimes the least idle of pursuits: it may be a wise passiveness in which the ideas germane to accomplishment are being engendered. Everybody dreams and has illusions, but as Hans Sachs sings in Wagner's *Die Meistersinger:*

> *My friend, that is just the poet's job*
> *To note and attach meanings to his dreams.*

And de Maupassant has said that the great artists "are those who can make other men see their own particular illusions."[7]

With this idea of imposing an illusion on the audience, we change the emphasis away from the creative artist as dreamer to the appreciator whose dream, it might be said, is fabricated and conducted by the artist.[8] Let it be said once again that in speaking now of the likeness between dreams and art, we are not thinking merely of such obvious cases as *Alice In Wonderland* and Kafka's novels and *A Midsummer Night's Dream* and the *Nutcracker Suite*, but even of realistic, wide-awake works. The work of art is *not* a dream: it has a permanent physical embodiment; it aims (usually) at having a certain public relevance and appeal: it has (usually) a highly structured form; and it aims at affording a stimulus and a reward for a contemplative attitude. The dream, on the other hand, is ephemeral, private, frequently loose-jointed even though permeated by a single feeling or mood, and it is typically subjective. But art experience, like dream experience, is sensuous, emotionally charged, imaginative, and, above all, it is the self's attempt to symbolize some matters that are not easily expressed in everyday ways.

Like a dream, a work of art may have both a manifest and a latent content. Suppose a sleeper to have had the following dream:

> *I walked into a forest. It was twilight and growing cool. As I penetrated deeper and deeper, the path grew dim and I began to fear I had lost my way. Still I kept on. I began to hear whisperings. They were not threatening, but seemed amused, accompanied by quiet laughter and giggling. I was annoyed by these sounds. I could not see who was there, though some of the trees and bushes moved in ways that seemed somehow familiar to me. Finally I*

---

[7] Preface to *Pierre et Jean*, in *The Portable Maupassant*, ed. Lewis Galantiére (New York: Viking, 1947), p. 671.

[8] See Kenneth Burke, *Counter Statement* (New York: Harcourt, Brace, 1931), p. 47.

came to a giant tree, off by itself. It was the greatest tree of the forest. It frightened me, and yet I went to it and lay down at its base. It had moss or something furry hanging from its high boughs. When I did that, the whisperings stopped, and I rested.

Now let it be supposed that this dreamer, a twelve-year-old girl, was by her dream symbolizing, among other things, these feelings of hers:

I am getting older. Things are not as clear to me now as they used to be. Sometimes I don't know what to do. People aren't always nice to me. They laugh at me and make fun of me, though I don't always know what they mean. They probably don't mean any harm. Still, I don't like it—whoever they are. I don't have anybody particularly in mind, just the people I'm around. But my father will protect me. Though I'm sometimes afraid of him, he's very powerful. Sometimes I look at him standing over me, and I notice especially his beard. Then I forget about the people who annoy me. I'm able to go to sleep and not worry any more.

The first account would be the dream she might remember and tell. It is the manifest content, the plot, the dream as it appeared on the surface. Below these images and events were some feelings, perhaps feelings she had never quite formulated or recognized by herself. These feelings, then, would be the cause for the dream taking the form it did. To be sure, she might have really gone for a walk in a forest lately, and this experience supplied her with the material for her dream, but the special character of the dream would be determined by her feelings.

Now, let us look briefly at a famous stanza from a Shakespearean elegy:

> *Fear no more the heat o' the sun,*
> *Nor the furious winter's rages;*
> *Thou thy worldly task hast done,*
> *Home art gone and ta'en thy wages.*
> *Golden lads and girls all must,*
> *As chimney sweepers, come to dust.*

If this verse may be likened to a dream itself, then the following paraphrase will express the manifest content of the dream:

Now that you are dead, you need be no longer concerned with the sun's heat or the winter's storms. It is as if you had finished your

*work, collected your pay, and gone home. All must die, be they
rich or poor.*

The latent content of the poem may be said to be the difference
in total experience between the actual poem and the prose paraphrase. To any sensitive reader, this difference is very great. There
is no adequate way of rendering this difference except by returning
from the poor substitute to Shakespeare's own words, but something may be set down to suggest that which is left out by the
paraphrase.

> *There is this consolation in death: that it is a cessation of fear, the
> fears of all the extremes in life; it is a cessation too of the drudgery
> and the strife which is man's lot, and is thus a rest from weariness.
> And there is consolation too in the fact of death's being the great
> leveler: it ends worldly discriminations.*

Thus baldly stated this suggestion of the latent content of the
poem is hardly better than the first paraphrase until it is further
pointed out that the special poignancy of the full poetic experience is brought about by the irreplaceable imagery, by the home-
liness of the diction, by the "binding" quality of rhythm and
rhyme, and by the richness of the contrast between "Golden lads
and girls" and "chimney sweepers." The word "golden" means
not only wealthy, but also glorious, shining (like the sun), fortunate—fully opposed to the poor, inglorious, grimy, benighted
"sweep." Opposed except in death. The soot of the one is no
closer to dusty death than the gold of the other.

In the poet as in the dreamer, then, we may say that there are
feelings and attitudes and a host of experiential materials which
are pushing toward symbolization. The poem (or other work of
art) or the dream constitutes a more or less adequate symbolic
expression, but both are such that they may be taken literally, in
which case they are especially likely to seem absurd and frivolous.
But both permit of a deeper understanding.

IS THE ARTIST NEUROTIC?

Understanding of what? The answer in the case of the dream
is perfectly clear. Everyone knows that dreams are analyzed and

interpreted (particularly, of course, by professional therapists) in order to facilitate better understanding of the psyche of the dreamer, an understanding that is strongly, sometimes desperately, needed when the dreamer is a neurotic. But scarcely is that word "neurotic" uttered, when the question springs to mind: Is the artist a neurotic personality? There is a considerable segment of the population that would be inclined to answer an immediate Yes. We think of the cartoonist's conception of the fiercely-bearded and oddly-smocked sculptor, the dreamy poet, the painter starving in his attic amid piles of "unintelligible" abstractions. And we think of the stories of artists who were suicides and alcoholics and dope addicts and homosexuals—and ill in all the other ways flesh and soul are heir to. Then we remember that such studies as Freud's on Leonardo da Vinci and Ernest Jones' on Shakespeare have tried to show that even these supremely great artists left evidences in their works of neurotic fixations and complexes.

Freud in particular has taught that phantasies of all kinds—dreams, daydreams, art-works, various kinds of wishful thinking —are the products of unsatisfied desires. When one is blocked in the direct attainment of his wishes, he compensates by building phantasy in which, though perhaps in elaborately disguised ways, the wisher has his way. Particularly, Freud says, do we see two kinds of wishes function in this way, ambitious wishes and erotic wishes. When the artist is frustrated in his attainment of "honour, power, riches, fame, and the love of women," he turns away from reality to an art medium he finds more malleable, and there he builds his dream castle.

But, even if this account of artistic motivation is adequate, does this fact establish the neuroticism of the artist? Unless one is willing to use the word "neurotic" in an unhelpfully broad way, the answer must be No; no person is neurotic just by virtue of being an artist. Indeed, Freud believed that the activity of art is the artist's escape from neurosis. His phantasy "works"; it affords an at least temporary release from his repressed desires. Further-more, his molded phantasy may very well work for others, and to the extent that it does he may even become "successful"—that is, win in reality the money and power and love which he had theretofore been denied.

Yet even though Freud did not say that all artists are neurotics, there perhaps remains for the art lover something unsatisfying in the above account. It seems, for all of the qualifications, to be too morbid, too reductive, too substitutive.

Carl Jung has said flatly and justifiably, "The art work is not a morbidity."[9] That is, it is not necessarily a morbidity. There are sick works of art as there are sick dreams. Schizophrenics may paint pictures and model clay and write stories, and these works will not fail to bear the marks of their sick creator. And even the finest works of art—say Beethoven's $C\sharp$ *minor Quartet* and Rubens' "Descent From The Cross"—may well be partially accountable in terms of personality deviations of the artists. But works of art and dreams may be healthy. They may be joyful, glad, vigorous, strong, reasonable, life-affirming—or anything else. To fail to see this is almost certainly to fail the works of art, to fail to experience them as they perhaps deserve to be experienced. To treat the work of art as a symptom or as merely a device for getting at the repressions of its creator may be justified in a therapeutic context, but is scarcely to be recommended as ideal art appreciation. For one thing, this approach to art makes of it too personal a thing. As Jung says, "Indeed the especial significance of the genuine art-work lies in the fact, that it has successfully rid itself of the restraints and blind alleys of the personal and breathes an air infinitely remote from the transitoriness and short-winded excursions of the merely personal."[10] It is especially to be noted here that Jung is speaking of the *genuine*, the good work of art. It may be said to be part of the artist's job to effect a transcendence of the restrictively personal, to get out and beyond the confines of his own unique self, to dream not only for himself but for his fellows—at least some of them.

A Freudian account of art-as-phantasy inclines to "reductiveness," the fallacy of explaining something complex by an inadequate simplicity. This is particularly apparent in its attempt to reduce all wishes to two, the ambitious and the erotic. Surely, to the extent that art creation has a basis in wishes and desires, these

9 *Contributions to Analytical Psychology*, trans. H. G. and C. F. Baynes (New York: Harcourt, Brace, 1928), p. 168.
10 *Ibid.*

wishes and desires are of *every* kind. It is perhaps possible to establish one or two or three great catch-all classifications, but such a practice is more likely to mislead than to conduce to better understanding. But it seems unfortunately reductive, too, to say that art invariably springs from frustrated desire, that art is nothing but a "sublimation" of repressed wishes. Apparently when Freud thinks of art he often thinks particularly of picaresque romances where there is a swashbuckling hero—a transparent get-up for "his majesty, the Ego" of the author—who wins out over numerous hardships to attain to the esteem of men and the adoration of women. The similarity between this kind of art and the daydream of the office boy truantly musing in the boss's chair is evident. But the wish basis of Mozart's *Jupiter Symphony* or Rodin's "The Old Courtesan" or a Mondrian abstraction or Shakespeare's "Fear no more the heat o' the sun"—this is not so easy to establish. *Fear* would seem to have something to do with many of Poe's short stories, *love* (not just desire) with Donne's marriage songs, *scorn* with Blake's "Mock On, Mock On," *joy-in-nature* with Beethoven's *Sixth Symphony*, *awe-in-majesty* with Michelangelo's "Moses"—and so on. By heroic effort one can squeeze down all of these and the million other psychic dispositions discoverable in art-works to wishes, but the effort seems not justified by any great gain in understanding.

Finally, in this criticism of Freudian aesthetics, mention needs be made of the tendency to regard art activity and art work as always a substitute for something else. "Happy people never make phantasies. . . ," Freud once wrote, but what kind of happiness is that! Why is it that the most fearful phantasy of all is that of a brave new world that has no place for dreams and play and art? Schiller taught that man is completely human only when he is playing, and even allowing for a certain rhetorical exaggeration, there is profundity in this recognition that play is an achievement, not just something which fills in gaps between work. Dreaming may be a *moving ahead* by our deeper powers, not just a somnolent visit to the rogue's gallery of repressions. And the creation of a great work of art is such an almost superhuman achievement as to make ironic any explanation of it as "what the artist did because he couldn't do what he really wanted to." Especially significant is what Rank has termed the artist's greatest work of art—his own artist-self. That is, the genuine artist is one whose creative activity is so positive, so strong, so omnivorous that every experience is grist come to the mill.[11]

Art work, then, is not a morbidity, not necessarily just a sublimation of erotic and ambitious wishes, not just a substitute for action. The artist is not necessarily a neurotic; indeed, it is almost but perhaps not quite fair to say that to the extent that a person is an artist he is not a neurotic, for "neurosis" means blockage and stoppage and destruction; whereas "art" means dynamic flow and productive achievement.[12] From the time of Aristotle to the present men have recognized that art has a kind of healing power, that it is a harmonizer of jangling nerves, a cathartic to undigested emotions, a resolver and synthesizer of warring elements, a balm to rawness, and for lethargy, deadliest of diseases, an awakener and a call. And sometimes the artist practices a homeopathic medicine; every lover of art knows that in sadness, for instance, what we often crave are not joyous art-works, but dirges, *Pietàs*, elegies, and pathetic sonatas and symphonies. Jung has said that "A psychoneurosis must be understood as the suffering of a human being who has not discovered what life means for him."[13] And it is most certainly true that it is from such suffering that the creation of art arises. But the issue of that creation, the art-work, at its best represents the alleviation (often *through* an intensification) of that suffering. The question, finally, is not whether there was sickness but whether there is achieved healthiness. Nietzsche put it this way:

> *Health and disease—be careful! The standard must always be the*
> *efflorescence of the body, the resilience, courage and cheerfulness*
> *of the spirit—but naturally also* how much morbidity it can absorb
> and conquer—*in other words,* make healthy.

[11] If a loyal Freudian should complain that these criticisms are not quite fair, his complaint may be honored; like other great creative geniuses, Freud was uneven in his work and perhaps not altogether consistent. What is here criticized is at least a popular "Freudianism."

[12] See Otto Rank, *Art and Artist* (New York: Tudor, 1932), p. 41; Daniel E. Schneider, *The Psychoanalyst and the Artist* (New York: Farrar & Straus, 1950), pp. 103-11; and Carl Jung, *Psychological Reflections*, ed. Jolande Jacobi (New York: Pantheon, Bollingen Series XXXI, 1953), pp. 179-82.

[13] *Contributions to Analytical Psychology*, p. 224.

And he adds: "That which would destroy more delicate men is a stimulant for *great* healthfulness."[14]

MYTH AND ART

The artist has been called a dreamer and a maker of dreams, a player and a conductor of the play of others, and he has been called a recorder and inventor of myths. To those accustomed to regarding myths as strange superstitious stories studied by fifth-grade children, it comes as something of a surprise to learn of the immense interest in our time on the part of the most serious and advanced philologists, anthropologists, literary critics, psychologists, and philosophers—as well as of imaginative writers, dancers, painters, and other artists—in mythology. Why this burst of new interest? The answer is different for almost every type of student. The agreement is in the *importance* of myth.

There is by no means perfect agreement as to what a myth is. We may start with Charles M. Gayley, writer of the famous textbook, *The Classic Myths*, used by generations of students. He makes a distinction between fable and myth:

> *Myths . . . are stories of anonymous origin, prevalent among primitive peoples and by them accepted as true, concerning supernatural agencies. . . .*
> *Fables are vessels made to order into which a lesson may be poured. Myths are born, not made. They owe their features not to any one historic individual, but to the imaginative efforts of generations of storytellers.*[15]

It has long been supposed that myths are like folk songs in being dependent for long times upon nonliterate recording, and alter not only with the personality of the transmitter but also with times and circumstances. In our time, with the collection of numerous versions of a single basic myth and with the direct field observation by anthropologists of peoples still employing live myths, much more is empirically known about these changes. If, as Gayley says, myths are born, they also grow and even, sometimes, wither

14 Quoted by Thomas Mann in his Preface to *The Short Novels of Dostoevsky* (New York: Dial Press, 1946).
15 *The Classic Myths* (Boston: Ginn, 1893), pp. 1-2.

and die. Franz Boas recorded a myth current among the inhabitants of Vancouver Island in 1888 and it was still going strong twelve years later, but by 1931 investigators could find no one who remembered the story.[16]

Myths have been widely regarded as (1) just stories—literature, (2) prescience, (3) primitive religion, (4) primitive philosophy, and (5) collective dreams. Our account will be shamelessly eclectic in saying that myth is all these things—and doubtless more too. We will call myth an "ur-phenomenon" by which will be meant something which predates our sophisticated distinctions of literature, science, philosophy, religion, and dream—something out of which these very distinguishable activities arise. Ernst Cassirer has gone further to suggest that myth and language are closely correlated, being both sprung from the primal root of metaphorical activity. That is, the very activity of *naming* is no more ancient than mythologizing: both represent the expression of a "spiritual excitement" which issues in likening and explaining.[17]

For us a myth about Thor or Jupiter may be "just a story," but for their originators and for many descendants of the originators these myths were live, real, believed accounts. They represented a meaningful orientation in a universe inexhaustible in its confusingness. They enabled the primitive to clarify his own being and status by relating himself and his environment to an original and higher state. In affording answers to how this or that got started, myths were assigners of meaning and justification for ritualistic and moral behavior. I. A. Richards has put it this way:

> The saner and greater mythologies are not fancies; they are the utterance of the whole soul of man and as such, inexhaustible to meditation. They are no amusement or diversion to be sought as a relaxation and an escape from the hard realities of life. They are these hard realities in projection, their symbolic recognition, coordination and acceptance. Through such mythologies our will is collected, our powers unified, our growth controlled. . . . Without his mythologies man is only a cruel animal without a soul.[18]

[16] See Richard Chase, *Quest for Myth* (Baton Rouge: Louisiana State University Press, 1949).
[17] See Ernst Cassirer, *Language and Myth*, trans. Susanne K. Langer (New York: Harper, 1946), chap. vi.
[18] *Coleridge on Imagination* (New York: Harcourt, Brace, 1935), p. 173.

He goes on to say that for every myth "The scope of its relevance and therefore of its proper influence upon action must be limited." That is, it is perhaps not, even for the primitive, a simple matter of belief, absolute and entirely literal belief. Primitives are not necessarily disturbed by "contradictions" that seem to us intolerable,[19] at least partly because the variant "beliefs" meet different needs, apply in different circumstances. Even a sophisticated philosopher like Socrates was not either quite a believer *or* a disbeliever in the Olympian mythology. There were times when it seemed appropriate to him to offer up a prayer to "the gods that haunt this place," but other times he was sceptical. Here is Socrates discoursing with Phaedrus:

> *Phaedrus: I should like to know, Socrates, whether the place is not somewhere here at which Boreas is said to have carried off Orithyia from the banks of the Ilissus?*
> *Socrates: Such is the tradition.*
> *Phaedrus: But I beseech you to tell me, Socrates, do you believe this tale?*
> *Socrates: The wise are doubtful; and I should not be singular if, like them, I too doubted. . . . Now I quite acknowledge that these allegories are very nice, but he is not to be envied who has to invent them; much labour and ingenuity will be required of him; and when he has once begun, he must go on and rehabilitate Hippocentaurs and chimeras dire. Gorgons and winged steeds flow in apace, and numberless other inconceivable and portentous natures. And if he is sceptical about them, and would fain reduce them one after another to the rules of probability, this sort of crude philosophy will take up a great deal of time. Now I have no leisure for such inquiries; shall I tell you why? I must first know myself, as the Delphian inscription says; to be curious about that which is not my concern, while I am still in ignorance of my own self, would be ridiculous. . . . Am I a monster more complicated and swollen with passion than the serpent Typho, or a creature of a gentler and simpler destiny?*[20]

In our own time there are men as diversely wise as Yeats and Santayana and Jung who have taught that modern man no less

---

[19] I leave it to the hard-bitten reader to think of our own, somehow more tolerable contradictions.

[20] *Phaedrus*, Jowett translation, Steph. 229.

than the primitive *needs* myths. Not that they advocate superstitious belief—Richards for one wants to call science itself a kind
of myth whose application and relevance like that of all other
myths is limited—but they think men of every age require certain
great overarching systems of narrative explanation.

Where Socrates' scepticism was a bit misplaced was in his supposition that a myth is merely objective—however mistaken—
rather than subjective; that is, that it tries to afford knowledge of
outer rather than inner life. Recent students see myths as "pro-
jections," as attempts to understand oneself by fanciful cosmology.
Freud's comparison of myth and dream has become very popular:
"It seems probable that myths . . . are distorted vestiges of the
wish-phantasies of whole nations—the age-long dreams of young
humanity."[21] Richard Chase has suggested that "myth is the reposi-
tory of repressed wishes and that part of the magic power of myth
stems from its ability to furnish 'recognition scenes' in which we
have the thrilling experience of coming face to face with a disin-
herited part of ourselves."[22] Carl Jung has put it this way:

> *The mind of the primitive is little concerned with an objective
> explanation of obvious things; it has an imperative need—or, rather,
> his unconscious psyche has an irresistible urge—to assimilate all
> experience through the other senses into the inner, psychic hap-
> pening. The primitive is not content to see the sun rise and set; this
> external observation must at the same time be a psychic event—
> that is, the sun in its course must represent the fate of a god or hero
> who dwells, in the last analysis, nowhere else than in the psyche
> of man.*[23]

However naive and unsatisfactory myth may be, compared to
developed science, philosophy, and religion, it remains important
as a collective phantasy which helps a people understand themselves. Furthermore, in spite of the different forms that myths
take from time to time and culture to culture, there turn out to be
surprising near-uniformities among myths from very different parts
of the world, so much so, indeed, that Joseph Campbell in his

[21] "The Relation of the Poet to Day-Dreaming," trans. I. F. Grant Duff, in
Eliseo Vivas and Murray Krieger, *The Problems of Aesthetics* (New York: Rinehart, 1953), p. 159.
[22] *Quest for Myth*, p. 101.
[23] *Psychological Reflections*, p. 15.

fascinating *The Hero with a Thousand Faces* finds a "shapeshifting yet marvelously constant story" that is *the* myth, or as he says "the mono-myth" whose basic formula for the adventures of the hero may be represented as "separation—initiation—return." But even without going this far in reducing myths to myth, it remains the case that even the myths of a far-away and exotic people have a strange power to move as well as to charm us provided only that we inhibit the condescending attitude that accompanies our taking them as merely false science, pagan religion, and childish philosophy.

If "literature" is understood in a deeper sense than just "amusing stories," myth may be called both literature and the great seed-bed of literature. The mythology of other peoples is literature directly for us—as it perhaps cannot quite be for those to whom it is a way of living—in the retelling by Bulfinch, Gayley, and Robert Graves. And it is the seed-bed of a literature stretching at least from Homer to James Joyce. It might be interesting for our purposes to bring these two great authors together as T. S. Eliot has done in his critical essay, " 'Ulysses' Order and Myth," where he analyzes Joyce's use of the Ulysses story and defends and recommends it as "a way of controlling, or ordering, of giving a shape and a significance to the immense panorama of futility and anarchy which is contemporary history."[24] Instead, let us take another tack, showing something of the relation between Greek tragedy and Greek myth, with special reference to the Oedipus story.

The Athenian citizen hardly expected on his visits to the theater to be surprised, even by a brand new tragedy. He went knowing the plot, at least in its main outlines, just as today we might go to see a new film based on the life of Joseph and his brothers or Jesus, knowing pretty well that there would be no unexpected ending or any entirely unfamiliar episodes, but going to see how the familiar story was handled this time, going to see if there were any new nuances of character or any subtleties of motivation introduced. The Athenian playgoer, hearing of a new play by Aeschylus called *Seven Against Thebes*, remembered the essentials of the myth—though perhaps he would know two or three versions.

[24] Reprinted in *Criticism*, ed. Mark Schorer, Josephine Miles, and Gordon McKenzie (New York: Harcourt, Brace, 1948), p. 270.

By the same token a playwright in that culture had at hand a considerable body of material on which to work, material which he and his audience alike took to be right and proper for his uses.

The great Athenian tragedians whom we know and honor today lived and prospered in the fifth century B.C., and not long before their time drama was entirely choric, not altogether unlike today's church choir chanting and hymning, now sitting, now standing, now in dignified processional. Their chants told the stories of Dionysus, Zeus, Athena, and Apollo; of Odysseus, Ajax, Perseus, and Medea; of the Eumenides, and stealing fire from heaven, the judgments of Minos, and the golden fleece. And perhaps as ancient as the plots themselves were certain manners of telling: a certain metrical arrangement for this episode, a different one for that; a quick tempo in describing this, and a slow one elsewhere; a sprightly movement here and a mournful one there. These forms, never arbitrary, came to seem so appropriate as to be inevitable. Doubtless the same expectations and even requirements of regularity were made in form as in story itself, yet in both there were from time to time innovations. With the appearance of artists better fledged than the legendary artificer Daedalus, artists like Aeschylus and Sophocles who were acknowledged as professional shapers of the old mythic stuffs, innovations doubtless became commoner, as well as did a certain specializing of effect and a consequent narrowing of audience appeal. That is, if the myth itself is genuinely collective, speaking of and for an entire people, a work of art as the deliberate contrivance of an artist, however solidly based it be in mythology, will be also individualized. It will express, if we may put it so, not only the dreams of man but also the dreams of *a* man.[25]

The myth of Oedipus may now be summarized:

To Laius, King of Thebes, it was prophesied that he should be killed by his son, yet despite his vows of chastity he was lured to the marriage bed by Jocasta, to whom was born Oedipus. Lest the child grow to fulfill the promise, he was handed to shepherds with instructions to pierce the infant's feet and leave him exposed to

[25] Nietzsche thought of Greek tragedy as a synthesis of two moments, the Dionysian and the Apollonian, where Dionysus represents the dark, seething, "drunken" ecstatic forces, and Apollo represents the pictorial, formed, controlled dream forces. See his "The Birth of Tragedy from the Spirit of Music."

the hillside to die. The shepherds took pity on the child and reared him, and later he was adopted by the childless King and Queen of Corinth, whom he regarded as his parents. When a soothsayer told the Oedipus grown to manhood that he was fated not only to kill his father but to marry his mother, he fled, as he thought, his horrible fate, only to have an altercation at a crossroads with Laius, a stranger to him, and to leave him dead; whence he journeyed to Thebes, which city he found under the dominating curse of the Sphinx, a cruel lion-woman. The Sphinx could be conquered only by him who should solve her riddle: What is it that goes on four legs in the morning, on two at noon, and on three in the evening? Oedipus correctly answered, "The human being," for in infancy he crawls, in maturity he walks, and in old age he employs a cane. The curse was lifted and Oedipus was received as hero and married to the queen dowager, thus fulfilling the conditions of his own curse. Two sons and two daughters were born of this union before the city again fell under an evil spell. Tiresias, a blind seer, revealed to Oedipus that the city had to be rid of its pollution, whereupon the King pronounced a curse upon the cause of this pollution, which gradually he came to realize was himself. Jocasta hanged herself and Oedipus in his agony stabbed out his eyes with his wife-mother's brooch. In due time he was banished by his successor, Creon, brother of Jocasta, and left the city to wander over the world, guided by his daughter Antigone. When Creon learned that that nation would be honored and profited by the gods which finally interred the remains of the expiated hero Oedipus, he sent an armed force to capture and return him, but this force was defeated in battle by Theseus and his Athenians, who claimed Oedipus for their own. In death Oedipus was thus again exalted into an almost divine status, from which he blessed the new land and helped establish its glory and its might.

Something like this represents the story with which Sophocles *began;* it was his heritage from mythology. What he ended with cannot, of course, be displayed here—the plays *Oedipus the King* and *Oedipus at Colonus*—but something may be briefly suggested about the interweaving of the universal elements with the more individualized.[26] As has already been seen, a work of art—and now we will say a myth, too—has more to it than meets the eye

[26] Interpreting Oedipus is a hazardous and polemical task. What follows is *one* interpretation, not entirely in accord with others.

and ear: it has a certain latent content that is both revealed and concealed by the symbols. What is the story of Oedipus in addition to being "a good tale"? Three themes may be found implicit in it: the theme of parents and child, the theme of the achievement of a national glory, and the theme of the emergence of the artist. The first is the pure mythic content, the second is the poet speaking through mythic materials for his own people, and the third is the more personal expression of Sophocles.

(1) Every male child, Freud has famously taught, is jealous of its father and desirous of its mother. If, as sometimes happens, the child does not outgrow these attitudes toward the parents, it becomes sick, develops a "complex"—the Oedipus complex, for Freud sees this myth and Sophocles' *Oedipus the King* as symbolic of this universal human problem. Let us, however, state the theme rather more broadly. Starting with Laius' fear of having a child who will replace him (the prophecy that the child will kill him) and Jocasta's urgent need for a child (her seducing of her husband), we go on to the child's feeling of early alienation from his parents (Oedipus' guardian-shepherds and foster parents). Then there grows the jealousy-desire with which Freud has made us familiar. After struggle and guilt and many other pains, the child rids himself of his parents, becoming independent of them (Laius' murder and Jocasta's suicide). Then in maturity he begins to feel the encroachment of his own time of superfluity, is alienated from his sons, who gradually replace him in high status, and in his extreme old age becomes a ward of his own daughter (his banishment from Thebes, the rule by Creon and later by one of Oedipus' sons, and his wanderings guided by Antigone).

(2) The second theme is political. Sophocles is writing for an audience that is riding high on the winged steed of mighty Athens. Here is a people yearly more conscious of their separate identity and needing help in understanding what they are thus conscious of. So Sophocles gives them a play, *Oedipus at Colonus*, that depicts the origin of Athens. The background is furnished by the state of Thebes, alternating between patriarchy and matriarchy, sick at the core, torn by internal internecine strife, until finally it falls. On its ashes arises the new, vigorous, masculine Athens with a farsighted, just, decisive, and humanitarian ruler (Theseus),

an enlightened citizenry (the chorus of Elders of Colonus). It is
a city—and this is perhaps most important of all—that is ruled
not by the caprice of the ruler, but *by law*, with due reverence
paid the gods, yet preserving a high degree of autonomy for the
people.

(3) The third theme has two parts: one of them as universal as
the parent-child theme with which it is closely bound up; one of
them more particularized. This theme might be called "the achievement of personal autonomy." It is partly a matter of knowledge.
One senses some things about himself which he fears and does
not understand (the prophecy in Corinth). In early manhood he
scores an intellectual victory, rising in understanding above his
parents (solving of the Sphinx's riddle). But there is a deeper kind
of wisdom yet to be found, a wisdom that consists in turning one's
perception from the outer world to the inner world (Tiresias, the
blind *seer*, teaches him some of the truth about himself; Oedipus
blinds himself, and starts anew on the journey of life).[27] In the
end he attains that kind of knowledge of himself which is at the
same time knowledge of the ways of gods and men (the beatifica-
tion of Oedipus at Colonus). Now, the particularized aspect of
this theme shows Oedipus as a personification of the artist—
Sophocles himself; still, even we may find ourselves personified
here too. The artist has to emerge from anonymity by distinguishing himself as hero, as spokesman for the people (solving
the riddle and being acclaimed). But even as he gains distinctive
independence—say, the emergence of the tragic playwright and
the individualized actor from the more ancient chorus—the independence that is the absolute requisite of artistic achievement, he
remains subject to the whims of his audience. They may reject
him even after he has scored successes (renewal of curse upon
Thebes, Oedipus' disgrace and banishment). But as he deepens
his insight and fares abroad, he may yet come to be acclaimed as
a prophet and a spokesman for the people and the gods (again,
Oedipus' glorious acknowledgement—amounting almost to apoth-
eosizing—at the end of his life).

And throughout the play on all levels is the alternation of two

[27] Compare the Norse myth in which Odin, father of the gods, gives one of his
eyes in return for winning insight into the future.

symbols: walking the road and the succession of lightness and·
darkness. Oedipus (the swollen-footed one) walks the road of
life painfully but sometimes gloriously. Oedipus, who would be
a seer, must go from light into darkness in order gradually to
attain the light of highest knowledge.

From the mythic dream of his people, then, Sophocles, himself
a dreamer, has fashioned a great work of art which through
phantasy guides us as well to the better understanding that is our
soul's best health.

And so with all artists. Whatever the medium in which they
work out their dream-myth, they effect a return to reality in
that they work a change upon the actual world, a world that we
inherit. As Santayana has said, "An artist is a dreamer consenting
to dream of the actual world; he is a highly suggestible mind
hypnotized by reality."[28]

[28] *Reason in Art* (New York: Scribner, 1906), p. 39.

• *Chapter 6*

EXPRESSION

 • *One* intelligent answer to the question "What is the creative act?" is: "It is an expression." One intelligent answer to the question "What is a work of art?" is: "It is an expression." The word "expression" sometimes refers to the act, the process; sometimes to the product, the *thing* which issues from the expressive act. Both uses are useful, but it may be wondered whether perhaps *all acts* and *all things* are not expressions. Somebody frowns and we note this expression of displeasure. Somebody raises his hand and we respond to his expression of friendship. We say of an acquaintance, "What an expressive face she has!" or of her new hat, "It seems somehow to express her personality." We may find a way of walking or sitting or standing, a way of arranging objects on a table, or items in a conversation, a way of being cautious or coy or witty—we may find any way of doing anything, expressive. Nor is it too much to say that objects and events of nature may be found expressive, or at least—if this is different—be regarded as expressive: the lowering cloud glowers, the daffodils dance, the jagged peak juts up. And many men have thought with the poet Hopkins,

> *The world is charged with the grandeur of God.*

The whole world, everything, would then be expressive.
  Yet if this is so, then nothing helpful is said about a work of

art when it is said that it is expressive unless there can be discovered some special way in which art expresses or at least some special power for expression that it has. Let it be asked first what is meant by "expression" in general, and then whether there is a peculiar, artistic expression.

EXPRESSION AND SYMBOL

Perhaps the best synonym for "expression" in the sense of a product is "symbol," and for "expression" in the sense of a process, "symbolizing." If a facial gesture is expressive it is symbolic. If a certain decision may be said to express our friend's character, we could also say that his decision is a sign of or that it symbolizes his character. If it is appropriate to say that a storm expresses divine disapproval, it is equally appropriate to say that the storm is a symbol of divine disapproval. If I express myself in word or deed, that word or deed is a symbol of me. The value of providing this synonym is that the word "symbol" probably better calls to mind the relationship between *what* is symbolized and to *whom* it is symbolic. But it will be still better to make a four-way distinction: there is the symbol itself, the one who symbolizes by means of it, the one who receives and interprets the symbol, and that of which it is a symbol. Each of these deserves a brief expansion.

(1) There is no object under the sun which cannot be a symbol —indeed the sun itself is one of the most ancient and most powerful of symbols, standing for power, masculinity, the source of knowledge and life, and so on. Words and their combinations are the commonest and most obvious kinds of symbols, but gestures, smiles, grimaces, lights, flags, bells, and whistles are equally familiar. The word "sign" is often used today in a broader meaning than the word "symbol," a sign being, roughly, anything that "stands for" something else or anything that serves as a substitute stimulus for something else. In this usage, then, a symbol will be a certain kind of sign, namely that which is produced by some sentient being. Not all signs are so produced. For instance, there is the clear sunset as a sign of fair weather or the smoke which is a sign of a forest fire. Such signs as these are found and interpreted without

having been made in order to signify. This distinction between symbolic and nonsymbolic signs is not perfectly precise because it is not always possible to decide whether a given sign was intentionally produced, but for purposes now at hand, further precision in this matter is not needed.[1]

Some artists employ verbal symbols; some, tonal symbols; some, the symbols of gesture and bodily movement; some, symbols of stone or bronze, or of pigment on canvas. The equestrian statue, the cathedral, the ballet, the landscape, the rondo—all will be symbols just as the poem, more obviously, is a symbol.

(2) Anyone who speaks or writes words, rings bells, flashes lights, sends up distress flares, blazes trails, or flashes a smile at a pretty girl—anyone who does these or any of a thousand other activities is a symbolizer. He is employing some *medium*, some sensory intermediary in order to send a message or to call out a response in someone or to record or memorialize some feeling or idea. The creative artist is a symbol-producer.

(3) That person is a receiver and interpreter of symbols who finds a message in a bottle, picks up an SOS on his crystal set, studies a Post Office portrait, reads his newspaper, jumps when a school bell rings, steps on the accelerator when the light flashes green—and so on. Not infrequently he will ask about the symbol, "What does it mean?" or about the producer of the symbol, "What does he mean?" Sometimes he will know, sometimes he will know in part or at least have a plausible hypothesis, sometimes he will sense the meaning but not in such a way as to be able to tell in precise words what it is that he senses. And sometimes he will be left puzzled. The number of gradations between a complete grasp of a meaning and complete bewilderment is great. Perhaps no less great is the number of ways in which a symbol *can* mean and therefore in which "understanding" of a symbol is possible. The art-appreciator is a symbol-receiver and interpreter.

(4) What may be symbolized? What are symbols about? It does not help to say they are or can be about anything and everything, except as this blanket claim confutes the supposition that

[1] For a fuller treatment of this subject, see Robert T. Harris and James L. Jarrett, *Language and Informal Logic* (New York: Longmans, Green, 1956), chap. ii.

only tangible objects—chairs and seas and cabbages, etc.—can be legitimately meant by symbols. Ideas and feelings and attitudes and events and institutions and qualities and classes and relations as well as *things* may in their different ways constitute the meanings of symbols. The word "sun" and an orange disk in a child's drawing both symbolize the sun, but they may symbolize much else too about the producer's state of mind. "Love" means something different in the mouths of Don Juan, a puppy lover, a mother, and a nun "breathless with adoration." "Justice" and "freedom" may seem to some tough-minded persons such vague abstractions as to be virtually meaningless, but to others they are among the noblest of words in symbolizing the noblest of human relationships. And once again, as dreams and myths are symbolic of matters that seem to require these indirect outlets, so art at its deepest symbolizes that which without the artist would go unremarked, to our loss.

It is at this point in discussing what it is that symbols symbolize that a significant difference between the words "express" and "symbolize" emerges. It would be inaccurate and misleading to say of a Crucifixion painting that it *expresses* Jesus or Calvary or a cross or even Jesus crucified, though it certainly *symbolizes* these. There can be no expression of objects and events in themselves but only of someone's particular feeling or—to try to find a word more general—someone's psychic disposition, perhaps about and toward this object and that event. To say this another way: what is expressed is always someone's *reaction*, say to the Crucifixion.

Although common usage permits us to say, "He expressed an interest which he didn't really feel" or "He expressed another man's point of view, but not his own," we will find it useful to exclude these meanings of "express," reserving the word for the narrower meaning of "manifesting one's own psychic disposition." There is no doubt that I can *say* I hate war even if I do not, but —as the term is used here—I can *express* my hatred of war only if I feel it. There is no doubt either that I can report someone else's expression as in saying, "His grimace reveals his contempt," but this report will not be an expression of mine except insofar as I in turn reveal some reaction to what I have observed. What Jung has said about the psychologist applies equally well to the artist:

> *One person will stress the forms into which this material can be worked, and will therefore believe that he has created what he finds within himself. Another will lay most weight upon the fact that he plays the part of an observer; he will be conscious of his receptive attitude, and insist that his subjective material presents itself to him. The truth lies between the two. True expression consists in giving form to what is observed.*[2]

In these restrictions of meaning, we have already begun to move from the broadest meanings of "expression" to the somewhat narrower "artistic expression." Another step in this direction is taken when we say that for an expression fully to qualify as artistic it must be embodied in such a way as to be repeatable; it must be externalized in some reasonably durable form. This stricture is comparable to the usual insistence upon "public verifiability" in the case of scientific knowledge: it would be dubious wisdom to deny the possibility of fleeting intuitions, or ineffable glimpses, but there is no good reason for calling these cases of knowledge unless they are successfully preserved in symbols. So too, there may be idle discoveries of "lost chords" of incomparable beauty, but until these chords can be found again and notated, there will be no purpose served in speaking of artistic expression. The spontaneous snort of laughter may be effectively expressive of a person's feeling state, but in lacking a more enduring embodiment is not yet artistically expressive.

May it not be correct to locate the kind of expression relevant to art between these two extremes: the spontaneous, automatic, and fleeting reaction, such as a heartfelt sigh or a cheer; and the deliberate, contrived evocation of a response from some other person, such as a faked sigh or cheer? These extremes, indeed, suggest ways in which works of art often go wrong—but this must wait for development at a later stage. For now let it be said only that the work of art at its best seems to be effective in evoking

[2] *Modern Man in Search of a Soul* (New York: Harcourt, Brace, 1933), p. 116.

a strong and deep response from others precisely *because* it is a strong, deep, and sincere expression of the artist's own self.[3]

In saying this, there is no intention of favoring so-called "subjective" art over "objective" art. In order to be expressive it is not required of a work of art that it be in some obvious way autobiographical or personal. It need not, for instance, be a lyrical love poem in which the poet himself is the lover. No, it may be as nonpersonal ("impersonal" would scarcely be the word) as *Oedipus the King* or *Macbeth* or Chartres Cathedral or a Scarlatti sonatina or a Chinese painting,[4] and yet be marvelously expressive, not in symbolizing certain events in the life of the creator, but in bringing to a formed utterance something greatly felt.

It has come out in previous discussions of the creative process that for the creative artist there is a certain nagging compulsion about his work. He says to advice-seekers, "Do not be an artist unless you have to!" or "You don't choose art; art chooses you!" or again "One doesn't make art-works just for fun but out of necessity, an inner necessity." We may now call this the necessity to express.

It would be a mistake to suggest that this necessity is known only to a Schumann or a Tintoretto or a Rodin. It is known, in some measure, to everyone. Who has not felt the absolute requirement to tell or write about a momentous event? Perhaps it is to the first person who comes along, the mailman or a trolley passenger, that one unburdens himself. Perhaps it is to one person only—no one else will do. Perhaps it is only to one's diary. But in any case this internal pressure to *tell* is surely universal. "Art begins," says Tolstoy, "when one person, with the object of joining another or others to himself in one and the same feeling,

---

[3] "One suspects that most of the finest works of art have been produced in a sort of middle state between pure expression and a desire to share experiences with others. Pure expression for expression's sake may lead to technical carelessness and a vehicle that does not precisely control its responses. Too much concern for the sharing with others can lead to the demoralizing temptations of popularity. The best result probably comes when the artist becomes absorbed in the expression for its own sake but feels that it is so fine and significant that he wants everybody else to share it with him." From Stephen Pepper, *The Work of Art* (Bloomington: Indiana University Press, 1955), p. 117.

[4] Jacques Maritain cites oriental art as contrasting with subjective, individualistic, expressive art. See *Creative Intuition in Art and Poetry* (New York: Meridian, 1955), pp. 11-17.

expresses that feeling by certain external indications. To take the simplest example: a boy, having experienced, let us say, fear on encountering a wolf, relates that encounter. . . ."[5]

Children have a very common and usually effective way of expressing the exciting things which happen to them: they *play* them, organizing games—perhaps with one person taking all the parts—in which there is a reliving of the encounter with the wolf, or the first day at school, whatever the big event was. They also draw with crayons and watercolors, mold clay, sing little songs and do dances; and the sharp observer will often be able to detect that the content of these activities is also that big event, though perhaps its presence will be less evident than in the case of the direct relating of what happened. As children grow up they learn to inhibit—even perhaps to become ashamed of—these natural outlets for their excitement, but they never lose the need for such expression, and their needs are satisfied, sometimes in the direct kinds of relating, sometimes in finding someone or something else which expresses for them.

EXPRESSION AS FORMED

Now if expressive needs are universal, we must ask again what is so special about the artist-as-expresser. The answer at its simplest is this: the artist is one who has developed ways of expressing *in* some such medium as musical tones or paints or stone or bodily movement,[6] and of expressing in such a way that the medium becomes under his shaping *an expression*—an expression *of* and *for* himself and *for* someone else, an expression about which he can say, "Yes, that's it!" and about which another person may say, "Yes, it does it for me, too."

Not always does the artist have complete control over his creation; indeed, it had better be said that never does he have

---

[5] *What is Art?* (New York: E. R. Dumont, 1899), p. 386.

[6] John Dewey has written, in *Art as Experience:* "Etymologically, an act of expression is a squeezing out, a pressing forth. Juice is expressed when grapes are crushed in the wine press. . . . It takes the wine press as well as grapes to ex-press juice, and it takes environing and resisting objects as well as internal emotion and impulsion to constitute an *expression* of emotion." (New York: Minton, Balch, 1934), p. 64.

complete control, for the very medium in which he is working makes its own demands and sets certain limitations, to say nothing of the human restrictions of the artist's experience and knowledge and technique. But not infrequently there will be practical circumstances too that dictate in part what the creator must do. The portrait painter and the architect cannot very well neglect the special desires of their patrons. A poet laureate may have the official duty of composing an ode for a national holiday or a birthday salute to the queen. A composer may be commissioned to write a work for harpsichord and viola da gamba—those two instruments and no substitutes. The sculptor may receive an order for an appropriate statue to grace Robert E. Lee Park. But it is one of the wonders of the history of art how often such limitations have *not* stifled the free creative powers of the greatest geniuses. John Donne wrote for money a long elegy on the death of a young and rich maiden whom he had not known, filled it full of the most extravagant praise, as was expected by the bereaved father, and yet succeeded in making it one of the finest achievements of the seventeenth century. Caravaggio, when his painting of Saint Matthew writing the first Gospel was rejected by authorities indignant at his original but not conventionally respectful conception, turned around and gave his patrons what they wanted, yet not a shoddy but a fine work. Bach, in common with the practice of musicians of the day, would accept a fugue subject from a noble patron and then work up the mediocre raw material into breathtaking counterpoint. Examples could be multiplied beyond necessity; the point is simply that whether a commissioned, externally-motivated work is good or bad depends as does the purest work upon whether the creator has something to express and can succeed in expressing it.

As we have repeatedly said in this book, there is no absolute chasm between artist and nonartist. We are all, like poet and novelist, artists in words, in that all of us can express our feelings and ideas verbally. All of us can tell a story. And probably all of us at times, perhaps especially at times of crisis, fall into highly rhythmic modes of utterance. There is good reason to believe that all of us could, if we liked and were willing to take some pains, be also musicians and painters and sculptors, and so on. In an interesting book,[7] Henry Schaefer-Simmern has recorded the results of his experiments in teaching refugees, businessmen, delinquents, and mental defectives to paint. He has proved that almost no matter how strange be a person's background, how set he be in his ways, how antisocial or how unintelligent, he can nevertheless learn to paint and model quite competently. This of course does not say that just anybody can become a Michelangelo; even if everybody became a "Sunday painter" there would still be only a comparatively few really fine painters. But it does show that these artistic modes of expression are not by nature ordained for only those who become professional, certified, union-card Artists.

When artists, big and little, are accused of failing to communicate, failing, that is, to make their works intelligible and meaningful to others, they are in the habit of replying that such a failure is a matter of indifference to them, for communication had been no part of their intention. They were not creating for other people but for themselves, not trying to get across to someone else but only trying to clarify some of their own feelings and ideas.[8] Not communication but expression is the aim of the artist, they often say, perhaps not without a touch of defensive disdain. Is such a reply to be discounted as mere self-consolation and rationalization? In the individual case it may be little more than that, but still there is a very large element of truth in the defense.

Wordsworth has said that the poet—and we may include other kinds of artists too—"is chiefly distinguished from other men by a greater promptness to think and feel without immediate external excitement, and a great power in expressing such thoughts and feelings as are produced in him in that manner." What are those thoughts and feelings? Not a peculiar poetic sort, answers Wordsworth:

[7] *The Unfolding of Artistic Activity* (Berkeley and Los Angeles: University of California Press, 1948).

[8] Thus Montaigne: "And if no one reads me, have I wasted my time, entertaining myself for so many idles hours with such useful and agreeable thoughts? In modeling this figure upon myself, I have had to fashion and arrange myself so often to bring myself out, that the model has to some extent grown firm and taken shape of itself. Painting myself for others, I have painted my inward self with colors clearer than my original ones." From "Of Giving the Lie," in *Selected Essays*, trans. Donald Frame (New York: Van Nostrand, 1943), p. 171.

But these passions and thoughts and feelings are the general pas-
sions and thoughts and feelings of men. And with what are they
connected? Undoubtedly with our moral sentiments and animal
sensations, and with the causes which excite these; with the opera-
tions of the elements, and the appearances of the visible universe;
with storm and sunshine, with the revolutions of the seasons, with
cold and heat, with loss of friends and kindred, with injuries and
resentments, gratitude and hope, with fear and sorrow. These, and
the like, are the sensations and objects which the Poet describes, as
they are the sensations of other men, and objects which interest
them.[9]

It will be instructive to follow a little further Wordsworth's reflections on poetry, which he famously described as "the spontaneous overflow of powerful feelings." He continued:

It takes its origin from emotion recollected in tranquillity: the
emotion is contemplated till, by a species of reaction, the tranquil-
lity gradually disappears, and an emotion, kindred to that which
was before the subject of contemplation, is gradually produced,
and does itself actually exist in the mind. In this mood successful
composition generally begins, and in a mood similar to this it is
carried on. . . .

Several points here may be underlined: the element of recollection,
the contemplation that proceeds from tranquillity to an excitement
of the same sort as was being recollected, and the powerful feelings
that spontaneously overflow into art.

Holding on to these points, let us set down some other statements by artists. Here is one by the painter Rouault: "In truth,
I have painted by opening my eyes day and night on the perceptible world, and also by closing them from time to time that
I might better see the vision blossom and submit itself to orderly
arrangement."[10]

Next we hear from a composer, Arnold Schoenberg:

Those who compose because they want to please others, and have
the audience in mind, are not real artists. They are not the kind of
men who are pressed to say something whether or not there exists

[9] Preface to *Lyrical Ballads* (1800).
[10] Quoted by Julian Levi, in "Before Paris and After," *Magazine of Art,* December 1940. Reprinted in Ghiselin, *The Creative Process* (New York: Mentor,
1952), p. 56.

one person who likes it, even if they themselves dislike it. They are not creators who must open the valves in order to relieve the interior pressure of a creation ready to be born. They are merely more or less skilful entertainers who would renounce composing if they could not find listeners.[11]

Picasso has said this:

A picture is not thought out and settled beforehand. While it is being done, it changes as one's thoughts change. . . . When I have found something to express, I have done it without thinking of the past or of the future. If the subjects I have wanted to express have suggested different forms of expression, I have never hesitated to adopt them. Different motives inevitably require different methods of expression. This does not imply either evolution or progress, but an adaptation of the idea one wants to express and the means to express that idea. . . .[12]

And for still another notion, we go to Yeats:

We make out of the quarrel with others, rhetoric, but of the quarrel with ourselves, poetry. Unlike the rhetoricians, who get a confident voice from remembering the crowd they have won or may win, we sing amid our uncertainty. . . . He only can create the greatest imaginable beauty who has endured all imaginable pangs, for only when we have seen and foreseen what we dread shall we be rewarded by that dazzling unforeseen wing-footed wanderer.[13]

From Rouault we derive the important point that expression is not just a matter of outward perception, but even more a matter of inward forming and arrangement. From Schoenberg we learn of the interior pressure on the creator: he expresses when he is "pressed to say something." Picasso tells us especially of the interplay between the *what* and the *how*, or—as it has been traditionally put—between content and form: the means of expression must be adapted to the peculiar something to be expressed. Yeats emphasizes in his beautiful words the importance for the creator of opening oneself to experience and of struggling with

[11] "The Musician," in *Works of the Mind*, ed. Mortimer J. Adler *et al.* (Chicago: University of Chicago Press, 1947), p. 69.
[12] Quoted in Alfred Barr, Jr., *Picasso: Fifty Years of His Art* (New York: Museum of Modern Art, 1946), p. 247.
[13] *Anima Hominis*, quoted in *Writers on Writing*, ed. Walter Allen (London: Phoenix House, 1948), p. 45.

this experience so as to convince and satisfy oneself rather than others. Perhaps now we can construct an account of the artist's expressive act that will take in these several important points.

The artist may be thought of, then, as one whose expressive needs are unusually great. If everybody needs to express himself, being somewhat uneasy about bottling things up inside himself, the artist *is* an artist largely because this uneasiness in him amounts to a passion. Virtually everything he sees and hears, everything he does, everyone he meets, every place he visits, is raw material for his art. To an extraordinary degree he is unsatisfied with mere experience, merely as *had*, but must forever be *using* his experience, shaping it, distorting it perhaps, connecting it up, seeing new significance in it, trying to understand it; as Nietzsche said, "exploiting it." But, and this is all-important, he goes about this process not by reflection and introspection primarily, but by *manipulating* some stuff or other, plastic stuff or tonal stuff or verbal stuff or still some other kind. Sometimes the artist will shape and reshape his particular medium and never satisfy himself that he has succeeded in making the medium "speak for him." He doesn't get the clarification and the understanding he seeks. He goes through the motions of expression but he doesn't get *the* expression. Other times he does succeed in bringing it off. The product of his expressive act satisfies him. It seems to him to be just that ordering of experience which he was after—though he didn't quite know *what* he was after until he had succeeded. Now, himself assuming the role of appreciator and contemplating his own product, he is pleased with it. Yet there are important ways in which he cannot wholly assume this role the way some other person can, for what the artist has before him is the memory of that pre-expressive state, of what it was he wanted to express before he had managed to express it.

WHAT EXPRESSION IS NOT

At this point it will be helpful to notice a few misleading ways of talking about this act of expression. One way is to speak of its "mirroring" the artist's experience. Another way is to speak of its "objectifying" or "externalizing" his experience. These are misexplanations precisely because they suggest that the artist's experience was already complete, formed, ordered, and understood *before* he began to express himself. They suggest that the expressive act is a simple matter of making public what was pre-existent in a private state, something like first saying to oneself the words of a sentence and then "expressing" them—that is, saying them out loud. But if one thing is clearer than another in this whole matter of artistic creation, it is that in the act of expression, the artist is fashioning new experience out of what may be called his experiential materials. When the work of art comes off, it is truly something that never was on sea or land, not even the internal sea of the artist's imagination. It is new, new even to the artist himself, a new vision, a new understanding.

One of the most influential interpreters of art in our time, the Italian philosopher Benedetto Croce, has made much this same point by identifying "intuition" with "expression." He makes light of those who claim that they are really artists, having real artistic insights and images and ideas, but lacking, somehow, the "technique" to give these internal works of art to the world. No, Croce says, if one has a genuine intuition or artistic grasp, the intuition *is* expressed. An intuition is not some vague, tenuous feeling or hunch, but is a realized, formed object. There is a great difference between having a notion of beautiful unheard tunes running through one's head and being a Mozart or Schubert who can truly compose even long musical works before a mark is made on a score sheet, or a piano key struck, for the great musician can make the marks when he needs to. To the person who says, "I know what I mean but I just can't say it," it is fair to answer "If you really knew, you would be able to say it." And it is no less fair to insist that genuine expression is the test, because it is part and parcel, of artistic creation.

Croce's is a fair reminder that *what* is to be expressed does not already exist, signed and sealed, ready to be delivered. It comes into being or at least comes into the *formed* being that its expresser requires in the very process of expression.[14] "Poetry," Wallace

[14] If anything, Croce exaggerates the "internality" of creation. Creators differ greatly in whether they carry forward their expression to an advanced point without any actual manipulation of their material in an overt sense, or whether they are experimentalists who do their devising and revising while they "dabble" in the very stuff of their art.

Stevens has said, "is of what does not exist without the words." And even the most realistic painting is of what does not exist without the paints, for however much the work of art may symbolize that pastoral scene or this rock-bound coast, it *expresses*—if it is truly a work of art—something its creator had to express, but something which not quite yet *was* as long as the painting itself was unfinished.

Not quite yet—but still something. There is an equal and opposite danger to that of exaggerating the degree to which *what* was to be expressed existed before it got expressed, and that is an underestimation of the *specific* quality of each expressive act. When a creator needs to express himself, this is not just a need in general, a kind of abstract hunger; no, he needs to express *this*, this very special something. What sort of something? A feeling? Well, yes, a feeling. And an attitude, a perception, a way of fitting together, a quality, an idea. If one asks, what feeling, what idea, and so forth, then again it must be answered that except in rather vague terms (a feeling of awe, a theme of revenge, the advance and retreat of the green sea, etc.) one can't *say* until the expression itself is made. Everyone has heard the story of the composer who when he had finished playing his new composition and was asked what it meant, turned around and played it again. It may be thought that he was unduly severe, but his reaction indicated his strong belief that what he had to express could not be adequately expressed in another way—for instance by words—than his art-work.

Now, it may seem strange to insist on the one hand that very little can be said about what is to be expressed in advance of the actual expression and on the other hand that this to-be-expressed is highly specific, yet is this fact not common to the experience of everybody? Who has not looked for a word to say something, been almost helpless to say what it is the unfound word means, strongly rejected proffered substitutes, and then suddenly greeted the *right* word with instant recognition and welcome? This familiar circumstance is closely related to artistic expression. The creating artist makes his choices and rejections (this line but not that, this chord but not that) according as each possibility appeals to him as faithful or not to the to-be-expressed. When he has achieved a satisfactory expression, he feels, "Yes, this is what I wanted to say," all the while knowing that he has brought something new into the world.

For all of this it is common for the artist to share the mystic's recognition that that which he is trying by means of his art to glimpse cannot finally be seen, that what he is trying to say is unsayable. Whitehead has put it that the philosopher and poet alike are trying to put in words what lies beyond words.[15] And Stephen Spender has written:

> *At the moment when art attains its highest attainment it reaches beyond its medium of words or paints or music, and the artist finds himself realizing that these instruments are inadequate to the spirit of what he is trying to say.*[16]

Yet for all its being foredoomed to failure—a failure of perfection—the artist's drive toward expression remains the most important of his characteristics. It is the need to "come to terms" with some aspect of his experience, the need to resolve into a work of art the quarrel with himself.

EVOCATION AND COMMUNICATION

Notice has already been taken of the artist's typical insistence that above all he is creating for himself, that if he succeeds in expressing himself, that *is* success in art, and the acclaim or neglect of the world matters little. Certain it is that some artists tend to lose interest in their creating once they are finished, having to call on some entirely different store of energy, as it were, to market their products. And it is certainly true that many an artist has been able to persist in his creative effort in spite of indifference or abuse from the public. Indeed, the biography of many a great artist suggests that a very high degree of faith in oneself, an indomitable confidence in the importance of one's own expressive urges, is an important component of success, however usual it be for artists also to have moments of despairing doubt.

Still, it would be plainly false to say that artists as a type are

[15] Whitehead has also said that ". . . expression is the one fundamental sacrament. It is the outward and visible sign of an inward and spiritual grace." *Religion in the Making* (New York: Macmillan, 1926), p. 131.
[16] "The Making of a Poem," *Partisan Review*, Summer 1946.

indifferent to wordly success or that they have no interest in reaching and pleasing other people. Artists sometimes pretend that they care nothing for the public, just as some of the public sometimes pretend that artists care for nothing else. Probably there are a few genuine artists near each pole: a few highly independent spirits and a few who have a positive craving for acclaim; but a study of the lives of the finest artists of all ages reveals that more typically they have been concerned with their public[17] at the same time that they have been to a high degree "inner-directed." But the word "public" here is misleading. It is probably more usual for artists to be genuinely concerned to reach some certain segment of the public, the ones they regard as discriminating, sensitive, intelligent, than to try to please everybody. It is not uncommon for an artist to be truly popular but still highly frustrated because he has not been praised by the critics he most respects.[18]

Whatever be the character of the artist's motivation, the interest of the artistic consumer or appreciator cannot but be in the communicative qualities of art. It is hard to be greatly interested in the fact that work of art Z has met the expressive needs of its creator, Mr. Q, unless it also does something for me. And if it does do something for me, it doesn't much matter (to me) whether the artist was aiming at such a result or not.

But what do we want art to do for us, its beholders? Please us? Yes, of course. But perhaps not just please us anyhow. Is there not art that pleases us without gaining our praise, for the reason that it fails to go beyond idle amusement? Perhaps the best answer to our question is that we want art to do for us something very like what its creators want it to do for them—that is, to be expressive of and for us.

Everyone, as we have seen, has expressive needs which he more or less satisfies by engaging in acts of expression, but all of us rely to some extent upon others to express for us what we cannot with entire satisfaction express for ourselves. It is unusual to put it so, but

[17] This is in disagreement with John Stuart Mill, when he says, "All poetry is of the nature of soliloquy. The peculiarity of poetry appears to us to lie in the poet's utter unconsciousness of a listener." *Dissertations and Discussions,* Vol. I, 71.

[18] See Ernst Kris, *Psychoanalytic Explorations in Art* (New York: International Universities Press, 1952), p. 60, on artists' needs for a public.

it is strictly the case that the professional artist is a provider of an important service to the community: he provides expression.[19]

In order for an artist's expression to serve not only for himself, but also for others, he must communicate. That is, he must somehow get across to someone else. His work must be understandable, intelligible; it must not merely baffle and confuse. Communication is not, of course, a simple yes or no matter, but varies both in spread and extent, where by "spread" is meant the number of people reached and by "extent" the degree to which a given work of art is understood by a given appreciator. It is sometimes thought that the over-all value of a work of art is a matter of its popularity, the spread of its appeal, but it should be quite apparent that its value to any given individual does not depend upon whether it communicates to other people but only on whether it communicates to him. This statement should perhaps be softened a bit: all of us do like to be able to talk with others about a shared art experience, so in fact it would be easy to lose one's enthusiasm for a work of art which, since no one else could understand it, would have to be enjoyed in pure solitariness. Nevertheless, generally speaking, each person in confronting an art-work is concerned to see whether it communicates to *him*, and if it does, whether it is valuable to him as an expression, for it is of course possible that though a particular work is perfectly intelligible to me, it is still expressively worthless to me. In our time there has been a great deal written about the "unintelligibility" or "meaninglessness" of modern art, especially poetry but hardly less music, painting, sculpture, architecture, dance, and prose fiction, the critics of modernism often manifesting an extreme annoyance at the art which has not communicated to them. Such criticism is likely to be well received by those in a similar plight, but of course to seem unintelligent and worthless to those who have had no such difficulty.

[19] "Art cannot be helpful through our artists' trying to help and specially concerning ourselves with the distresses of others, but in so far as we bear our own distresses more passionately, give, now and then, a perhaps clearer meaning to endurance, and develop for ourselves the means of expressing the suffering within us and its conquest more precisely and clearly than is possible to those who have to apply their powers to something else." Rainer Maria Rilke, *Duino Elegies*, ed. and trans. J. B. Leishman (London: Hogarth, 1939), Introduction.

More will be said in a different context about the appreciator's
job of interpretation and his "obligation" to bring the full resources
of his mind to the aesthetic experience, but for the present let us
raise a question about the artist's "obligation" to communicate.
Two contrasting failures of artistic communication may be examined. At one extreme may be put what R. G. Collingwood has
called "magic art," that is, art which has a palpable design on its
receiver, art which is calculated to have such and such an effect.
The perpetrators of such designs (propaganda art, sensationalism,
topical art made to cash in on a current news item, faddishness,
etc.) should perhaps be called "confectioners" rather than artists
proper. They conceive their job more in *evocative* than in expressive terms, their question being, "How can I call out this
particular response in the audience?" and not the true artist's
question, "How can I say what I have to say?" Evocative art
fails in communication because for there to be communication,
something must carry over from creator to appreciator. What
has been thought and felt and realized by the one comes through
the medium of the art expression to be thought and felt and realized
by the other. But the evoker's job is to make his audience experience *without* himself experiencing.[20]

The other kind of failure of communication may be artistically
more respectable. It springs from the artist's isolation of himself
from others, so that what he says may make sense for himself
without making sense for others, or for so few others as to keep
communication to a minimum spread. The story is told of the
poet Edith Sitwell that when questioned about the phrase in one
of her poems, "Emily-coloured hands"—what color *was* Emily
color?—the poet confessed that Emily had been a family maid,
with a highly distinctive complexion. Now in such a case—the
particular story may not be authentic, but the point remains—the
artist's means may well have been more expressive for herself and
perhaps for her brothers and a few old family friends than any
others available, but there has certainly been a sacrifice of com-

---

[20] Goethe: "I have never affected anything in my poetry. I have never uttered
anything I have not experienced, which has not urged me to production. I have
only composed love-songs when I have loved. How could I write songs of hatred
without hating!" *Conversations of Goethe with Eckermann* (London: Dent, 1930),
p. 361.

municative spread. It need not be maintained that this is immoral on the artist's part;[21] but only that there is in such instances a loss of shared value, perhaps a regrettable loss. Still, nothing is more common in the creation of art than that some value must be sacrificed. Every time a novelist uses a three-syllable word, he is limiting his audience to those who can handle such complications. Every time a composer introduces an exotic chord, he runs the risk of offending those whose expectations are more traditional. How many concessions he can make to his audience without seriously weakening the expressive force of his art for himself and perhaps for a comparatively small number of others is a question not to be settled by formula nor by exhortations to the artist either to "remember his obligations to his audience" or to "be faithful to and mindful of himself alone."

[21]This matter will be discussed further in Chapter 12.

• Chapter 7

AESTHETIC ATTITUDE

• *In the* three preceding chapters our attention has been chiefly, though of course not entirely, upon the creative role, upon the maker and the making of art objects. Now we will turn more particularly to the appreciative role, focussing our attention upon the beholder and the beholding of objects of art. We begin with the aesthetic attitude, a kind of attitude, that is, that will be shown to be indispensable to the full aesthetic experience.

A naive account of perception and reality might hold that when a human being turns his attention toward his environment he either perceives it as it is or makes mistakes in his perception, the reality itself being wholly objective and determined and definite. But consider a case. Our dramatis personae: four men. Our setting: a meadow. Enter first man. He speaks:

"Now that's interesting. I didn't expect to find manzanita bushes at this altitude. And look at that clover. There must be more rainfall than I had supposed. Either that, or the soil is less sandy than the last I examined." And the man reaches down to pick a small blue daisy which he presses in his notebook along with a brief notation. Exit.

Second man enters and says to himself:

"Say, that's pretty good pasturage. In fact about the best clover I've seen in these parts. That ought to take care of my cattle for a week anyway." And he makes a mental note of where the meadow is in relation to his herd, and leaves.

The third man is murmuring to himself as he comes in:

"Now what did that fellow say? I'd come to a big meadow split right down the middle by a small stream. And then if I'd follow the creek up, I'd come to Crystal Lake about a mile . . . Oh, this must be the meadow he meant. Well, here I go; it's a big one." On he continues, carrying his rod, creel, tackle box, lunch, and hip boots.

The fourth and final visitor strolls onto the scene most leisurely and in a rapt manner. He notices a gnarled piñon pine and stops for a moment to look at it. He glances at the clouds warmly scudding along in the June breeze. Then his eye falls on the meadow. He too soliloquizes:

"Say, that's nice! The way that stream bends right there—such a long, smooth curve. And the border of cream-barked trees over there to back up this mottled green texture." And he sits on a boulder to look for a while.

What is the reality which is the common object of these perceptions? We have called it, neutrally, a meadow. But how different it is for our four observers. To the botanist it was an herbarium, a group of specimens, some problems in cause and effect. To the rancher it was a place to employ, an object of use. To the fisherman it was a space to be traversed and a signpost. To the last visitor—call him a nature lover or perhaps a painter (though we are presently interested in him as observer and not as a maker) —the meadow was a thing of beauty. Shall we say that the four observers all had different objects of their perception or that there was a single object seen from four differing points of view? It matters little so long as it is noticed how much difference is made by the observer's *attitude* toward what is observed. No one of the men took exclusive charge of reality; none of the perceptions was unreal; certainly there is not just a single true or right way of regarding the meadow and three or more wrong ways. True and false, right and wrong, adequate and inadequate, correct and incorrect, real and illusory, appropriate and inappropriate—all such judgments relate to the circumstances of an experience and especially to the needs and interests of the experiencer at a given time.

Another thing worth noting about the four-scene playlet (somewhat wanting, it must be confessed, in dramatic complication) is that one person—not just one actor, but one integrated person—could easily be imagined taking all four parts. The scientist is not a scientist twenty-four hours a day; there are times when a scientific approach to experience is not feasible or appropriate or desirable. Not the most single-minded aesthete can constantly palpitate with his appreciation of beauty. The housewife may examine the sirloin tip twice, first with an eye to her family palate, and then again with an eye to her family budget. Should we say then that "it is *all* a matter of attitude"? No, but it—what we experience—is most certainly in an important part a matter of attitude.

A psychological dictionary defines "attitude" as "a more or less stable set or disposition of opinion, interest or purpose, involving expectancy of a certain kind of experience, and readiness with an appropriate response."[1] Put slightly otherwise, an attitude is a manner of approach to experience, the way you regard something and the way you prepare yourself to meet it. One way of distinguishing attitudes is by the polarity: good-bad, or favorable-unfavorable. It is a rough common-sense rule that if we sit down to a meal or a movie expecting to like it—that is, having a favorable attitude of anticipation—we are not likely to be disappointed. And if our attitude is initially sour we are also not likely to be disappointed; we'll probably get what we expect. But attitudes may be classified in many other ways, for instance by such other polarities as advancing-withdrawing or optimistic-pessimistic. Or they may be more specifically characterized as belligerent, suspicious, generous, analytic, worshipful, or humorous—to name a few. Take an attitude of humor. We are all sometimes surprised into a laugh when we least expect it, but most of the time, apparently, we laugh or smile when we have already set our faces in anticipation. When someone starts to tell us a joke we nearly always know it's a joke and prepare ourselves to appreciate its humor, but if something "funny" happens when we are unprepared, we may be embarrassed by conflicting emotions: we do not know what is the

[1] *A Dictionary of Psychology*, ed. James Drever (London: Penguin, 1952).

appropriate response. This is not to say that the attitude wholly determines the experience. A husband may sit down at the table with the best will in the world only to discover that his bride has salted the ham. We may be ready and willing with our laugh but find the joke falls flat. But the housewife and comedian soon learn that their chances for success are better if their clients are first prepared in an appropriate attitude.

Nowhere is attitude more important than in the appreciation of beauty. Yet what is an *aesthetic attitude?* Is it the attitude one takes toward a work of art? But here are some questions that may be asked about a work of art in different circumstances by different persons:

1. What does it weigh? (post office clerk)
2. How much will it sell for? (art dealer)
3. What does it reveal about the personality of its maker? (psychologist)
4. What can be learned from it of the place and time in which it was created? (historian)
5. How effective will it be in advancing our Cause? (propagandist)
6. What techniques did its artist employ? (art student)
7. What of interest to the art-devotee can be said about it? (critic)

Each of the questions tells us of a certain attitude toward the common work of art. Yet none of them can be called a genuine aesthetic attitude, not even the last two, though they perhaps come closer than the others.

Let us suppose an earnest, intelligent man who has made a great success in the business world but who suddenly comes to see himself as a man "without culture." This bothers him and he wants to improve himself.[2] So among other things he decides to go to a great museum and study its pictures and statues. But he feels a little uneasy about just setting off on his own, so he comes to us for advice, saying:

"Now tell me how I should go about looking at these things. There must be certain things to look for, a certain approach, an attitude. What is it? What's the aesthetic attitude I ought to adopt as I prepare to look at the masterpieces?"

It is an honest and important question that deserves an answer

[2] Someone, for instance, like the hero of Henry James' *The American.*

neither misleading nor trivial. But it is a very hard question, as hard as a question about the religious attitude or the scientific attitude. Still, it mustn't be dodged, and we might give a short answer such as this:

One takes an aesthetic attitude toward a work of art or some part of nature when he deliberately *opens himself to the qualities of the experience*. Three kinds of qualities are especially important. They may be called the *sensory* qualities, the *formal* qualities, and the *symbolic* qualities. Perhaps the simplest illustration of sensory quality is taken from eating or drinking. If one takes a bite or a sip with his whole attention devoted to savoring the taste, his attitude is, insofar, aesthetic. In the case of a painting, attention to the colors, in sculpture and architecture to textures, in music and poetry to the sound presently in one's ears; but also a pure regard for the blue of the sky, the odor of a gardenia, the feel of a piece of driftwood—all these exemplify openness to sensory quality. When sensory materials are considered in their spatial and temporal patterns, we have passed on to the second type of quality, the formal. Here our attention is upon arrangement, organization, design, form. As was noticed in an early chapter, the so-called "lower senses," touch, taste, and smell, do not so readily admit of arrangement into regular, identifiable, and interesting sequences and orders as do the materials of hearing and sight, but when we admire a chair, say, we usually are noticing not only the wood and fabric of which it is constructed, but also the lines of the chair, the way they intersect and bend and flow and in doing so make up a single whole. And even if we concentrate upon the depth of the rose's color and the delicate softness of its petals, we can scarcely fail to attend also to the shape of the petals and the relationships they have to each other, and in turn, to the stem and leaves. And in listening to music it is next to impossible, even for those without well-developed musical memories, to hear just one note or one chord at a time in isolation from what has gone before and what is anticipated. No, instead we group the tones or, if you prefer, *discover* the groupings of tones that are there; and we hear the music in rhythms and as returns of familiar sounds. We have been emphasizing the virtual inevitability of at least a minimal notice of form, but not everybody has his eye or ear out for the form, not everybody is prepared to concentrate upon form, to sensitize himself to its special qualities. It is part of a proper aesthetic attitude so to do.

What remains is so-called "symbolic qualities." We will leave it an open question whether *all* works symbolize—perhaps some are purely self-contained and "mean nothing but themselves," as the saying goes—but at least a great many do. The landscape painting is not just arrangements of colors on a canvas but is about something; so too the statue in the park and certainly stories and plays. Now the qualities that are symbolized may be the same sorts of qualities that a work of art presents directly and immediately, namely, sensory and formal qualities. For instance a writer cannot, normally, *show* colors and shapes but he can describe them, perhaps with sufficient vividness that we can see them "in the mind's eye." As we have noticed earlier, prose fiction particularly, but poetry too, depends heavily upon these secondary, imaged qualities of sense and form. There are also qualities other than the sensory and the formal which reach us through symbolization. For instance character qualities, the way somebody is: Rembrandt's Noble Slav with his peculiar worried dignity, or Milton's Satan with his all too human, impatient ambition. Again, there are symbolized emotions: the holy ecstasy of Bernini's St. Theresa, the cold defiance of Antigone addressing Creon, or the wistful disappointment in Emily Dickinson as she writes:

> *A shady friend for torrid days*
> *Is easier to find*
> *Than one of higher temperature*
> *For frigid hour of mind.*

A third sort of symbolized quality is the dramatic, where the emphasis is upon the relationship between person and person, as in *Tristan and Isolde;* between man and a supernatural agent, as in *Faust;* the relationship of a man to himself, as in the self-deprecations of Dostoevsky's *Notes from Underground;* or such a struggle between man and society as Ibsen liked to portray. Finally mention may be made—and this list makes no pretense to completeness —of the quality of symbolized ideas, ideas taken not as "plans for action" primarily but as thoughts to be entertained. As an example consider Yeats' tantalizing question about Leda after she had been raped by Zeus, who had assumed the form of a swan:

> *And did she put on his knowledge with his power*
> *Before the indifferent beak could let her drop?*

Now in all these cases there is representation of qualities which we are asked, quite as much as in the case of the sensory and the formal, to respond to. We are taking the aesthetic attitude when we prepare ourselves to have a full experience of these qualities *as* qualities.

NONAESTHETIC ATTITUDES

Another approach can be made to the nature of the aesthetic attitude by considering some of the alternative attitudes that must be avoided or inhibited or at the very least suppressed into a secondary position if a rich aesthetic experience is to be encouraged. One is the *practical* attitude, the attitude that concerns itself with usefulness, with doing and accomplishing and getting on. We recognize the boorishness of asking about something that is prized exclusively for its beauty—perhaps a rock found on the hillside or an engraving—"What's that good for?" It is far from true that everything beautiful is useless, but it is far from false that many things which are beautiful have no use external to their beauty. Immanuel Kant, who made much of the "disinterestedness" of our relationship with beauty, held that anything we prize for its usefulness must be regarded in terms of a purpose, but that this is not necessary to beauty; we do not even care whether the object represented by a painting or a poem exists. However much the exquisiteness and inevitability of a thing of beauty suggests "purposefulness" as against the merely accidental and haphazard, our satisfaction in it is genuinely disinterested and free. But there are some people who pride themselves on being of a practical bent, who out of ingrained habit examine objects in terms of their usefulness and money value. Such people may have particular difficulty in assuming an aesthetic attitude when such an attitude is appropriate and may have to practice inhibiting the attitude that seems more natural to them.

Another attitude sometimes necessary to inhibit is what might be called a *personal* attitude, that is, an approach to objects in terms of one's own life and one's own special personality. It may come as a surprise to some that such an inhibition should even be desirable, for works of art are of course often used as vehicles for conducting one's own daydreams and memories. This may be a very pleasant pastime indeed, and may even be for a given person at a given time, *more* pleasant than any aesthetic experience he could reasonably expect to get; nevertheless it is distinguishable from the aesthetic experience in being self-regarding rather than other-regarding. In the aesthetic experience we are attentive to the object, letting it have its way with us (though this is not to say that ours is a passive role) rather than letting us have our way with it. Schopenhauer found in this ability of works of art and other beautiful objects to take us out of ourselves their chief value. "When we say that a thing is *beautiful*, we thereby assert that it is an object of our aesthetic contemplation, and this . . . means that the sight of the thing makes us *objective*, that is to say, that in contemplating it we are no longer conscious of ourselves as individuals, but as pure will-less subjects of knowledge."[3] And in this escape from our will-driven singular selves, we attain, at least for the time being, a noble peace.

A third attitude that wars with the aesthetic is the *common-sense* attitude, by which is meant here a stubborn tendency to reject all representations that do not apparently accord with one's own everyday experience. Strange as it may seem, some persons cannot get comfortable in the theater for thinking that the play or the movie is not *real*. Others may draw the line only at fantasy, where the playwright takes us to heaven or hell or the gnome king's palace. Others balk at any deviation from "realistic" representation, resenting any liberties a painter or a sculptor might take with human beings or beasts or trees that make them at all eccentrically different from those he has encountered or is likely to encounter in his walks. But it is a requirement of the aesthetic attitude that one free his imagination, be willing to go along with the artist, at least part of the way, to see whether the artist really does make some gains that way that would not have been available to him on more com-

---

[3] *The World as Will and Idea*, trans. Haldane and Kemp, Bk. III, §41.

mon-sense ground. It is just as ridiculous to hold the artist to a strict conformity with "reality" as it would be to object to the rules of chess because "knights really can go in a straight line if they want to and besides they don't look like those wooden pieces."[4]

The dream-like, mythical, "as-if" character of art remains closed to the literalist. However marvelous the imagination of the creative artist, his art product requires for its re-emergence into living experience a liberal imagination in the beholder. The imagination appropriate to the appreciative attitude may be called both active and passive. It is passive in letting itself—even in requiring itself—to follow the lead of the art object instead of roaming at will. It is active in being probing, searching, vivid, alert: the mere everyday, common-sense recognition of objects and happenings must give way to an imagination that tries to match that of the art creator, an imagination that, in Coleridge's words, "dissolves, diffuses, dissipates, in order to recreate. . . . It is essentially vital, even as all objects (*as* objects) are essentially fixed and dead."[5]

Because there is abroad a general fear of imagination, not merely on account of its tolerance of heterodoxy but perhaps even more because of its reputed kinship with neurotic and psychotic phantasy, it is worth remarking that in fact a certain healthy sense of security appears to be necessary for the aesthetic employment of imagination. This point is sometimes made in psychoanalytic writings, as for instance:

> *The more secure the writer is in his own emotional stability, the more freedom he has to identify himself with and write about the persons who become his readers. Similarly, the less fearful the reader is in his contact with life, the more courageously he can "flow out" toward the writer and identify himself with him.*[6]

A fourth attitude that may and sometimes does interfere with aesthetic experience is the *analytic*. It is easily possible to become so taken up with asking and answering questions about how a work of art came about, what it's made up of, what special techniques

---

[4] It is tempting to say that it is just as ridiculous to hold the artist to a strict conformity with "reality" as it would be so to restrain the scientist.

[5] Samuel Taylor Coleridge, *Biographia Literaria*, chap. xiii.

[6] Beulah Kanter Ephron, "The Reader and the Writer," in *Explorations in Psychoanalysis*, ed. Robert Lindner and Clement Staff (New York: Julian Press, 1953), p. 117.

were employed in its making, or how it is being performed or exhibited that one loses sight of the work itself. Often, however
curious the fact may seem, it is those who are especially close to a
certain art who substitute an analytic for a truly aesthetic approach
and so stifle their own aesthetic reaction. It is natural that architecture students, for instance, should be interested in the technical
problems of building construction, and that theater people should
be hyperconscious of the problems of play production; therefore it
is not surprising that they sometimes are carried away by their
analysis—that is, carried right away from an aesthetic relation with
the art-work. However, making this point is risky, for it is easy to be
understood as saying that in our aesthetic commerce with objects of
beauty we ought to be uncurious, nonintellectual, and entirely
unanalytical. Though it sometimes happens that an object's beauty
will just whirl us away into a dream world and we will almost
forget to breathe in our rapture, surely such a state is far from usual
even in the most highly developed sensibility. More commonly we
keep our critical and analytic powers awake and functioning, our
minds and imaginations active, without neglecting the primacy of
appreciation and enjoyment.

AESTHETIC DISTANCE

Perhaps no more influential idea has been introduced into modern
aesthetics than that of "psychical distance," a concept first named
and described by the British psychologist Edward Bullough, in
1913. It will be fruitful to spend some time with this idea, even
though it means using a new plow on some ground that has been,
at least in part, already worked.

Whenever we have to do with any object or event, our relationship may be said to be more or less distanced. *Less* if the object or
event is very intimately bound up with our own personal interests,
more if it is not. Take the case of a newspaper headline reading
"Ten Killed in Plane Crash." Our interest caught, we read further
and discover that the plane crashed in the Himalayas and that all
the passengers were Nepalese. In all likelihood, we will read this
account with great objectivity and detachment, feeling no very
personal involvement with the accident. But let the accident turn

out to have happened near our home and the passenger list to include persons of our acquaintance, and instantly we are greatly involved. It comes, as we say, close to us. In the other case, it was a long way away, both in space and, metaphorically, in our concern.

Now in order to enjoy, aesthetically, a work of art we must have a certain optimum "distance" in our relationship to it; or more accurately the distance must be neither too great nor too small, though it may vary between the two limits. If we are "underdistanced" in our attitude, we will be unduly subjective or practical; if we are "overdistanced," we will be too cold and withdrawn. Either way, the art loses, or we lose the art. But let us look at some hypothetical cases. There is the classic example of the country bumpkin at his first stage play rushing up onto the stage to save the heroine from the clutches of the leering villain. He has mistaken the play for reality, failed to adopt an attitude of "as if."

Or suppose a gentleman tipping his hat to a lady, the lady being, however, a statue. Or a listener to a radio drama about a Martian invasion getting up and locking his door. But these are gross instances of underdistancing. For a more subtle case, consider one of Bullough's: a man who is jealous of his wife fails to enjoy a production of *Othello*, the play throughout bringing home to him his own "real-life" problem. But underdistancing is not always unpleasant: a young man seeing "Swan Lake" may be carried in memory back to the first time he had witnessed the ballet, in company with a charming girl; the dancers fade from view to be replaced by the welcome memories.

To avoid the aesthetic destructiveness of "underdistancing" we must be able to hold the art-work off at arm's length, as it were. We must be conscious of the fact that it *is* an art-work, an artifact,[7] that it does not make the same kinds of demands upon us that the objects and events in the nonaesthetic world make, that it belongs, however important it may be to us, to a world of imagination, that we are not called upon to do anything about it except contemplate it. We could enjoy more of our dreams if it were not for the fact that inside the dream we do not know we are dreaming.

---

[7] Or, if it is not an art-work but some other object toward which we seek an aesthetic attitude, we must somehow pull it or even wrench it out of its more ordinary context in order to contemplate it.

But in order to be found beautiful, an object must move us. A person totally ignorant of and inexperienced in music may be simply baffled by a Brahms symphony, so that it seems unimportant or meaningless to him. It may be that most of us would find great difficulty "getting into" a novel whose plot concerned the niceties of court politics in the China of the Ming dynasty, especially if the maneuvers were quite different from those we know closer to home. Many persons fail to react, except in indifference or a slight annoyance, to much abstract or nonobjective art; it seems to them, and leaves them, completely cold. "Mobiles" have only slowly made their way, for until people became somewhat accustomed to the idea of moving shapes suspended from the ceiling, they were inclined to regard these objects as affectations or as simply foolish. Again, modern readers often have difficulty enjoying some of the highly rationalistic, formal verse of the eighteenth century, so austerely argumentative does it seem. These are all cases of over-distancing.

It will have been already apparent that failures of proper distance, whether on the over or the under side, can be a fault either of the work of art itself or of the beholder; usually they are a function of both. It may be called part of the artist's job to help the beholder keep in mind that a work of art is a work of art, that is, a specially created and therefore "artificial" something. If, on the other hand, in his enthusiasm for "realism" he gives us too convincing an illusion of nonart reality, the art suffers precisely because it has not invoked in us the beholders the kind of attitude that is necessary for art to function aesthetically. Think of a playwright who has decided that it is stuffy to keep his actors up on a stage and that it will be a nice realistic touch to distribute them throughout the audience. Then when in the middle of the play some stranger sitting next to me starts to talk, I'm annoyed and confused—and hardly less so when I decide that he does belong to the play, to that different world, and not to the everyday world of the audience. Or think of a sculptor who decides to bring his statues down off pedestals, to make them perfectly life size, and to give them a life-like color. Or of a painter who makes a picture look like one of a series of windows, showing indeed the same scene you would see through an adjoining window. Or of a composer who decided the best music was that which he could capture on a tape recorder on a busy downtown corner or in the forest. But no, typically there are many helpful signs of artificiality in a work of art: the frame of the painting, the pedestal for the statue, the stage for the actors and dancers, the instruments of the orchestra which sound like themselves but not like nature, the distinctive conventions for capitalizing in poetry. These all issue an invitation to the beholder to take an aesthetic attitude toward the work, to prepare to enjoy it as art and not as something else.

The Spanish philosopher, Ortega y Gasset, has found and praised in modern art a tendency he has called "dehumanization." After saying that "the artistic object is artistic only in so far as it is not real," he goes ahead to say that doubtless most people depend upon the human interest elements in paintings and novels to make the art palatable, but the ideal is to overcome this human weakness:

> *Even though pure art may be impossible there doubtless can pre-vail a tendency toward a purification of art. Such a tendency would effect a progressive elimination of the human, all too human, elements predominant in romantic and naturalistic production. And in this process a point can be reached in which the human content has grown so thin that it is negligible. We then have an art which can be comprehended only by people possessed of the peculiar gift of artistic sensibility—an art for artists and not for the masses, for "quality" and not for hoi polloi.*
>
> *That is why modern art divides the public into two classes, those who understand it and those who do not understand it—that is to say, those who are artists and those who are not. The new art is an artistic art.*[8]

To many of us this seems to go too far, in making an aristocracy of true art lovers, but of course it is perfectly correct in saying that works of art are often liked for the "wrong" reasons—that is, for reasons that have little to do with a genuine aesthetic response—and that works of art are often resented because the resenters are unprepared to take an aesthetic attitude. As Bullough points out, it often happens that a subject matter that is perfectly aesthetic for an artist may be seriously underdistanced by his less sophisticated

[8] *The Dehumanization of Art* (Princeton: Princeton University Press, 1948), pp. 11-12.

audience. For instance, the statue of a nude may quite truly alarm and shock and appear obscene to persons unused to seeing the unclothed human body, a response that will be incredible to the sculptor himself.

But there are many more subtle clues to the "unreality" of a work of art than its frame or its being on a stage. Its selectivity and its form are especially important in this way. Some "naturalists" in drama and fiction have taken for their ideal the "slice of life" motto, but if art is ever a slice of life, it is a very carefully controlled slice. Our ordinary experience goes on and on, its separate incidents sliding over into each other, with many false starts and anticlimaxes and redundancies and irrelevancies and few clearly demarcated events. But contrast a good work of art, with its regular rhythms, its well arranged sequences, its balances, its interconnections, its impressive coherence. A tragedy, said Aristotle, has a beginning, a middle, and an end; but these are what real slices of life so seldom have. Now, this essential orderliness, this unification of art, is a constant, if often unconscious, reminder to us its beholders that it *is* art with which we are dealing, and that therefore a certain attitude on our part is appropriate. If the artist fails to impress us with the *artistic* qualities of his productions then he will fail to help us to attain and sustain the attitude that is indispensable to his art's success with us.

The artist has a special responsibility in this way if his subject matter is one that we, his audience, are likely to have strong feelings about already, one toward which we are especially sensitive. Thus topical art, touching upon political or economic affairs of our own time is notoriously difficult to handle with sufficient distance, and so is sex. And violence and death. A concrete example comes to mind: James Thurber's famous cartoon of two duelists, one of whom having just completely beheaded the other exclaims "Touché!" Now humor tends to be especially highly distanced, and here the cartoonist has achieved his distance by making the figures extremely un-lifelike. Indeed they are scarcely more than match figures: no blood, no pain; but only a stylized head and a stylized body with daylight showing between. The word "stylized" is suggestive of the fact that "style" itself as well as "stylization" is a distancing factor: the singleness of the style of a work of art contrasts with the multiplicity of styles and the lack of styles in non-aesthetic life.

In tragic and pathetic art we are enabled to look with satisfaction upon scenes of horror—Goya's display of an execution, for instance, or Othello's smothering of his wife—precisely because the artist has helped us keep in mind that this is not some actual scene that we have unluckily stumbled upon, but the imagined world of art, however much that world is based upon starker reality.

Sometimes we blame the artist for not *decreasing* somewhat the distance we feel between ourselves and his work. He has been too austere, too reserved, too esoteric, and we *feel* too little about what he has done. He has insufficiently tied it to our experience, to the life we live, to what we know. However much Schoenberg himself may have been moved by his string quartets, and however much we may feel initially sympathetic to musical innovation and to the need to escape from the confines of tonality, we may very well find the works cold and far away. Again some poetry or a novel like *Finnegans Wake* may impress us without soliciting in us an aesthetic appreciation. They may seem more like puzzles to be solved, complications to be unravelled, and allusions to be looked up than like works of art; and if so, they invite not an aesthetic but a severely analytic approach.

Yet if we are fair, we will not by any means always blame the artist for distance failures. Someone who has suffered great evil at the hands of the Nazis may be excused for not being able to maintain a certain aesthetic detachment toward a book about Germany under Hitler, whether the treatment be friendly or unfriendly. A person who is tone-deaf may not want to blame Mozart for failing to write music that is winning. Or one who personally knows and dislikes a certain sculptor may disqualify himself as a judge of his work, recognizing that his animus prevents an adequate distancing. We are not always able to decide what exactly causes a given failure of distance, but it is often worth trying to decide, for if the fault is our own, it may be something we can overcome or mitigate, such as ignorance.

Psychical distance is a highly variable factor, of course. A play that starts a political riot in Argentina may seem to Englishmen just a play. A symphony that struck its first audience, fifty years ago, as frigid, cacophonous music may be a warmly appealing favorite of ours. A symbol in a Chinese print that traditionally elicits a deep sorrow may for some reason be funny to us. An abstract dance that bores me may have you rapturous with delighted involvement. A movie that profoundly moves Mrs. Jones may just puzzle Mr. Jones. A work that I like today may tomorrow, because of something that has in the meantime happened or merely because of a change in mood, be unendurably painful.

The question may be raised as to whether there is an optimum distance between under- and overdistance. Bullough has answered this by his principle of the "antinomy of distance." He states it as a normative rule: "What is . . ., both in appreciation and production, most desirable is the *utmost decrease of Distance without its disappearance.*" And he says too: "The flowering periods of Art have . . . always borne the evidence of a narrow Distance." This position is directly contrary to the one taken by Ortega, who might easily be imagined to state the ideal as the "utmost *increase* of Distance without its disappearance." But both rules may be criticized as more the manifestations of personal preferences than anything else. Bullough apparently *likes* art that is warmly and personally expressive, whereas Ortega's taste is more austere. One way of putting it is that Bullough apparently inclines toward Romantic art, Ortega toward the Classic. This is only a very rough characterization, but in general we do think of the Romantic movement in all the arts as inclining toward the underdistance pole, and of the Classical movement as inclined in the opposite direction. But of course there are very great achievements in both Romanticism and Classicism—as well as in other "isms." A person of catholic taste may simply refuse to choose between, say, Haydn and Chopin, or Marvell and Keats, or Giotto and Tintoretto. He may greatly enjoy the very rigorously formed music of a Bach invention as well as the shifting moods of a Liszt rhapsody. He may upon occasion choose the slightly distanced love poetry of Shelley, but at another time, the cooler numbers of Ezra Pound. Nor is it at all necessary to reject Klee merely because you also like the sensuality of Renoir. No, there do seem to be upper and lower limits of distance for any one of us at any one time, but between these limits we may want to move freely back and forth, choosing now that which touches our own lives closely, now that to which we can make scarcely any personal, subjective reference.

In spite of the great importance of doing what we can to achieve distance in our relationships with art-works, this factor in itself does not guarantee a successful experience. To say it another way, distance is not the sole desideratum. We may find that a given object does engage us without losing its status as artifact, and still we may not appreciate it, for any one of a great number of possible reasons. But since we may not aesthetically appreciate it without distance, and since, as we have seen, failure to achieve distance may be our own fault, awareness of this concept is valuable.

SENTIMENTALISM AND DISTANCE

Bullough interestingly considers the case where art that is highly distanced in being "Idealistic"—that is, in dealing with "general conceptions like Patriotism, Friendship, Love, Hope, Life, Death" —may by its very abstractness tempt the beholder to read very personal meanings into the ideals and hence to underdistance the relationship. But Bullough does not seem to have recognized an opposite tendency that is perhaps more usual.

Here is a much-reprinted and apparently widely-liked poem, "Little Boy Blue," by Eugene Field:

> The little toy dog is covered with dust
>   But sturdy and staunch he stands;
> And the little toy soldier is red with rust
>   And his musket moulds in his hands.
> Time was when the little toy dog was new,
>   And the soldier was passing fair;
> And that was the time when our Little Boy Blue
>   Kissed them and put them there.
>
> "Now, don't you go till I come," he said,
>   "And don't you make any noise!"
> So, toddling off to his trundle-bed,
>   He dreamt of his pretty toys;
> And, as he was dreaming, an angel song
>   Awakened our Little Boy Blue—
> Oh! the years are many, the years are long,
>   But the little toy friends are true.

Ay, faithful to Little Boy Blue they stand,
  Each in the same old place,
Awaiting the touch of a little hand,
  The smile of a little face;
And they wonder, as waiting the long years through
  In the dust of that little chair,
What has become of our Little Boy Blue,
  Since he kissed them and put them there.

Now it is entirely possible that many persons feel a quite satis-factory distance in their experience with this poem, though prob-ably nearly everyone in our culture would feel it to incline toward the underdistance pole; for even without having actually known what it is like to suffer the death of a beloved child, something similar must have touched most adults and they are therefore likely to feel the appeal to their heartstrings and tear ducts. But many readers of the poem have noticed that, in common with certain paintings exhibiting the fine character of the old-fashioned family doctor and certain songs celebrating the beauty of Home, it is to them embarrassing. They are likely to call it "sentimental," by which they will mean that it is too flagrant an appeal to a strong emotional response. It parades its sentiment, has too patent a design on their tears. This is what is embarrassing. And being embarrassed they are very likely to become somewhat contemptuous of the work. They dismiss it, shrug it off, perhaps even make fun of it. But these are "cold" feelings. They signify overdistance. From their early inclination to underdistance they rush to the extreme opposite end of the scale.

But if artists sometimes play the sob sister, exploiting for public consumption an everyday occurrence, they are perhaps even more often remarkable for their ability to take some incident, perhaps right out of their own lives, which would seem to most persons fraught with the poisons of sentimentalism, and filter it through their art into a draught at once hearty and sweet that satisfies with-out cloying.

• *Chapter* 8

FEELING
and
EMOTION

• *A sampling* of modern aesthetics reveals the great importance that feeling and emotion are thought to have in art, beauty,
expression, appreciation, and aesthetic experience.

Gentile: *"In a work of art the feeling is everything."*
Ducasse: *"Any object is to be called beautiful when, or in so far
as, the feelings which one obtains in the aesthetic contemplation of it are pleasurable feelings."*
Prall: *"It is only as works of art give specification . . . to human feelings, emotions, desires, and satisfaction, embodied in the sensuous surface and felt upon it as being
its character and quality—only so do they share in the
nature of actual concrete works of art."*
Fry: *"In the case of works of art the whole end and purpose
is found in the exact quality of the emotional state."*
Croce: *"What gives unity and coherence to intuition is feeling.
Intuitions are truly such because they represent feeling,
and only thence can they arise. It is not a thought but
a feeling that gives to art the airy lightness of its symbolism."*

Bosanquet: "*The aesthetic attitude is that in which we have a feeling which is so embodied in an object that it will stand still to be looked at, and in principle, to be looked at by everybody . . . 'Feeling expressed for expression's sake.'*"

Tolstoy: "*To evoke in oneself a feeling one has experienced, and having evoked it in oneself, then, by means of movements, lines, colours, sounds, or forms expressed in words, so to transmit that feeling that others may experience the same feeling—this is the activity of art.*"[1]

Everyone can testify from his own experience that a successful act of aesthetic appreciation is emotional, is moving; no more negative pronouncement can be made about a work of art than: "It leaves me cold."

But suppose it doesn't leave one cold. How does it then leave one? Feeling? Doubtless, but what does this mean?

MEANINGS OF "FEELING"

At least three meanings of "feeling" seem to be relevant to aesthetics. There is first of all feeling as *tactile sensation*. Such pairs as rough-smooth, warm-cold, wet-dry come to mind. And more specifically, the roughness of sandstone or burlap or a file; the smoothness of cream or silk or a kitten's fur or unblemished skin or rubbed wood—and so on. These sensations are relevant to works of art mainly as images. Upon occasion, in spite of the vigilant museum guards, we may touch the marble statue, but chiefly we *see* its texture, as we see the long smoothness of the red robe in El Greco's portrait of Don Fernando de Guevara or as we feel the paralyzing cold in a Jack London story of Alaska. This kind of feeling, though important to the sensuous nature of art, is not the chief concern of the present chapter.

A second meaning of "feeling" is what psychologists often call *affect*. Here there are two poles of feeling: pleasure and pain, (or as some would rather say, pleasure and displeasure—since pain may be pleasurable), or positive affect and negative affect. This kind of

[1] From E. F. Carritt, *Philosophies of Beauty* (Oxford: Oxford University Press, 1931).

feeling is relevant to the aesthetic experience in the sense that, roughly speaking, we all want pleasure from art and when we find beauty we are reporting pleasure felt. This claim as it stands, however, may easily be misleading. Take for instance the tired businessman's cliché: "When I read a book [see a movie, etc.] I want something pleasurable, not a lot of agony and tragedy and morbidity and gloominess."[2] Here "pleasurable" is being used in a narrower way than in the judgment that everybody wants a pleasurable experience from art, for the latter statement is consistent with the fact that many people do deliberately seek out tragic art and other art that incorporates pain within itself. Because of this ambiguity there is something gained in avoiding the use of "pleasure" or "pleasurable" in describing the successful aesthetic experience, and using instead some such term as "gratifying" or "satisfying"; it perhaps grates less to speak of finding satisfaction in the portrayed death of Iphigenia than of finding pleasure therein.

It is useful here once again to employ the old distinction between aesthetic surface and aesthetic symbolization in noticing that in a successful aesthetic experience the satisfaction may derive not only from pleasantness or (if the word helps to suggest the narrower sense of pleasantness) the delightsomeness of aesthetic surface or symbolized object and event, but also from a degree of painfulness in either or both respects. It takes no penetration to understand how gay colors or lissome movements or mellifluous sounds on the one hand, or the portrayal of joy and happiness on the other can evoke aesthetic satisfaction in the beholder; it is not quite so easy to perceive how it is possible to be gratified by the "difficult beauty" of somber colors, jagged lines, and dissonance, or by the portrayal of pain, disease, waste, cruelty, and premature death. But as Aristotle never tired of saying, what is actual is possible. This is not the place to try to explain how it is possible, but only to record the fact that it is.

We come now to the third meaning of "feeling": feeling states or *emotions*. There is little important agreement among psychologists or philosophers about what exactly the emotions are (either in the sense of the exact nature of an emotion or a classification) and what is their precise relationship to bodily states. William James

[2] In the terms of Chapter 3, this is a testimony for "easy beauty."

held that emotions are the feeling of bodily states which are themselves the direct effects of various perceptions; for instance we
see blood, our body reacts to this perception and *then* we feel the
emotion of fear (or whatever), which is nothing different from our
feel of our bodily reaction. Lange made a very intimate connection between emotion and vasomotor states. The physiologist
Cannon has greatly emphasized the importance of the thalamus in
emotional reactions. Others have insisted that emotions are primarily
psychic and only secondarily or concomitantly physical.

But for our purposes the best way of identifying emotion is perhaps to name some instances, hence: sadness and happiness, fear and
security, grief and joy, elation and depression, love and hate, kindness and cruelty, generosity and meanness, sorrow and gladness.
Such states as these typify emotions.

If now it is asked how emotions figure in the aesthetic experience,
there are two severe answers that must be first considered. One
answer says that the only emotion that may properly figure is the
"aesthetic emotion" itself. It is not popular in most circles today to
admit that there *is* any such entity as an aesthetic emotion, but if
the term is used in a liberal meaning, it is hard to see what can be
urged against it. That is, if there does seem to be a certain quality
that makes the expression "aesthetic experience" meaningful and
if, as must be admitted, this experience is a *feeling* experience, it
does not seem gratuitous to go on to speak of an aesthetic emotion.
However this be, it surely cannot be the case that this is the only
emotional constituent in our aesthetic reaction to a work of art,
for one's emotional reaction is certainly markedly different in the
case of Debussy's *La Mer* and the quartet from *Rigoletto*. So
however alike the experiences of these two works of art be, a
likeness which entitles us to speak of having an aesthetic reaction
to both, there remains a fundamental difference in the two experiences, a difference in part in emotional make-up.

The second severe answer occasionally given to the question of
how emotions figure in aesthetic experience is that the only appropriate emotional response to a work of art is approval or perhaps
admiration, or their opposites. Now, it is certainly very common to
feel approval and admiration in the presence of a work of art, as is
shown by our strong inclination to clap our hands enthusiastically

when we have enjoyed a concert or a play or to comment on what a fine work it is or on the consummate skill and perceptive depth of its creator. But to say that these are the only emotional constituents in an aesthetic experience seems to make this experience what it is not, exclusively a judgment. To be sure, one can imagine a seasoned teacher of painting or a veteran play producer expressing a word of admiration for this canvas or script and a word of rebuke for that, without having done more than to detect, with a craftsman's eye, certain signs of worth. But again, this is clearly not a case of an aesthetic experience.

The answer to the question of what emotions may be present in the aesthetic experience is then (1) the "aesthetic emotion" itself, by which is meant the total warm response to the thing of beauty; (2) emotions of approval or admiration directed toward the creator or the performers or the work of art itself; *and* (3) any other emotions among whatever emotions there are. Everyone not completely insensitive to art-works has known terror and pity and gratitude and mercy and sadistic cruelty and many, many other emotions within the aesthetic transaction. What in the entire range of human emotions is inherently disqualified?

Now the question may be changed to: how are the emotions we feel within the aesthetic experience—limiting ourselves from here forward to (3) above—stimulated by the work of art? Or, to what do these emotions relate?

One thing to notice right away is that emotions developed in response to works of art are sometimes "objectless." Whereas in ordinary experience when we experience fear it is fear *of* something —fire, high places, snakes, certain persons, etc.—this is by no means always so with art. Music, for instance, often *directly* stimulates emotions in its hearers without there being any known story to go along with the music. So, too, may nonrepresentational dancing and painting call out feelings that we cannot easily, if at all, attach to any objects or events. Something about the colors, we will say, or about the lines or the tune makes us feel a very special way. Now it may be that in such cases there is always some unconscious association at work. It is well known that neurotics often have irrational "objectless" terrors; they are afraid without there seeming to be anything to be afraid of. But psychologists point in such cases to some "buried" or repressed memory. A person who is puzzlingly afraid of bees without being able to recall ever having been stung is really always afraid for a perfectly adequate reason, perhaps some experience of early childhood that has entirely disappeared from the conscious memory. So in the case of art it may be that the so-called direct stimulation of emotions by the very surface of the art-work depends upon our unconsciously associating this shade of red with fire, that sort of line with a snake who one time threatened, the lilt of this tune with a forgotten lullaby. Even if this is always the case—and there does not appear to be anything absurd in a theory which holds that we do sometimes emotionally react directly to masses and lines and colors and rhythms without even unconscious connections with real objects and events—the fact remains that as the experience is available to our own introspection, the stimulation *is* direct and objectless. It is perhaps not wholly irrelevant to remark here that the experimental injection of adrenalin has sometimes been found to produce "as if" fear, fear without any content, so that the subject says, "I feel as I would feel if I were afraid." Perhaps the bare elements of art-works also affect our bodies so as to produce reactions we can liken to the human emotions normally directed at objects.

If some art-works such as "absolute" music and nonobjective painting and sculpture employ only this direct stimulation, all art-works employ it one way or another, but very frequently in com-bination with the symbolic or representational function of art. For instance, there is the representation of a scene. This, of course, is the landscape painter's stock in trade: he shows us Mt. Fuji piercing up through the clouds, or a wind-tormented sea, or a sagging, splin-tered old house, or a field of leaning daffodils—and if we are alive we respond feelingly to what we see. But such an appeal is not the monopoly of the painter. We sometimes detect bird calls and storms and passing parades in music and respond accordingly. And of course famous settings in literature and theater come to mind, Egdon Heath in *Return of the Native,* the farmhouse framed by the two trees in O'Neill's *Desire Under the Elms,* and the long succession of scenes revealed to the journeying poet in *The Divine Comedy*—all of which evoke emotions.

Usually when a human being is introduced onto the scene, another factor becomes important, and that is the represented emotion of the portrayed person. Then the emotions of the aesthetic beholder are conditioned by the emotions he detects in or ascribes to the person within the art-work. Thus it is perfectly obvious that looking at "Laocoön," one sees not just a man, two boys, and a great serpent, but one sees as a principal datum the hopeless terror[3] in the faces and in the struggling, straining bodies; and that one's own feeling in this perception is in very large measure stimulated by these expressions. The whole experience of the beholder would be different if he found registered in the faces ironic amusement or ecstatic joy.

Still, this is not to say that one's own feelings are always the same or even closely similar to the represented feelings. A general distinction can be drawn between *sympathetic* and *antipathetic* responses. Doubtless it is commonest for the beholder to feel pain in seeing pain, feel bewilderment in seeing bewilderment; when one reads of Miranda exclaiming, "Oh brave new world that has such marvels in 't!" one sympathetically experiences her bright-eyed, naive delight. But the citation of an example from drama should be enough to remind us that we often react against the expressed emotion. After all when the *villain* says "Aha!" we are apprehensive and when he says "Curses!" we rejoice. Yet there are many times, too, when our own reaction is neither just sympathy nor just antipathy. After all, *we* may know something that the dramatized character does not know: we share Romeo's grief at seeing Juliet apparently dead, but our grief is modified by knowledge that is not his, modified, indeed, by our *recognition* that such knowledge is not his. Or again we mourn for Dido as she laments, but all the while are also pleased that Aeneas did not linger longer. Or we laugh with Franz Hals' Cavalier, but we also laugh a little *at* him.

The situation is only slightly different when the emotion expressed is not that of a character but more directly of the creator, as in lyric verse. Keats writes of a drowsy numbness and his words, both in meaning and in sound, tend to engender in us a like feeling. When Andrew Marvell wittily admonishes his coy mistress, we too

---

[3] It does not matter if one should at this point disagree and say no, not terror, but . . . some other feeling. The point is that *some* emotion or combination of emotions is immediately discovered in the faces and bodies of the statuary.

experience the special poise of this impatient but logical lover. Lyrical expression is even less different from represented character than is sometimes supposed, for after all the "I" of the poem is not quite the "I" of the author's personal letters, for in a poem a character is assumed, a role is played, only more or less like that which is real life for the poet.[4] The protagonists in the novels of Stendhal and D. H. Lawrence and Thomas Wolfe are surely not less autobiographical than many a lyric poem. But even when the artist is speaking very much for himself, we still may react against rather than with him, though such a reaction will usually if not always signify a failure of the aesthetic experience. If the poet gets so carried away with his mistress's kisses that like Shelley he must rhymingly characterize them as "slippery blisses," we may laugh, a most unsympathetic response to a love poem.

Another constituent of the art-work which may beget an emotional response is the *symbol*, where this word is now taken not to name just any device by which the work signifies, but in the narrow sense of an artistic symbol, that is, some element in the art-work which is intended to have a special meaning beyond its apparent one. Sometimes artistic symbolism is highly regularized and conventional. For instance in Hindu art, Vishnu is typically shown holding in his four hands a discus, a mace, a conch-shell, and a lotus bloom. In the first place these devices assist recognition that this figure *is* Vishnu; but more, they tell of his royal power, his magic, and his purity. In Christian art the dove symbolizes the Holy Ghost and the symbolism has its effect precisely because there is felt by the devout to be a special appropriateness to the symbol. A turtle, say, would not do just as well. The dove suggests peace, gentleness, and descent from the heavens, at the very least, all qualities thought to be particularly consonant with the third member of the Trinity. Still, however appropriate these symbols be, they have become so highly conventionalized that one who knows the conventions reads them off almost as he would an inscription. A different kind of symbolism is that which is invented by an artistic creator (though possibly unconsciously in some cases) for

---

[4] See John Crowe Ransom, "A Poem Nearly Anonymous," in *The World's Body* (New York: Scribner, 1938); and E. M. Forster, "Anonymity: An Enquiry," in *Two Cheers for Democracy* (New York: Harcourt, Brace, 1951).

his unique purposes. For instance there is Lady Macbeth who washes her hands and in so doing tells us of her fruitless efforts to rid herself of her guilt. Or again there is the much-repeated light symbolism of *Oedipus the King*, with the alternation between light and dark, seeing and blindness, relating to the quest for wisdom. Dante symbolizes lust by a leopard. And there is James Joyce's use of bird and flying symbolism in *Portrait of the Artist as a Young Man* to say more about the proposed flight of the fledgling artist from family, religion, and homeland; though this particular symbolism draws heavily upon the Greek myth of Daedelus and Icarus, and thus to a degree shares in the nature of partially conventionalized symbolism as well. Students of the language of symbolism would probably agree that the most effective symbols that an artist can employ are those which are neither wholly conventional nor wholly singular. The conventional tends to lose its power, and that which is contrived for the occasion may have only a superficial, too exclusively intellectual, appeal. Many of the great artists have made their symbolism powerful by the unique use of traditional symbols, as does everyone in his dream life, where the meaning of symbols is sufficiently constant to permit the compilation of a virtual dictionary of dreams, but where for full interpretation it is always required to examine the individual context for the occurrence of the symbols. And such symbolism, in dreams and in art, tends to be invested with strong emotions.

A final source of emotional response is named by the word "ideas." Though not a universal element in art-works, ideas can be discounted as an important aspect of art only if one is willing to disqualify for the aesthetic fraternity huge blocks of fiction, poetry, and drama, including much of the literature most highly esteemed by critics and public alike. Since this is a topic which will be more fully examined in a later chapter, it will suffice here to cite an example. Let it be a famous one, *Paradise Lost*. However magnificent the imagery, the scene, the characterization, and the measured sweep of the verse, a full appreciation of this poem is quite impossible without hard thinking about the moral and theological issues with which Milton here grappled. There are those who respond to such a statement by objecting that this is to take the poem as *philosophy*, not as *poetry*. Now, it is perfectly true that if the philosophi-

cal content of this or any other work of literary art is separated and
given distinct consideration as a bare, abstract argument, then there
has been an overdistancing, a departure from an aesthetic attitude
and an arrival at an analytic, intellectual attitude. But this is by no
means necessary, as it most certainly is not desirable in the case of
a work such as *Paradise Lost*. The greatness of the poem derives
from its intimate fusion of the ideational and the sensuous, a fusion
it is in the highest degree important to preserve in one's reading.[5]
Only as one understands Satan's rationalization of his revolt can one
understand his character and his predicament—only so can one experience the poem feelingly, only so can the poem truly move the
reader.

> *The mind is its own place, and in itself*
> *Can make a Heaven of Hell, a Hell of Heaven.*
> *What matter where, if I be still the same,*
> *And what I should be, all but less than he*
> *Whom thunder hath made greater? Here at least*
> *We shall be free; th' Almighty hath not built*
> *Here for his envy, will not drive us hence:*
> *Here we may reign secure; and, in my choice,*
> *To reign is worth ambition, though in Hell:*
> *Better to reign in Hell than serve in Heaven.*[6]

It has been said that one of the chief characteristics of a great writer
is his ability to *feel* an idea as directly and as powerfully as the smell
of an onion. In exactly the same way it is incumbent upon the reader
of literature to feel the ideas with which he is presented, neither
ignoring them in the false supposition that they are an extra-
aesthetic element nor extracting them for quite separate, coldly intellectual perusal.

Long before this point in our discussion it will have occurred to
many in this "relativistic age" to say, perhaps with some annoyance,
"Doesn't all this assume that everybody's emotional response to a
work of art is uniform? But this ignores individual and cultural differences!" Now it is most certainly true that any theory about the
place of emotion in art that does assume such a uniformity and does

[5] This is the nub of the Hegelian aesthetic, the principle of the *concrete universal*.

[6] *Paradise Lost*, 1, 254-263.

neglect differences, or any theory that assumes a narrowly circum-scribed one and only one *right* emotional response to a work of art is clearly untenable. In our day, the evidence for considerable and to a certain extent unavoidable variety of emotional response among people—evidence afforded by anthropologists, sociologists, histo-rians, physiologists, and psychologists (among others)—is plainly overwhelming. But in discussing some of the factors of emotion in art, no assumption to the contrary of this evidence has in fact been made. Individuals not only differ from each other but they differ in themselves, from time to time, in the emotional quality of their art (or any other) experiences. Nor can it be safely assumed that, say, a romantic movie ending upon the kiss of the lovers will draw an identical audience response in Kyoto and in Memphis. Nevertheless, let it also be said here that it is possible to exaggerate the variety of emotional responses to a given work of art within the relevant limits of (1) a common culture[7] and (2) the aesthetic attitude. The distancing discipline necessary to full aesthetic appreciation does itself eliminate or at least greatly diminish many of the idiosyncratic responses, so that a seasoned playgoer, to revert to an earlier ex-ample, may be able to suppress his personal suspicions of his wife sufficiently to enjoy a performance of *Othello*.

It would be a mistake disastrous to the understanding of art to suppose that the area of emotional reaction to a work of art is a chaos of variety. The fact is that there appears to be a very impres-sive degree of similarity of feeling among the members of an audi-ence listening to Yehudi Menuhin play the Beethoven *Violin Con-certo*—not unanimity, not uniformity, but a significant coming to-gether. To put it another way, if an able painter should want those who were going to view his work to feel a certain way, for instance gaily ribald, he would not by any means be at a complete loss as to how to go to work; he would not suppose for a minute that it was

[7] Those who dote on contrasting cultures with each other ought not to neglect the interesting fact that occidental twentieth-century people in large numbers still read with avidity and excitement the stories produced in ninth-century B.C. Attica; that the sculpture of primitive Africa has had a profound effect upon European and American artists; that the illuminated manuscripts of seventeenth-century India are prominently displayed in New York's Metropolitan Museum and the London Museum—to mention a few of very many significant examples of cross-cultural appreciation. Nor may the answer that "this is so only because different people see different things to enjoy" be given with dogmatic assurance.

simply a matter of chance whether he would have better success
with a picture of a sailor with a parrot on his shoulder or a picture
that resembled Whistler's "Mother."

Before passing on to a different topic, it will be well to pause on
one more qualification of the discussion so far. It may have seemed
at some places in the exposition as if emotions were being thought
of as purely ready-made, like little pellets to be discharged when the
right trigger was squeezed. And it may have seemed too that we
have treated our emotional responses to art-works as wholly conditioned by our previous experiences. On the first point John Dewey
has made the telling corrective:

> *We are given to thinking of emotions as things as simple and
> compact as are the words by which we name them. Joy, sorrow,
> hope, fear, anger, curiosity, are treated as if each in itself were a
> sort of entity that enters full-made upon the scene. . . . In fact
> emotions are qualities, when they are significant, of a complex ex-
> perience that moves and changes. . . . Experience is emotional but
> there are no separate things called emotions in it.*[8]

There *is* a danger in supposing that emotions are rigidly distinct
entities. They are *states*, shifting, developing, diminishing, evan-
escent, shading off into other states, returning, growing now intense,
now meek. They are only very roughly susceptible of the conventional labels—joy, fear, jealousy, love and so on; each such category
covers not only a multitude of sins but a multitude of emotions.

As Susanne Langer has said, "What a work of art sets forth—the
course of sentience, feeling, emotion, and the *élan vital* itself—has no
counterpart in any vocabulary. . . . But what it conveys is really
just one nameless passage of 'felt life,' knowable through its incar-
nation in the art symbol even if the beholder has never felt it in his
own flesh."[9]

Furthermore, great works of art should be thought of not only as
invoking familiar emotional responses, but as *extending*, too, our
emotional lives. But the point can easily be filled out by anyone who
has deep experiences with art; he knows to what extent the best art
has sometimes seemed to contrast with the often narrow range of
his own life. He knows his debt in emotions to the great artists.

8 *Art as Experience* (New York: Minton, Balch, 1934), pp. 41-42.
9 *Feeling and Form* (New York: Scribner, 1953), p. 374.

EMPATHY

So far little has been said about the means, the mechanisms by which the sounds, the daubs of paint, the typographer's marks, and the other elements of aesthetic surface do arouse emotional responses of an aesthetic sort. For these purposes the most useful word in the aesthetician's vocabulary is "empathy," a word coined of Greek metal that it might thus have a more familiar ring to ears accustomed to English than the German "Einfühlung." A literal English translation is "in-feeling" or perhaps better "feeling into." Put at its simplest, empathy is endowing the external thing with our own feelings; or, regarding the object of perception as having the feeling-qualities which it arouses in us. Suppose, for instance, that looking at a tall church steeple we seek words to describe it. We might say, "It's straining toward the heavens." Or it seems natural for us to say with Wordsworth that the daffodils are dancing. But it is we who strain and we who dance—or almost dance. Yet it is as if what we see is itself feeling what it makes us feel.

Empathy is analyzable into three distinguishable steps: mimicry, feeling, and projection. (1) In perception there is, at least often, a tendency to dispose the body or part of the body in imitation of what is perceived. We see a bird swooping and swaying and we may make little movements with our head and shoulders in imitation. We watch boxers and we may ourselves punch and duck in miniature. Sometimes, in seeing the sea swell and recede, we expand and contract our chests. And it is almost impossible to watch someone eating a lemon without ourselves pulling a sour face; perhaps our mouth waters too. (2) These movements and bodily attitudes are felt, each having a distinct quality. They are felt as lightness or heaviness, strain or ease, awkwardness or grace, advancing or retreating, quickness or slowness; and also as reluctance or eagerness, gaiety or sorrow, fear or confidence—to name only some of the possibilities. But these feelings are not directly experienced as one's own; (3) they are projected into the object we began by imitating and are *seen* as belonging there. For the empathic experience not to be broken, it is of particular importance that one not become self-conscious during the process, for as soon as one notices his own feelings, he no longer makes the attribution to the object—and this is quite a different thing.

Empathy is of course not confined to aesthetic objects, as some of the examples already cited suggest, but it certainly is an important process in at least some of the arts, particularly those whose appeal is primarily visual. Perhaps the arts of dancing and sculpture most commonly and importantly invoke empathic responses, for though we may imitate anything we see, we seem to be especially prone to dispose our own bodies like other bodies. Possibly the three-dimensionality of the bodily presentation in dancing and sculpture also helps in this way, but the painter with his illusion of a third dimension is scarcely handicapped. Theater is not far behind in its empathic possibilities. Indeed, actors are often coached to solicit audience empathy by using their whole bodies in the delivery of their lines. In architecture, "stresses and strains" are not merely matters of engineering, but are as well matters of psychology; that is, in contemplating buildings the sensitive observer feels the pressures, supports, thrusts, leanings, spannings, and connectings in his own body.

In the case of music, empathy, though necessarily different, is still important. Offhand it might seem that it is impossible to carry through the mimicry step without actually singing or whistling, but what is much commoner is a kind of "silent singing," an incipient movement of the vocal chords in imitation of the sounds. We also experience the rises and falls of music in our body. Perhaps the reason high notes are called "high" and low notes "low," is because of our tendency to raise and elongate our bodies as we go up the scale, and to contract and depress our bodies as we go down, even if we are not actually singing aloud.[10] In addition, no one needs to be reminded of how we tap our feet, move our hands, sway our bodies, and regulate our breathing in accordance with music, though discreet concert-goers learn to keep these movements so slight as to be usually unnoticed by their companions.

Insofar as literature is rhythmic and dynamic it is similar to music in its empathic appeal. Of course, in its rich resources for imagery it broadens its possibilities, though perhaps for most persons empathy

[10] Doubtless other explanations for this terminology will occur to the reader.

induced by imagery (e.g., a dance as described in words) is rather slighter than that induced by more direct stimulation.

What has been so far discussed might be called "motor or kinaesthetic empathy" and there is even some reason for holding that this is the only empathy properly so-called. Still, this phenomenon relates so closely to a slightly different one that there is also good reason for broadening the term "empathy" to make room for the other species, what might be called "dramatic empathy."

It will have been noticed that the bodily changes so far described and exemplified have been muscular; for instance, as we look at a portrait we may slightly pull down the corners of our mouth and then react to the feel of that, see the portrayed face in terms of that. But suppose now that we are reading a play—make it Ibsen's *The Wild Duck*. We have reached the point where Hjalmar, the lazy, vain, rather stupid photographer has gone off to a splendid party, a social event quite above his petty little world, an occasion where there are to be famous politicians and men of the world, with champagne and expensive food, singing and dancing, and sophisticated repartee. He has left in an excited whirl amid the fussings and helps of his wife and their daughter, a withdrawn but loving girl, afflicted with an eye disease that is gradually worsening. Hjalmar has bounteously promised to bring a present to the girl, and when he returns, full of the imagined success of his debut, the daughter claims her present. Hjalmar has forgotten, but he has what he regards as a happy thought. He will produce the menu and describe in detail the progress of the dinner: this will be just as good as a present. The girl tries not to betray her disappointment, but it gets through even to Hjalmar and he begins to bluster, demanding to know why they begrudge him this outing, and so on. Now, as we read, we participate in the shifting emotions of the characters, and particularly as we get to the line where the girl tries to thank her father for the present's substitute, we experience a poignancy that may perhaps be described as a mixture of disappointment with her and a disgusted embarrassment for him. The question then is, as we turn aestheticians, how and why we feel as we do.[11] An answer in terms of muscular tensions seems plainly inadequate; surely there is more than that. *What* more is very difficult to say—perhaps it would not be

[11] It is not of course suggested that we should by any means always, or even frequently, interrupt our aesthetic reaction with curiosity about the nature of the reaction.

wrong to speak of vascular and visceral changes; but whatever be the actual physiological conditions, our own reaction is a function of a cumulative understanding of the characters involved and a grasp of the particular dramatic situation. Not, however, a sparely intellectual understanding and grasp—though intellect has much to do with it—but an emotional understanding that is made possible by our psychic identification with the characters of the play. Still, the word "identification" must be qualified to the effect that we do not identify the characters with ourselves, but ourselves with the characters. To the extent that we make the characters tell our own story or, to put it otherwise, make them the vaguely formed vehicles for the content we supply from our own autobiographies, the attitude is too subjective, is underdistanced for purposes of an aesthetic enjoyment. Still, in identifying with them, we of course carry along a considerable baggage of personal history; the identification is possible only if there is a certain coming together, a certain congruence, between our experience and that of the characters in the drama. The congruence need not be detailed or specific by any means: we must not underestimate the powers of the human imagination at its best. If it is often said that one mark of the educated man is his ability to entertain new ideas; it might be added that one mark of the person of aesthetic sensibility is his ability to entertain emotionally the drama of persons, places, and predicaments far removed from the circumscriptions of the particular happenings of his own life.

It remains to observe the relations between this "dramatic empathy" and the "kinaesthetic empathy" earlier described. How are they both empathy? It does not of course matter whether they are classified under the same name, but there is this important resemblance: in both, the object of the perception stimulates feelings in the beholder that are then read back into the perception as feelings or qualities of the object. In the one case, this is done by a motor mimicry; in the other, by an imaginative identification.

MODIFICATIONS OF AN "EMOTIONALIST" AESTHETICS

In the present chapter constant reference has been made to the place of emotions in art, and indeed the implication has been that "emotionless art" is a contradiction in terms. Only as the artist is *moved* to express does he create art at all; only as the beholder is *moved* in his contemplative perception is he having an aesthetic experience.

This emphasis may easily beget certain misunderstandings which it is well to forestall. Thus, the following propositions will be *denied:*

1. The artist is emotional and art is the spontaneous overflow of his emotion.
2. The artist's job is to evoke emotions.
3. The artist's job is to describe emotions.
4. The artist's job is to find a suitable vehicle for conveying emotions.
5. Since art is emotional, the more emotion the beholder feels, the better.
6. Art, being emotional, is therefore not intellectual or ideational.
7. Art, being emotional, is destroyed by analysis.
8. Art, being emotional, is properly the prelude to action.

(1) The artist is emotional and art is the spontaneous overflow of his emotion. One stereotype of the creative artist pictures him as a temperamental, unrestrained gusher of feeling and sentiment. If this position seems to have the support of Wordsworth, let this poet once again be quoted more fully:

> *I have said that poetry is the spontaneous overflow of powerful feelings: it takes its origin from emotion recollected in tranquillity: the emotion is contemplated till, by a species of reaction, the tranquillity gradually disappears, and an emotion, kindred to that which was before the subject of contemplation, is gradually produced, and does itself actually exist before the mind.*[12]

Art is seldom, if ever, the direct manifestation of an occasion's emotion. When the poet is at the death bed, he does not write a sonnet; when the composer is trying to stay out of the line of fire of a machine gun, he does not write a concerto. Sometimes even a fine writer, when angry or full of animus, will spoil his work; witness Swift in the last voyage of *Gulliver's Travels*. It is far more likely

[12] Preface to *Lyrical Ballads* (1800).

that such powerful emotions will beget art-works when they are "recollected in tranquillity," even though that recollection itself recapture in a contemplative context an emotion "kindred" to the previous one. The emotion proper to art creation exists "before the mind." If emotionally-toned experience is to be expressed and not merely ejaculated, it must be controlled by the artist's sense of form, and his spontaneity must be checked by a devotion to critical revision. A madwoman weeping and pulling her hair is not, after all, an artist.

(2) The artist's job is to evoke emotions. To the extent that the artist addresses himself to evoking certain emotions in his prospective beholders, he has "taken his eye off the ball" and is altogether likely to "miss." As deliberate evoker, the so-called artist might be better referred to as a propagandist if the emotion is aimed at action, or, if not, as a confectioner or a caterer or an entertainer. So put, the judgment seems unduly severe, and it must be admitted that the greatest artists most certainly have been aware of their audiences; they modify their works in terms of the audience's limitations and demands, and, generally, want to please their public. But what keeps them great in spite of such concessions is that they remain primarily concerned with their *expressive* task, that is, with trying to say what they are internally being pressed to say. This distinction is important for us, consumers of art, because it seems to be a sound empirical generalization that the best art shows marks not so much of being beamed *at* an audience as *out of* an artist, and onto the emerging object.

(3) The artist's job is to describe emotions. However much the artist may be or consider himself to be an authority on emotions, it is not his job as artist to describe or directly to tell *about* them. It has often been noticed that in expressing emotion adequately, it is unusual for the emotion to be itself named.[13] The playwright will probably have a character say, "I feel very angry with you," only if the audience is to understand that he doesn't. The artist will tell about the emotion only if he has decided not to induce it expressively—which is to say, has decided, insofar, not to be an artist. It is the psychologist who is in the best position to tell about emotions;

---

[13] For instance, see R. G. Collingwood, *The Principles of Art* (Oxford: Clarendon, 1938), pp. 112-13.

the artist may afford him a keener insight and give him much material, but as artist he is not a scientist.

(4) The artist's job is to find a suitable vehicle for conveying emotions. As has been noticed already in another context, one danger in speaking of the artist as "expressing emotions" lies in the encouragement of the notion already too prevalent that emotions are ready-made, ready-formed in the artist's consciousness, waiting to be unearthed and hauled out. The metaphor could be made usable, perhaps, by speaking of the artist as a miner and smelter in his own unconscious, concerned not merely to dig out but also to refine the ore; but in this figure "emotion" would need to be thought of as a certain quality of the metal and not as the metal itself. No, the artist is not just an emotion-dispenser or broadcaster; he is an emotion-discoverer. The process of expression is a process of discovery; the process of articulation, of forming, of selecting, is a process of discovery. Furthermore, unlike nearly all emotion-describers, he is concerned, usually, less with types of emotion than with highly specific emotions: not just love and hate, but this unique love and this unique hate. Furthermore, the specific sensory embodiment of an emotion is never a dispensable vehicle. As L. A. Reid has put it, "If pink is 'feeble' or 'vulgar,' it is not feebleness or vulgarity in general, but 'pinky-feeble' and 'pinky-vulgar.' Or if violet or blue expresses delicacy or mystery, it is not delicacy or mystery *apart* from blue, but 'blue-mystery' or 'violet-mystery.' "[14]

(5) Since art is emotional, the more emotion the beholder feels, the better. If the proper artist is not a howling madman, no more is the proper beholder. Aesthetic appreciation is not an orgy; perhaps even the word "ecstasy," so lovingly employed by art lovers, is not quite right, not at least if it suggests that the beholder's only requirement is a readiness to swoon. The value of a work of art cannot be measured by the intensity of emotion it arouses, a fact that is supported by the experience of every (even moderately) critical moviegoer. A work may, as it is guaranteed by its advertisements to do, produce "chills and thrills," without its seeming to us to merit much praise as art. Indeed it is not unusual to be embarrassed about one's own relatively intense emotional reaction to art, in some circumstances; nor is this a sign of effeteness. For instance a person may be conditioned to experience a very strong feeling whenever Old

[14] *A Study in Aesthetics* (London: George Allen & Unwin, 1931), p. 77.

Glory is unfurled, but he may not therefore consider a given un-furling in a movie to be necessarily a happy dramatic incident. From the fact that a work which leaves us cold has therefore failed as art it does not follow that the warmer its effect, the better it is as art. Generally great intensity of emotion is a sign of underdistancing. Sometimes in polemical reaction to classic or "academic" art, artists and critics will beat the gong for more emotional art, but this is to be understood as a Romantic battle-cry and not as an endorsement of "The more emotion the better!"

(6) Art, being emotional, is therefore not intellectual or idea-tional. So common is it to distinguish sharply emotion and thought, feeling and intellect, emotion and idea, that it has become a com-monplace that emotion is necessarily inimical to thought and thought to emotion. They are enemies. They can be brought into juxtaposition or mixed only with grave danger to both. There is a half-truth (or a little better) in this everyday wisdom: clearly, it is important for a scientist to keep a cool head when he is examining his data; clearly, art-works that appeal to us only as puzzles to be solved invite overdistancing. But it might be remembered that a purely emotionless scientist would not get out of bed and into his laboratory and a purely emotional artist would be too busy sighing or shrieking to produce any art. It is the part of another chapter to examine the place of ideas in art, but it may be remarked here that it is a great fault of "emotionalist" theories of art that they have often encouraged people to neglect or even to despise such ideas as they encountered, say, in literature; such theories stunt aesthetic experience.

(7) Art, being emotional, is destroyed by analysis. Those who resent art criticism and analysis often find comfort in a position that emphasizes the emotional nature of art. Emotions, they may say, cannot be analyzed. We murder to dissect. Art is to be enjoyed, not thought about. Now it has already been sufficiently admitted that art that is *just* thought about is not functioning aesthetically, but it needs equally to be emphasized that fear of analysis usually betrays a weak and unstable appreciation. Analysis, though not itself appre-ciation, is very often a most marvelous help to appreciation. How this can be will appear more fully in our subsequent investigation of the activity of criticism.

(8) Art, being emotional, is properly the prelude to action. It is

well known that emotions as they occur most simply and usually are tied up with action. In animals, for instance, the secretion of adrenalin is functional, permitting faster flight or more ferocious attack. It might therefore be thought that the emotions aroused by artworks also properly issue in overt action. But this is to neglect the impressive self-containedness of the aesthetic experience. In the artwork the emotions are balanced, harmonized, interrelated and interfused; thus one tends to rest *in* the work, rather than go out *from* it, as he would from an orator's harangue, into action. I. A. Richards has influentially argued that the very best art is that which accomplishes an integration, a "synaesthesis," of highly conflicting and contrasting emotions. But whether one agrees with this normative principle or not, it is hardly disputable that one must *stop* in order to enjoy art; the excitement it engenders is finally likely to be an excitement in repose. This, for some, is the case for damnation of art; for others, it is art's glory.

T. S. Eliot's classical voice has been heard in opposition to "emotionalist" theories, saying that art is not a stimulus to emotion but a release from emotion. Yet, fully to understand this warning, we must also remember him as saying: "If we are moved by a poem, it has meant something, perhaps something important, to us; if we are not moved, then it is, as poetry, meaningless."[15] That is, art is working for us aesthetically when it moves us within the confines of our aesthetic contemplation, not when it spurs us to emotional debauch.[16]

The emotion in art must be constantly thought of, not as a separate issue or as a distinct essence, but as a permeating quality. It is, at its best, highly particularized, exquisitely ordered, and contemplatively controlled. Art's emotion does not just shake us but informs us too; it is aroused in us in such a way that we can, through the exercises of our imagination, perceive and contemplate its qualitative expression.

[15] "The Music of Poetry," *Partisan Review*, Nov.-Dec. 1942.

[16] Compare D. G. James' statement: "Mere emotion in itself is something and nothing; what is necessary for poetry is the imaginative command of this emotion. The life of art is in this sense a strenuous effort after release from emotion on the very act of experiencing it. There must go on a certain depersonalization, a quietness in the midst of the speed of passion. It is from the 'balance of those opposites' that poetry is born. Hence in lyrical poetry what is conveyed is not mere emotion, but the imaginative prehension of emotional states, which is a different thing." *Scepticism and Poetry* (London: George Allen & Unwin, 1937), p. 114.

• Chapter 9

IDEATIONAL
CONTENT

(1) "This painting is done in oils on a white canvas, four feet by six feet. It is managed in a variety of gray tones, though with a small amount of purple and gold, the values in general lightening from bottom to top. Its composition is organized around two intersecting diagonals ascending from points near the two bottom corners."

(2) "This musical composition is a relatively free rondo, the repeating theme chiefly contrasting with the other materials in the regularity of its ¾ time. It is scored for small chamber orchestra: four violins, clarinet, oboe, flute, and cembalo."

(3) "This poem is an unconventional sonnet, consisting of four groups of three line units and a final couplet. Its meter is a fairly regular iambic hexameter."

Anyone encountering such descriptions as these would know that in all three it was the *form* of the work of art that was being concentrated upon. But what if he, remembering having heard some place that all works of art were made up of *form and content*, were to ask for further descriptions of these same works of art now in terms of content? What sorts of responses would he consider appropriate? These that follow?

(1-a) "The painting portrays a deadly combat between two

armor-clad, lance-bearing warriors, their chargers themselves rear-
ing and biting each other."

(2-a) "This music gives the predominant effect of a contained,
carefully controlled stateliness and formality, but with contrasting
interludes of frivolity, brooding melancholy, and wild abandon."

(3-a) "The poem suggests that though the universe is entirely
nonrational and impersonal, death is no evil but the welcome con-
summation of life."

If we add to the initial list of formal descriptions one of an architectural work (4) where the emphasis is upon building materials
and the play of lines and masses, could we then also add to our
second group of descriptions (4-a) one in terms of what the building was designed to do, whom to accommodate, what activities to
facilitate—in short, a *functional* description? If it should be agreed
that 1-a, 2-a, 3-a, and 4-a are all matters of content, it will be worth
noting how ambiguous the word "content" is; for 1-a has to do with
representation, 2-a with expressed and evoked emotion, 3-a with in-
corporated ideas, and 4-a with function. But the subject is even
more complicated than that, unfortunately—or fortunately for those
who like doing aesthetics. If we equate, as sometimes is done, "form"
with "manner" or "shape," and "content" with "matter," then it
must be noticed that "matter" has not only the meaning of "subject
matter" but also the meaning of "physical material." This is again
evident if we think of "form" as exemplified by a mold and "content" by a hardening agent such as gelatin or liquid bronze that is
poured into the mold.

In this chapter we will concern ourselves with 3-a, which will be
spoken of as "ideational content," and our questions will have to do
with the aesthetic importance or unimportance of such content and
with its relations with form and with other kinds of content.

SUBJECT AND SUBSTANCE

Critics and aestheticians have been known to say that in art the
"what" is of no importance, everything depending on the "how."[1]
This strong statement has at least a superficial plausibility deriving

[1] For instance, Victor Hugo: ". . . There are in poetry no good and no bad
subjects, there are only good and bad poets. . . . Examine how the work is done,
not on what or why." Preface to *Les Orientales* (1829).

from an undeniable fact, namely that there are fine, moving, impressive works of art about apples and fleas and other such trivial objects and, indeed, there are works of art that may be said to be "about" nothing at all, as for instance the Bach *Brandenburg Concertos;* then too there are trivial, dull, unimportant works of art whose subject matter is the fall of a kingdom, the advent of a new age, or even Providence and the Future State. However, this fact does not really imply that the "what" of an art-work is not of any importance but only implies that it is not all-important, for though it is certainly possible to write, say, a play which, though having a trivial theme, is "perfect in its kind," it is hardly possible to write such a play that will deserve the superlative praise of "sublime" or "great." It could perhaps be said that when the subject matter is especially exalted or of high importance, the risk of artistic failure is greater, but so is the possibility for the highest kind of success.

Still, it seems in general true that among the most devoted lovers of this or that art, there is a greater unwillingness to condemn an art-work for having to do with an unelevated topic than among those who want art to serve their special doctrinal interests, and who therefore are scarcely disinterested patrons. The latter group, for instance those who see art as a handmaiden of religion or of social revolution, are often contemptuous of all art that does not address itself to such momentous issues.

Since a work of art may in some sense be about a "big" subject without itself saying anything "big" about the subject, it is of importance to make a distinction such as that of A. C. Bradley between what he calls "subject" and "substance." Bradley proposes that by "subject" we understand

> *That which we have in view when, looking at the title of an unread poem, we say that the poet has chosen this or that for his subject. . . . If the title of a poem conveys little or nothing to us, the "subject" appears to be either what we should gather by investigating the title in a dictionary or other book of the kind, or else such a brief suggestion as might be offered by a person who had read the poem, and who said, for example, that the subject of* The Ancient Mariner *was a sailor who killed an albatross and suffered for his deed.*[2]

[2] "Poetry for Poetry's Sake," in *Oxford Lectures on Poetry*, 2nd ed. (London: Macmillan, 1909), p. 9. Reprinted by permission of the publisher and St. Martin's Press, Inc., New York.

The "subject," Bradley goes on to say, is not "inside" the poem (or other work of art) but "outside." That is, one can know the subject without in any but the most superficial sense knowing the work of art. The subject is just a general designation of what the work has to do with. It does not follow from this that it is always a matter of indifference what the subject is. For instance, poetry anthologists have a way of grouping their selections so that they appear in the table of contents under such headings as Death, Love, God, and so on; and it is presumably of some interest to readers to be able to read several poems one right after another on a common subject, even though it is in the highest degree likely that the poems will differ radically from each other in what they say about the subject.

It should be said further that the history of art makes it difficult to believe that there are any subjects whatsoever that are by their very natures unartistic, though there are certainly some which recur much more frequently than others; particularly if we confine ourselves to one age or one tradition do we get such recurrences, as in the themes of love and battle celebrated by Persian poetry.

Unlike "subject," the "substance" of an art work, according to Bradley, is internal to the work. It consists in what the artist particularly says about the subject, what he says beyond the common meaning known to all educated persons. One can be told in advance of reading the poem that *Paradise Lost* is about the Fall of Man, and can from that description know the poem's subject, but the substance of the poem can be grasped only in the very reading.

This is a useful distinction, but it is to be noticed that within the word "substance" we still find crowded together representation, emotion, idea, and conceivably function as well, so now we will need to concentrate on those parts of artistic substance that may be considered ideational. In what follows we will confine ourselves primarily to that art in which ideas are especially prominent, literature, with a short discussion of music at the conclusion of the chapter.

MEANINGS AND "ENTERTAINED" IDEAS

The plausibility of a program for "purity" of form in art with no dependence upon objects or persons or events or other meanings is based entirely upon thinking of the arts other than literature. As soon as one considers literature, it becomes apparent that *at least* one of the major arts derives its aesthetic value for the most part from its meanings. Consider the very medium of literature, words. Words are of course in the first instance marks and sounds, but marks and sounds are not words until, among other things, they signify, that is, act as signs or substitute stimuli. Consider the following candidate for admission into the ranks of literature.

> *Oppity oppoty, fleedle der flam,*
> *Sed ro mo, tas mer noo, trackosy twam.*
> *Steckvilly, teckreezee, wussery jie?*
> *Glie hep nor, Quie ret ness, tillecky Vry!*

If one reads this aloud, he may even get a certain amusement out of the sounds, as one does from the refrains of nursery rhymes or magic spells and enchantments, but no one would call it literature. It shares something with poetry, a rhythm of vocables and rhyme, but its obvious great deficiency is simply its lack of meaning. When we pass to

> *Diddle diddle dumpling, my son John*
> *Went to bed with his stockings on,*
> *One shoe off and one shoe on,*
> *Diddle diddle dumpling, my son John.*

one sees still a great reliance on elementary rhythmic effects, but even here there is a certain "content," a little story that is an essential part of its character. And when one goes to

> *Taffy was a Welshman, Taffy was a thief,*
> *Taffy came to my house and stole a roast of beef.*
> *I went to Taffy's house but Taffy wasn't home;*
> *Taffy came to my house and stole a marrow bone.*
> *I went to Taffy's house, but Taffy wasn't there—*
> *So I took him by the left leg and threw him down the stair.*

all manner of complexities have entered: a series of incidents, a feud, a surprise ending, two characters, and a national prejudice. All are meanings. They make this a poem—something "Oppity oppoty, fleedle der flam" cannot be.

Since the purely "nonobjective" qualities of literature are distinctly minor when cut off from the meaning qualities, no one has seriously argued that literature is and of a right ought to be meaningless in the way that nonsense syllables are meaningless.[3]

But there have been those who, like the so-called "Imagists," advocated a poetry kept close to the presentation of sharp images of nature. And George Moore once edited an anthology of "pure" poetry—that is, poetry which was nonphilosophical, nonreligious, nonpolitical, nonmoral, but which held itself to "objective" description and straight story-telling. Such programs may be understood and even welcomed as reactions to literary practice that verges increasingly on the abstract and the abstruse, but taken more seriously than that they appear to be quite gratuitous limitations on poetic possibility.

But if literature may go beyond image-creating ("Petals on a wet black bough") and simple narration ("The king has writ a letter and signed it wi' his hand / And sent it to Sir Patrik Spens was walking on the sand")—what *is* "beyond"? As a first step we may mention an author's use of causal connections. E. M. Forster once wrote that in itself a mere string of incidents does not constitute a *story;* what more is needed are some "becauses." "The King died and the Queen died" is not a story, but "The King died and then the Queen died of grief" is. It is to be noticed that every time an author presents a causal connection, he is presenting an idea for the reader's inspection; and the reader must find the connection plausible unless the story is, insofar, to fail. Aristotle observed that the dramatist's aim is to show a certain character saying and doing what such a character *would* probably or necessarily say or do. Of course the character and his actions may be entirely fictional, indeed they may be fantastic, but we require that they be plausible. Better a plausible impossibility than an implausible possibility. Some critics have taken this to mean that consistency is therefore all that is required. For instance, the author has been compared to the geometrician: as the latter lays down his postulates, not claiming for them truth, but only their power to yield certain theorems, so the novelist or dramatist

---

[3] Max Eastman in *The Literary Mind* has come close to arguing this in his fulminations against "modernism" and his proposals for returning poetry to the level of incantation. It may be incidentally remarked that it is far from easy to write apparent nonsense, even impossible to write absolute nonsense: there is an inescapable causal connection between what one *is* and what he utters, even if his program be to disguise this connection, and thus it is always theoretically possible to use utterance as a sign of the personality of the utterer.

asks us just to take unquestioningly his initial "givens" but then to see whether what is said to follow really does. Now, consistency within the work of art is certainly a desideratum: once we have granted an author the authority to give one of his characters wings we will not have him absent-mindedly let the character fall over a cliff and kill himself. But consistency just as surely is not the whole story; we readers want the author to be held responsible to the experience that is available to all as a check. It is merely impossible that the boy should fly, but it is downright implausible that he should think like an adult.

Beyond the causal linkages and characterizations of his work, the author may place in his work opinions, theories, speculations, reflections, observations—in short, ideas. One of the commonest ways in which to do this is to have a character express an idea. If we run our minds over a random sampling of the great characters of drama and fiction—Odysseus, Prometheus, Oedipus, Hippolytus, Aeneas; Panurge, Criseyde, Falstaff, Hamlet, Don Quixote; Ivan Karamazov, Anna Karenina, Leopold Bloom—we may ask, rhetorically, which of them was without ideas. And if we are reminded that the opinions of these characters are by no means necessarily those of the authors, our consent need be only laconic: the important matter, for present purposes, is that the ideas of such characters—perhaps ideas the direct contrary of those held dear by the characters' creators—are put before us for our consideration, and this consideration is no small part of our aesthetic experience.

Consider the famous lines: "As flies to wanton boys are we to th' Gods; / They kill us for their sport." This idea is something very different encountered here out of its natural context from what it is as a speech of Gloucester in Act IV of *King Lear*, but there too it is an idea, and requires of us understanding if we are to stay with the play. Gloucester is saying something very important here, and if we do not know what he is saying, do not know perhaps because of our notion that the ideas in a play are of no importance, we will be failing of an adequate aesthetic response. But more than a bare understanding is asked of us; it is very difficult to say accurately what more, but the word "entertain" is suggestive in the sense of "to entertain an idea." We do not perhaps have to decide—it may be questioned whether the author is finally asking us to decide—whether the gods wantonly destroy us; but we are required to hold the idea before our minds, to understand what it means and to know something of what the universe would be like if that were true, and of course to understand this further in Gloucester's terms as they are dictated by the tragic course of the play.

Nor is this appreciative entertaining of ideas confined to the speeches of dramatized characters in plays and stories. Very often a more directly expressed notion will "tease us out of thought as doth eternity." Take as an instance three lines that occur toward the end of Wallace Stevens' poem "Peter Quince at the Clavier":

> *Beauty is momentary in the mind—*
> *The fitful tracing of a portal;*
> *But in the flesh it is immortal . . .*

We read and are set to musing: it contradicts a more conventional idea and therefore in its quiet way disturbs us and we feel the need to turn it over in our minds—again, of course, not all by itself but in its setting.

It is part of the job of a cultivated reader to be able, not only in dealing with aesthetic materials but throughout the entire realm of ideas, to entertain without directly affirming or denying, accepting or rejecting. If we read philosophy—Plato, Aristotle, Kant, Hegel, Russell, Dewey—we probably read, at least much of the time, without saying after each thought, "Yes, that's right"; "No, he's wrong there." Reserving always our right to be critical, we often want from philosophy neither new truth, nor confirmation of our old beliefs—no, nor a whipping boy either; we want *food for thought*, ideas to play with, stimulation for our meditative capacities. And in the whole field of controversial opinion, it needs to be remembered that if one is to choose rationally and intelligently, it is of the greatest importance that he be able to hold before his mind, before choosing, the several candidates for the preferred position. This is to entertain ideas.

So in literature too, with extra incentives to preserve a meditative peace, do we practice Coleridge's "willing suspension of disbelief"; but now we must add, as many others have done, "and of belief." It is not only that we *will* not to disbelieve the fantasy that ill accords with our common sense, everyday notions; but also that we do the harder thing and refuse quite to believe what is perhaps most agreeable to our dispositions, refuse because of our interest in this more contained, unassertive entertainment of ideas.

SCIENCE AND LITERATURE

Since the seventeenth century it has become increasingly important to inquire of every human activity how it relates to science. Is there a special kind of religious knowledge that is quite distinct from scientific inquiry? Does conscience afford moral knowledge that is extrascientific? Is philosophy a branch of science or does it lie outside of science, and if the latter, is it then a legitimate activity or a mere vestige of an unscientific era? And what of art, particularly literature—how does it stand with respect to science? Is the literary author properly concerned with some other kind of knowledge than that known to scientists? Or is he, unlike the scientist, not at all concerned with knowledge, except as he is absentminded and forgets his proper role?

Everyone knows that science affords knowledge. Does art too? Is there any *knowing* in and through and by means of the aesthetic object?

One easy answer—so easy that it may seem to be a cheat—is that the very experience of a work of art or other aesthetic object is an instance of knowing. We hear a Beethoven piano sonata and in that hearing we are confronted with the object, we directly experience it, we enjoy its acquaintance. We *know* it in this sense—"knowledge by acquaintance."

Closely related to this usage is that wherein we ask, "Do you know Renoir's 'Mme. Charpentier and her Children'?" A person might reply that he had seen it once, or had seen pictures of it, but both of these would be taken for qualified affirmatives. He who could reply that he *did* know the picture, or that he knew it well, would no doubt be indicating thereby that he had had repeated experiences with it, that he had it well in mind in the sense that he could satisfactorily imagine it or describe it. And of course in the case of a musical work, to claim to know it would, in many contexts, constitute a claim to be able to perform it. But whatever it may mean to know the object *itself*, it is presumably a very different thing to know by *means* of the object. One might put it this way: in knowing this work of art, what *else* do you know? What can be learned from it?

Again there is an easy answer: From it I know better how to come at similar art. It has helped me perform the act of appreciation better. Now this might be thought a trifling answer, but all of us know what it is to come away from a work of art with the feeling that we are better equipped to deal with and to enjoy this or a similar art-work in the future. This, after all, is the principal means to the aesthetic education of all of us, not merely reading about art but confronting it and getting to know it so that next time such knowledge will be easier and more satisfactory.

If the question is now rephrased—"In knowing this work of art is there anything *else* you can know about the extra-aesthetic world?"—the answer is again *yes*. For one thing, an art-work can tell us something, even a great deal, if we know how to interpret its data, about its creator. From it we may learn that the artist was an introvert, or one who hated his mother, or an admirer of red-headed women, or a contented city dweller, or a critic of court life. It may tell us that the artist was a Christian or a friend of revolution or one interested in prison reform. Again, from a work of art we may be able to make astute inferences about the society and the times which produced it. Architecture is often pointed to as a very important index to the character of an age; for instance, consider the Gothic cathedral in relation to medieval France or the skyscraper in relation to twentieth-century America. It is perhaps more to the point that a work of art may, and not infrequently does, convey information or knowledge about persons, places and things. For instance, no one doubts that we know what Charles IV of Spain looked like, since we have Goya's portrait of him. In many a novel we are told directly, and often accurately, about this or that historic personage or institution or place or event.

But at this point someone may object that when he claims cognitive value for art, he does not mean these relatively unimportant and largely irrelevant kinds so far mentioned. After all, though from da Vinci's paintings a psychoanalyst may formulate hypotheses about the artist's attitude toward women, this fact is quite incidental to the quality of the art-work. A four-year-old child's scribblings may be valuable data to the trained psychologist without thereby having any artistic merit. And a hack cartoonist or an insipid poetaster may pen documents more revelatory of the times than are the works of masters. Again, he might say, if it turned out that the so-called portrait of Charles IV was really a Goya self-portrait, it wouldn't matter artistically, just as it doesn't matter that Shakespeare committed anachronisms and solecisms. What is important is that kind of knowledge that art communicates which is inextricably bound up with its aesthetic value; that knowledge, if any, which art alone can convey.

One answer to this objection is a flat denial that art, even literary art, does have any important cognitive content. For instance, Max Eastman, in *The Literary Mind*, traces the gradual but inevitable withdrawal of literature before the juggernaut of science. Science, he says, has replaced the artist-seer in quite the same way that astronomy has replaced astrology and chemistry has replaced alchemy. Today it is only a superstition that the poet as poet knows anything; if he knows anything at all, Eastman says, he knows it from the scientist. But it is not important that he know anything, for knowing and teaching are not his proper function. His job is to delight through the magic of his incantations.

A somewhat similar and more influential position is that of I. A. Richards in his early works, *Principles of Literary Criticism* and *Science and Poetry*, and in the pioneer work in semantics which he wrote with C. K. Ogden, *The Meaning of Meaning*. There are, according to Richards, two totally different uses of language, the referential and the emotive. Science employs referential language, that is language which makes verifiable assertions about the world of experience. But the language of literature is emotive; that is, its function is to arouse, sustain, and control emotions and attitudes in the reader.

> It will be admitted—by those who distinguish between scientific statement, where truth is ultimately a matter of verification as this is understood in the laboratory, and emotive utterance, where "truth" is primarily acceptability by some attitude, and more remotely is the acceptability of this attitude itself—that it is not the poet's business to make true statements. Yet poetry has constantly the air of making statements, and important ones. . . .[4]

[4] I. A. Richards, *Science and Poetry* (New York: Norton, 1926), p. 67.

An emotive utterance that looks like and may by the naive be taken for a genuine referential statement is called by Richards a "pseudo-statement." A pseudo-statement is not, as some have supposed, a false statement.[5] It is not a statement at all; it only appears to be a statement, perhaps because of a grammatical similarity to ordinary assertory prose. A pseudo-statement is *neither true nor false*, but is more or less effective emotively. Or if we insist on speaking of effective pseudo-statements as true, it should at the very least be recognized that "true" is now being used in a very different sense from the scientific. So, too, the state of repose and satisfaction that may result from an aesthetic experience may be mistakenly referred to as "knowledge," for "Any state of mind in which anyone takes a great interest is very likely to be called 'knowledge,' because no other word in psychology has such evocative virtue."[6] There are some, like the philosophical positivist A. J. Ayer, who would agree in a very general way with the early-Richards' views,[7] but who would deny that literature contains few if any real verifiable, referential statements; it contains many, but nearly all of them are false and the ones that are true are trivial. Ayer would hold for instance that the statements in *Tom Jones* about the leading character can be shown, if anybody should want to take the trouble, to be false, for the simple but sufficient reason that no such person ever lived.

If now we should look for the polar opposites from the debunking theories of Richards and the positivists, the following brief quotations would be helpful:

> Literature is the complete knowledge of man's experience and by knowledge I mean that unique and formed intelligence of the world of which man alone is capable.[8]
>
> Philosophy . . . has shown that all scientific knowledge leads us away from the real object, giving us merely its connections; that if we want the real object, we must separate it from all its connec-

---

[5] Allen Tate speaks of "*pseudo-statements,* Mr. Richards's most famous invention in scientese; that is, false statements, or just plain lies." "The Present Function of Criticism," in *Reason in Madness* (New York: Putnam, 1941), p. 12.

[6] C. K. Ogden and I. A. Richards, *The Meaning of Meaning,* 4th ed. (London: Kegan Paul, Trench, Trubner & Co., 1936), p. 157.

[7] Richards' later works in literary criticism reflect a considerable modification of the position here sketched.

[8] Tate, *Reason in Madness,* p. 19.

tions, must grasp it in its complete isolation; and that it is the function of art to bring about this isolation and to show us the object in its immediate truth.[9]

Truth! there can be no merit, no craft at all, without that. And further, all beauty is in the long run only fineness *of truth, or what we call expression, the finer accommodation of speech to that vision within.*[10]

Beauty is truth, truth beauty . . .[11]

These are expressions of a position that has been popular among art lovers for many ages. It is simply the position that art affords a higher, a nobler, a completer truth than science or philosophy. Science is disparaged (typically) as fact-grubbing, mundane, analytic, and utilitarian; art is commended as vision-inspiring, uplifted, synthetic, and free. Unfortunately, such remarks usually seem to be more animadversions than theories, and are too vague to deal with.

But there are others who, though they make a sharp distinction between two ways of knowing, do not make the distinction so utterly invidious. For instance, D. H. Lawrence wrote, "There are many ways of knowing, there are many sorts of knowledge. But the true ways of knowing, for man, are knowing in terms of apartness, which is mental, rational, scientific, and knowing in terms of togetherness, which is religious and poetic."[12] Bergson makes a similar distinction when he speaks of knowing from the outside and intuitive knowing from within. Intuitive knowing, the kind that the artist (among others) attains, is knowledge for its own sake, not for the sake of manipulation and control, the ultimate aims of all science. And above all, the knowledge that art affords is *concrete:*

Art always aims at what is individual. What the artist fixes on his canvas is something he has seen at a certain spot, on a certain day, at a certain hour, with a coloring that will never be seen again. What the poet sings of is a certain mood which was his, and his alone, and which will never return. What the dramatist unfolds be-

[9] Hugo Munsterberg, *The Principles of Art Education*, quoted in Melvin Rader, *A Modern Book of Esthetics*, rev. ed. (New York: Holt, 1952), p. 400.
[10] Walter Pater, "Style," in *Appreciations* (New York: Macmillan, n.d.).
[11] Keats, "Ode on a Grecian Urn."
[12] *Apropos of Lady Chatterley's Lover* (London: Mandrake Press, 1930), p. 55.

fore us in the life-history of a soul, a living tissue of feelings and events—something, in short, which has once happened and can never be repeated. We may, indeed, give general names to these feelings, but they cannot be the same thing in another soul. They are individualized. Thereby, and thereby only, do they belong to art; for generalities, symbols or even types, form the current coin of our daily perception.[13]

Further he speaks of artists as those who

When they look at a thing, . . . see it for itself, and not for themselves. They do not perceive simply with a view to action; they perceive in order to perceive. . . . In regard to a certain aspect of their nature, whether it be their consciousness or one of their senses, they are born detached; and according to whether this detachment is that of a certain particular sense, or of consciousness, they are painters or sculptors, musicians or poets. It is therefore a much more direct vision of reality that we find in the different arts; and it is because the artist is less intent on utilizing his perception that he perceives a greater number of things.[14]

Benedetto Croce similarly distinguished the intuitive knowledge of the artist from logical, conceptual knowledge. And, to content ourselves with one more authority, the poet and critic John Crowe Ransom has written, "The artist interests himself entirely in individuals, or he should; if he does not really, he should declare himself a scientist or a moralist."[15]

"Art always aims at what is individual." Bergson and many others *say* this, but is it true? Certainly as we stand before a portrait by Holbein, we have the conviction not only that he has caught the unique quality of the person who appeared before him, but that this particular combination of circumstances represented in the painting—just this age in his life, just this passing mood, his face in these particular shadows and lights—is literally unrepeatable. Matisse has been one among many artists to emphasize the necessity of returning to a kind of child-like innocence and freedom from the dictates of stereotypes if one is to do great creative work. He

[13] *Laughter*, trans. Cloudesley Brereton and Fred Rothwell (London: Macmillan, 1911), p. 161.
[14] *The Creative Mind*, trans. Mabelle L. Andison (New York: Philosophical Library, 1946), pp. 162-63.
[15] *The World's Body* (New York: Scribner, 1938), p. 206.

says somewhere that there is nothing more difficult for a truly creative painter to paint than a rose, because before he can do so, he has first of all to forget all the roses that were ever painted. All the other roses are not this rose and *this* rose is his object.

Or let one remember a character out of literature—it may be a big character like Cyrano or Tartuffe, or a little character like Hotspur's wife—and ask the questions, "In this person, has the author given us someone who is truly unique, who is, finally, just himself and nobody else? Is he just an assemblage of traits or a realized unity?" The answers will be important.

If this focussing upon the individual *is* characteristic of art, it may be asked whether this constitutes a point of differentiation between art and science. In answer, we might turn here to Sir Arthur Eddington's little story about the elephant sliding down the green, grassy hillside: In the physicist's language, the elephant is *just* a certain mass, the hillside *just* a coefficient of friction. The scientist and the philosopher too do seem vocationally inclined toward the abstract and the still more abstract. Any question about a given individual, man, rose, pencil, star, is answered, if possible, by putting the individual into his appropriate classifications. The pressure is always toward the formula and the law of nature, and this means away from the individual in his distinctness. To be sure, applied science represents something of a return to the individual; for instance, the practicing physician must deal with each separate case as at least potentially different from every other. Yet to the extent that this is true, and it is seriously limited in extent by the fact that the physician is still dealing with the individual as defined by converging classifications of symptoms, it is so precisely because in this respect medicine is not a science but a use of science, a kind of practical art. Consequently, if it can be made out that art is particularly directed at the individual and the concrete, it will insofar be contrasted with science, which is directed at the general and abstract.

But there is another side to this question. It is interesting, for instance, that Aristotle held poetic drama to be more philosophical and of graver import than history in that the poet was not primarily concerned with what Alcibiades *did* in fact but with what such a being in such and such a situation *would* do. Samuel Johnson once wryly remarked that it was not the poet's job to number the streaks of a tulip. And in artistic practice, the existence of classical drama, symbolic art, so-called abstract painting, the morality plays, problem novels, and such great philosophical poems as those of Lucretius, Dante, and Goethe, makes is difficult to sustain the thesis that the artist is interested in individuality *as against* generality, concreteness *as against* abstractness.

There is an anciently honorable way of adjudicating this dispute. For Plato it was the disgrace of the artist that he always must embody his vision of truth in a sensory material, for this was necessarily to soil and distort the quest for the pure forms of the universe. For Hegel, who would ultimately agree with Plato in elevating philosophical dialectic to the most sublime of ranks in human activity, it was art's unique glory that she could "present ultimate reality to our immediate perception in sensuous shape. . . ." Hegel goes on to say:

> But inasmuch as the task of art is to represent the idea to direct perception in sensuous shape, and not in the form of thought or of pure spirituality as such, and seeing that this work of representation has its value and dignity in the correspondence and the unity of the two sides, i.e. of the Idea and its plastic embodiment, it follows that the level and excellency of art in attaining a realization adequate to its ideal, must depend upon the grade of inwardness and unity with which Idea and Shape display themselves as fused into one.[16]

Put it this way: the painter, no matter how lofty his conception be, when he comes to address his canvas must use not just some color in general, but this color and that; he may not just draw a line in general, but must draw a line of this unique quality or that. The artist's use of sensory and imagistic appeal, then, is at least one factor that makes for the concreteness of art works; and we are likely to be critical of the artist who seems to us to slight this side of his work: Samuel Johnson, however great his contempt for the streaks of a tulip, might have been a better poet if he could have been more sensual. Sometimes a playwright will be criticized for making a character into a mouthpiece for the author's ideas; the character will

16 *Aesthetik,* "Introduction," in Bernard Bosanquet, *A History of Aesthetic* (London: Swan Sonnenschein, 1892), Appendix I.

seem to have too few individual human qualities, and proportionately too many abstract theories.

And yet may we not also criticize an artist for being too "thin," too slight, too eccentric in his work? The comment is heard: "Yes, but he doesn't seem to have anything to say." Or: "It is competent art, but certainly not great art—its scope is too narrow, its penetration too shallow." Or: "What an assemblage of characters! You would never mistake one for another, but neither would you mistake any of them for a human being. It is an excess of eccentricity." However it be with other artists, do we not ask of the literary creator that in his individuality he retain a certain universality too? Bergson wrote that it is only comic characters that are *types*, and he instances Molière's "Misanthrope" and "Bourgeois Gentleman," and his doctors and misers and debtors and valets. But surely this is a mistake: we do speak of "a Hamlet" and of course of "an Oedipus complex." Hamlet and Oedipus are singular characters, not to be mistaken for any others, living or fictional; but they are also characters we find in ourselves and in our fellows, characters who reveal to us something about man and his ways. We want not just images but suggestive images. John Crowe Ransom, whose words were quoted above to the effect that the artist must interest himself entirely in individuals or frankly declare himself a scientist or moralist, goes on to say, however, that if the artist "Is of a mature or observant mind his individuals are likely to be rich and suggestive. . . ."

Of course literary practice is by no means uniform in this respect. It is often taken to be characteristic of Romantic and of Classical literature, respectively, that the one features the strange, the exotic, the unusual, the distinctive, the aberrant, the unique, while the other is likely to present the normal, the characteristic, the typical, the standard. Then again there is a great range from imagism and simple narrative on one side to the large-scale dramas of God and man, heaven and hell, on the other. And still another range exists from the art of pure amusement, let us say, to didactic art.

This problem can be approached from another angle, the consumer's. Let us for a moment think not so much of what the artist was trying to do as of what the appreciator can be best counseled to do when he confronts works of art. It is most certainly good advice to say, Do not be hasty in making generalizations from the works. Do not lose sight of Hamlet himself in your eagerness to understand the *sort* of man he is. Do not let your explanations of Don Quixote come to seem adequate substitutions for the inexhaustible richness of his personality. Beware of such easily applied categories as "Christian," "atheist," "pessimist," "optimist," "reactionary," "liberal," and so on—no artist of importance can be adequately reduced to these pigeonholes. And much more along this same line. Yet, is it any harder to think of occasions when the advice needs to be in the opposite direction? Many readers and playgoers perform satisfactorily on the level of straight narration and the more overt kinds of drama, but seem content to miss the play of ideas, and to neglect the fact that Dostoevsky here and Ibsen there give every evidence of wrestling with the weightiest philosophical problems of man, problems of a high level of generality.

Now, in commenting thus on that theory which confines art to individuality, partial refutations have implicitly been made out of the two previously discussed theories, namely, that art in being emotive is entirely noncognitive, and that art sometimes contains propositions, but propositions which are usually false and in any case trivial. As has been abundantly shown, art is never, except when it miserably fails as art, emotionless; that is, it always aims at inducing reactions which in being aesthetic are emotional. This fact seems to some to make plausible the notion that therefore all cognitive elements in art are so strictly subordinate to emotional effect as to be insignificant and to merit being called "pseudo-statements." But this mistake comes, apparently, from either or both of two assumptions, neither of which is warranted: (1) that the only use an art work has is in inducing a *residual* emotional release or satisfaction; (2) that only that is properly cognitive which is wholly dissociated from feeling states. The first assumption mistakes in a way that might almost be called the most heinous of aesthetic heresies, replacing the full-bodied aesthetic experience, where there is close and feeling attentiveness to all the elements of the object, with something that is the *result* of this aesthetic perception—an afterglow, as it were. The second assumption rests upon a much-popularized anathema: emotionally-toned thinking, wishful thinking. It may well turn out that our age will be looked back upon as one in which there was a great overselling of the idea that feeling is always an enemy of intelligent behavior. There is not space here to deal with this large subject beyond alleging that any adequate examination of the good reader's experience when he is reading, let us say, *The Brothers Karamazov*, will reveal that he is dealing not with mere "pseudo-propositions" but with real and meaningful assertions—dealing with them in a manner different from that appropriate to science or moral harangue or even metaphysics, but dealing with them no less seriously and with no less employment of his mind.

But the hardest job yet remains for us—and it is in this that a fuller answer can be made to the emotivist position and to the theory that literature's propositions are either unimportant or false —the job of explaining how the cognitive elements can function not only so as not to militate against but so as even to enhance the aesthetic value of a work of art.

KNOWLEDGE BY IMAGINING

George Santayana has written:

Where literal knowledge is possible . . . is in literary psychology. Here we often conceive our object exactly as it was or may be: because it is no more improbable that two brothers should feel and think alike than that two similar leaves should sprout on the same tree. Therefore poetry is, in some sense, truer than science, and more satisfactory to a seasoned and exacting mind. Poetry reveals one sort of truth completely, because reality in that quarter is no more defined or tangible than poetry itself; and it clarifies human experience of other things also, earthly and divine, without falsifying these things more than experience falsifies them already. Science, on the contrary, the deeper it goes gets thinner and thinner and cheats us altogether, unless we discount its symbols.[17]

What Santayana calls "Literary Psychology," "the art of imagining how animals feel and think" (as distinct from scientific behavorial psychology), is of course at the very center of at least

[17] "The Realm of Matter," in *Realms of Being* (New York: Scribner, 1940), pp. 232-33.

the literary artist's art. When Keats tells of the song of the nightin-
gale, he is being a literary psychologist:

> *Perhaps the self-same song that found a path*
> *Through the sad heart of Ruth, when, sick for home*
> *She stood in tears amid the alien corn. . . .*

The kind of knowledge that is here communicated is not historical:
nothing could be more irrelevant than any question about the
identity of the original Ruth. But when we read the lines we learn
something about homesickness through having the feeling quickened in our imaginations. It is far from a detached and analytic
knowing; on the contrary it is warm, inward, and above all feeling.
It is not like being ourselves homesick, which is normally a state
not conducive to learning—even about homesickness—but it is a
kind of direct knowing within the poetically controlled context of
the imagination. It is, to put it slightly differently, a presentation to
our consciousness of an experience, but a presentation so ordered
that the experience is available to us for direct inspection and contemplation. Sufficiently distanced that we are not carried from the
emotion into action or into an "emotional disturbance," it is at the
same time not so distanced that our attitude is one of pure intellec-
tion and detached observation. The experience is both ours and not
ours: ours in the sense that we have some of the pang, the tang,
the savor, the direct qualitative feel of it; not ours in the sense that
it is only indirectly related to the flow of our workaday lives, its
origin and cause and focus remaining in the object and not in ourselves.

Now, one may go along with this explanation but then come up
short against the question of whether all this is *knowledge*. Many
say no. But there is at least this much justification for saying yes:
it sometimes happens—and lovers of literature will not grant such
to be only a rare happening—that from a poem or a story or a play
one feels that he has extended the breadth of his experience and has
refined his discernment of the particular quality of a certain experience. It seems not inappropriate to speak of this as "coming to
know" and as "learning."

It is important in this type of discussion that we think not only
of successful but also of unsuccessful cases. If it really is so that

literary works afford knowledge in the way described, can it then be said that they sometimes fail so to do, even when it seems that they mean to? Two sorts of failure may be noted. The first is the case in which a work leaves us cold; it does not succeed, for any one of a large number of possible reasons, in arousing in us the imaginative experience which is its *sine qua non.* "I read the words," we might then say, "but they were just words." But the second case is quite different: let us work from an illustration, though remembering that not all readers will react the same way, or even with sufficient similarity for this or any other to be a thoroughly convincing illustration. Consider "Trees" by Joyce Kilmer, a very popular poem, and an even more popular song.

It need not be quoted. Everyone will remember that the poet starts right off with a comparison and contrast between poems and trees, goes on in a series of couplets to liken a tree to a nursing infant, to a meditative and prayerful woman, to a dressed-up woman, and to a chaste woman. The concluding lines express a sharp disparagement of poetry because of its merely human and even foolish origin. Trees, however, can be created by God alone.

It may be supposed that a certain reader would read this sympathetically, letting the words build in him a feeling of humility in comparing the works of man with the works of God. He had conjured up in his imagination the picture of a tree nourished by the "earth's sweet flowing breast" and a tree who devoutly prays with its uplifted leafy arms. He has considered the impotence of man to create a living being. But then, it may be supposed that this experience is jolted, perhaps by the word "fool" in the next to last line. "Why 'fool'?" he may ask himself. Is man a fool for not being able to make a tree? And it may seem to him that the expression is forced and insincere and inexact: it is not the expression of a genuine but only of a trumped-up humility. The reader may be embarrassed or annoyed at this conclusion, and may on rereading even find that the whole poem confirms his new impression.

In such a case it seems appropriate to speak of a failure that is in part at least cognitive. The reader was prepared to learn, to extend his awareness of a certain way of feeling, but he had been disappointed. He had found that the work of art had nothing to teach him. The author seemed to be claiming knowledge that he did not succeed in expressing.

But there is another kind of implicit knowledge-claim in some literature that is probably more nearly what people are thinking of when they affirm or deny the cognitive value of art. It is exemplified by so-called *philosophical* poetry and novels and plays; that is, literary works in which the author is working out of or into a more or less comprehensive view of man and the universe, usually with implications as to the nature of good and evil, right and wrong, in such a scheme of things. No one would pretend to have disposed of Dante in calling him a Catholic poet, or of Hardy in describing him as a writer who believed there was no divine interest in man's fate—no, these are woefully inadequate accounts of complex matters; still, they are, as far as they go, accurate. For instance, it would be absurd to reverse the two descriptions just given, making the second apply to Dante and the first to Hardy. These authors, and many others—for instance, Milton, Donne, Lucretius, Zola, Turgenev, D. H. Lawrence, to name a few—we identify with a position, perhaps one very distinctly original, perhaps one which they express for an institution or a tradition. We cannot meaningfully read them without taking their philosophy into account.

Does this, then, mean that we have to *believe* the philosophy we find in a work in order to appreciate it? I. A. Richards' answer is forthright:

> . . . *Poetry conclusively shows that even the most important among our attitudes can be aroused and maintained without any belief entering in at all. . . . We need no beliefs, and indeed we must have none, if we are to read* King Lear. *Pseudo-statements to which we attach no belief and statements proper such as science provides cannot conflict. It is only when we introduce illicit beliefs into poetry that danger arises. To do so is from this point of view a profanation of poetry.*[18]

The justification for Richards' position proceeds from an examination of the habits of sensitive and intelligent readers. The fact is that mature readers can and do read with appreciative enjoyment works differing so markedly from each other in their philosophical orientation that it would be impossible to believe all of them. Many readers will sometimes prefer one work whose philosophy is antipathetic to their own to a work whose philosophy they find con-

[18] *Science and Poetry*, pp. 72-73.

genial; for instance a naturalistic reader might like and admire the intensely religious poetry of Gerard Manley Hopkins and prefer it to that of Robert Frost. It seems to indicate an incapacity of the imagination when somebody reports that being a Moslem he cannot appreciate George Herbert, or being scientific-minded he cannot enjoy *Peer Gynt*, or being Catholic he cannot abide Nietzsche, or being a communist cannot read Henry James. Such an attitude betrays a habitual underdistance to at least some literature. As we noticed before, everyone needs to develop his capacity to *entertain* ideas, even those which, if he were called upon to take a stand, he would emphatically reject.

There is this much truth in the theory that we must suspend our disbelief when we are taking an aesthetic attitude. But there are important qualifications to this theory. Although a good reader will admit his own aesthetic duty not to reject out-of-hand a philosophical attitude or idea he finds expressed in a work of art, but to go along with it at least in the aesthetic context, to entertain it, to savor it, and even to "believe" it in an as-if way, he will feel it his *right* to require of the author in turn not only that this position be consistent (as we have hitherto noticed), but that it be relatively (1) adequate or broad, (2) deep, (3) freshly insightful. The word "relatively" is used here to take account of this important fact, that the extent to which we make these requirements of the author will depend very much upon the nature of the claim that he seems to us to be making. That is, we probably do not feel at all dissatisfied with the philosophical position expressed in Gilbert and Sullivan's *Mikado,* even though it is scarcely profound, because we easily detect the very serious limits within which it seems intended to apply. It would be pedantic indeed to deprecate the whole area of "light" verse, musical comedies, and the like for not being what it does not mean to be and even for not being what we scarcely want it to be.

Indeed, we do not always scold relatively superficial philosophy in literature; we may be willing to take it for what it is and recognize its merit within its obvious limits. Nevertheless, we will also admit that its final failure to move us deeply is precisely because of these limits. If an example is needed, we may cite the *Rubaiyat:*

XXVII

Myself when young did eagerly frequent
Doctor and Saint, and heard great argument
About it and about: but evermore
Came out by the same door where in I went.

XXXV

Then to the Lip of this poor earthern Urn
I lean'd, the Secret of my Life to learn:
And Lip to Lip it murmur'd—"While you live,
"Drink!—for, once dead, you never shall return."

XCIC

Ah Love! could you and I with Him conspire
To grasp this sorry Scheme of Things entire,
Would not we shatter it to bits—and then
Re-mold it nearer to the Heart's Desire!

There can be no doubt that this is philosophical verse, and even philosophical verse which many people throughout their lives (and many more people when they are at a certain stage of adolescence) richly enjoy. But to others it seems, though not utterly untenable nor a position unpleasant to dwell within for a while, unsatisfying in their search for wisdom and so not in the same order of greatness as, for instance, *Faust* or Shakespeare's sonnets. It has neither an adequate breadth—which is to say that it fails to provide any answer at all to many of our questions—nor much depth of penetration—which is to say that such answers as it does give are only very partial ones. For further illustration of the last point, we may look again at the first quatrain quoted above, number xxvii. Everyone has had the experience of going out by the same door through which he came, in the matter of philosophical argument, and so may feel a certain chuckling recognition of a truth in the Omar Khayyam-Edward Fitzgerald words. But everyone not totally averse to ideas has also had the experience of exiting by another door or hacking one through for himself, and so cannot find this answer very deep.

Sometimes the philosophical position of a literary work may be unexceptionable on the matters of breadth and depth, but may seem wanting in originality. Originality is never enough in art, but without it the art is never enough, the principal reason being that it is too hard to attend to the stale or the commonplace, too hard to maintain the peculiar vigilance of the aesthetic attitude. There have been many works written out of one or another of the great religions of the world, faithfully giving voice to these religions; but, though such works will always command a ready audience among the appropriately faithful not because of their aesthetic value but because of their rightminded piety, they may, some of them, be nothing more than a slight rephrasing of perfectly familiar items of creed. But let John Donne start off

Batter my heart, three-person'd God

and we can hardly do other than sit up and take sudden notice.

These considerations indicate that the matter is not so simple as to permit a cavalier exclusion of all belief from aesthetic reading. When Richards writes, "We need no beliefs, and indeed we must have none, if we are to read *King Lear,*" he reveals the absurdity of this extreme doctrine, for what would our experience of reading *King Lear* in a perfectly beliefless state be? We could not then believe that one ought to beware of flatterers and seek more dependable evidence of love than glib protestation, that the actions of Regan and Goneril were ungrateful and vicious, that through suffering it may be possible to gain wisdom; such beliefs on Richards' dictum would have no part in our reading—but what then is left of the play? In the absence of these standard moral beliefs of the audience, *King Lear* would be hardly more than a senseless succession of noises.

Admittedly there is a certain danger in thus speaking of and even defending the audience's beliefs: the danger is that the work of art may come to seem merely a testimony-strengthener, a pat on the back and a confirmation of what one already believed. Doubtless works of art are often so prized, but when they are, their aesthetic value must usually be very slight. The Browning Societies may have been too harshly scorned by sophisticated critics, but one of the pitfalls on the path to aesthetic adequacy is the "stock response." The stock response is the disposition to react with undiscriminating approval toward what one detects as on the side of the right and with equally undiscriminating disapproval toward what one detects as on the other side. Nearly everyone develops certain stock responses during times of international tension, so that we delight in even the crudest disparagement of the enemy and shudder at even the most qualified praise of him. But some people seem to be hardly more than neat stockrooms of such ready-made responses, and these people it is who have been responsible for the successes of aesthetic "know-nothingism."

If the work of art does nothing more than say what we already know, give somewhat elegant articulation to what we already believe, then it is insofar aesthetically worthless. But if, like *King Lear*, it starts from certain counted-on beliefs of the audience in order to make advances into hitherto obscure regions, it may merit our praise for the beauty of its ideational content.

TRUTH

It is very common in our day to lay down the following stipulations:

(1) No statement about the world is cognitively meaningful unless it is at least theoretically confirmable by empirical observation; i.e. shown by experimental evidence to be true or false.

(2) No statement may legitimately be called true unless publicly available evidence of a substantial amount may be cited in its support.

These rules have been principally used in order to rid philosophy of what many have taken to be idle metaphysical speculations, but they have also been used more recently to lump poetry and other forms of literature with metaphysics in a file bluntly labeled by some "non-sense," by others "pseudo-statements," by others something like "cognitively unimportant but often interesting and valuable utterances."[19]

It is of course true that on the perfectly literal level, a great many of the statements of literature are either meaningless or false. Thus, if we decide that a certain book of the *Odyssey* says "There was a man named Odysseus whose ship was wrecked by the god of the sea," it is open to us to debate whether such a statement could in any

[19] Richards, who uses the "pseudo-statement" terminology, was, even in his earlier books, a strong, even excessive advocate of literature, which he confidently expected to replace religion as an orderer of human attitudes.

sense be verified. If we decide that it cannot, the utterance will then be called *meaningless;* if it can, we will likely decide that the evidence is decidedly disconfirmatory, so the statement will be called false.

All of this may be admitted and the feeling continue that it is not to the point. What *is* to the point is this complex question: Is there some more subtle sense in which literature, at least sometimes, makes statements; some more subtle sense in which such statements may be confirmed; some more subtle sense in which such statements may be true or false? A decisive answer is forthcoming from some quarters: There is no warrant for using such words as "meaningful," "true," and "knowledge" except in the context of strict, controlled scientific procedure. This position is at least not wishy-washy and seems to settle some problems, but will be here rejected as not really a solution, as using these terms in an unusually narrow way, and as inviting disparagement of literature and other arts.

As we have already said, though not quite in these terms, there is a kind of verification process that operates in the reading of literature. It is, if you will, armchair verification, involving memory and imagination, "thought experiments" and the like; but for all its nonscientific character, it seems not inappropriate to speak of it as verification.

Suppose that we are reading an adventure story in which a desperado is described as blowing open a safe with a home-made explosive consisting of equal parts of salt, flour, and cayenne pepper. If the story is apparently intended to be serious—not a fantasy or a farce—it is easy to imagine being annoyed at this fake chemistry. We might say, "But that wouldn't explode. What's the matter with this author?" If the story were good enough otherwise, this might not be sufficient for us to condemn the work; but it can hardly be thought other than a blemish.

But now suppose the more likely and important circumstance in which a fictional character gets *out* of character, or in which his actions are explained in a way that seems to us plainly insufficient or wrong. A hardened criminal suddenly, and apparently without sufficient reason, becomes a sweet and kind gentleman. A stupid and inarticulate charwoman discourses learnedly on Marcellus of Padua. A refined society woman for no reason made known to us takes to chewing tobacco and talking like a top-sergeant. These are of course crudely exaggerated examples, but they point to the *kind* of thing we can test by our own experience and find mistaken. For obvious reasons, the world's most prized literature does not afford us many clear-cut instances of such damaging errors, but one *possible* instance comes to mind from the play recently referred to, *King Lear*. It will be remembered that at the start of the action, the King is shown dividing his kingdom among his daughters. He asks them first to express their love for him, after which he will apportion to each her just share. But when Cordelia balks at this open avowal, refusing finally to say words which her sisters have used with such hypocritical glibness, Lear cuts her off from her bounty, suddenly and ruthlessly. We realize that this opening scene must be very economically handled to allow room for the main action of the play, and we realize that Lear must be made out to be headstrong and obtuse in order to show the progress of his sensitivity and awareness; but the scene seems forced and exaggerated. We can hardly believe that even Lear would be so easily and utterly deceived. We are shocked at the disparity between his intelligence and ours, for we, who are newcomers, take in the situation at a glance, and poor Lear is hopelessly obtuse. This is doubtless an interpretation that will encounter many objections, but our point is this: *on* this interpretation, the play is at fault. Why do we feel that Lear wouldn't be that easily taken in? Partly from the evidences about his character afforded by the rest of the play. But partly, and this is the major point for the present, from our own psychological understanding, or if another phrase is preferred, our knowledge of life. When we read such things, we cannot but consult our own experience, and our experience will somewhere be relevant, for though we have not hobnobbed with kings and been in on the divisions of empires, we know something about fathers and daughters, about hypocrisy and honesty, about gratitude and greed. And what we know is intimately involved with what we read. We are not just looking for a confirmation of what we already know, but we are looking for actions that are convincingly compatible with what we know and for insightful extension of our own knowledge.

Some descriptions of scientific observation seem to suggest that the scientist goes into the experiment with a *tabula rasa* mind. But if he did, he would be altogether certain to come out with the tablet still unmarked. He of course carries with him to any observation a great deal that he already knows, and except in rare cases this knowledge is not itself up for correction: he is looking to extend what he knows but in ways consistent with his accumulated knowledge. The case is not entirely different with either artist or appreciator. Nevertheless, the verification that is relevant to the aesthetic processes is only what may be called "incipient verification." It is partial, likely to be unsystematic, taking place in imagination and memory; and still it is important.

Let us look for a moment at a favorable example, having glanced at a case in which the verification is negative, leading to disapproval. Here is a very brief instance. In *Crime and Punishment*, the murderer Raskolnikov is finally brought to the very brink of confession through the offices of a gentle, pious, and uncondemning girl, Sonia. And just before he opens his lips to tell his awful story, Raskolnikov feels a violent hatred for his confessor. And then the author says, "It was not hatred at all; he had mistaken one feeling for another. It merely meant that *the* moment had come." Here is a comment that might bring us up short with questions; for instance: Could he, can anyone, be *mistaken* about his own feeling? Can one have a feeling that seems like hatred but is not hatred? The notion that one can may be rather startling. But now what is one to do with such a question? The author says no more at least directly. He is not writing a systematic psychology. It is at precisely such a point as this that one may, even quite deliberately, *think*, think about one's own feelings and the interpretations of those feelings. And thinking, one may decide that it does sometimes happen: a feeling is not really what it first seems to be. And with that, he returns to the story.

This particular example may make the process of question-raising and verification sound more like an interruption of the aesthetic transaction than a continuation of it—and there are instances, to be sure, when an author or other artist leads us clear out of our aesthetic experience (perhaps into a voting booth) to the neglect of the art—but typically this imaginative turning of a question proceeds within the aesthetic spell; is, in fact, often one of its most deepening enhancements. Frank Lloyd Wright once wrote, "The artist's perception science later verifies."[20] Scientists (Sigmund Freud being an important example) have sometimes said the same. But the word "later" is important. The kind of verification that is scientific is not something appropriate to the special, self-contained, and delicate space of the aesthetic experience. But there often is verification of a more imaginative, remembering, and tentative kind, and its pronouncements are of particular importance to the quality of the experience itself.

THE LANGUAGE OF POETRY

The notion is commonly encountered that since poetry particularly, and prose literature to some extent as well, employs metaphorical and emotionally-toned language, it thereby forfeits any claim to cognitive significance. The scientist, it is pointed out, has to be exceedingly careful of his terms, making sure that each one is precisely and unambiguously definable; he must make sure that his propositions express very exactly the relations between the terms which he has in mind. He must take great pains to avoid any emotional red herrings in his language, sometimes even going out of his way to choose the most colorless, dull, scholarly words possible in order that the reader's attention may not be distracted from the point at issue.

The poet, on the other hand—so this common idea goes—is interested only in the emotional impact of his words. His job is to create a mood, to weave a spell, by his rhythms and images and harmonies. This being so, his language is necessarily *subjective*, contrasting sharply with the objectivity of scientific exposition. Poetry is therefore inexact, nebulous, shifting, vague, ambiguous—meaning now one thing to this reader, now something else to another—and who is to say which meaning is right? No, they're *all* right: poetry is whatever happens to you when you read the words on the page.

This account, while essentially correct in its description of scientific language, is essentially incorrect in its description of poetic language. Although there are many poets whose practice exhibits the use of vague, inexact language, and even some whose creed endorses such a practice, probably most poets would insist that their aim, however much they may fall short of it, is to use language in

[20] *Genius and the Mobocracy* (New York: Duell, Sloan & Pearce, 1949), p. 23.

the most precise, exact, controlled manner possible. If this is so, it may be asked why, then, the scientific and poetic uses of language are so strikingly different. The answer lies in an understanding of how the poet tries to express the full qualitative richness of an experience, and to do this must draw upon *all* the resources of language, its sounds, its beats, its suggestiveness, its denotation, its allusiveness. Scientific language, it must be understood, is not *the* model for language usage, but only the model for certain purposes. Scientific language is language stripped down to an aseptic austerity —perfect for some functions, sterile for others.

One of the most perceptive accounts of the difference between poetic and scientific language is that of Philip Wheelwright. Wheelwright makes out a contrast on three levels. First of all, the ultimate ingredient of scientific language is the "monosign"; of poetic language the "plurisign." A monosign is a term with a precisely defined, independent, and invariant meaning. A plurisign tends to carry a "plurality of meanings in any given instance" and to vary its meanings with every new context. For scientific purposes monosigns are combined in certain rigorously prescribed ways to make "propositions"; for poetic purposes plurisigns are combined to make "poetic statements." A proposition is an assertible, true or false entity. A poetic statement, on the other hand, is only "quasi-assertible," only true or false in a special sense. A proposition, it may be said, asserts "heavily," its monosign constituents being "solid." A poetic statement, however, asserts "lightly" (though not necessarily weakly, or unimportantly, or unseriously), its constituents being more fragile and delicate, and the relations between them more tenuous.

At the third level of semantic complexity, there is a contrast between the whole poem and the whole scientific work. In the case of the poem there is, or tends to be, a special organic quality; it is much less analyzable into its separate statements than is the scientific work; it has an inviolable unity in its completeness.[21]

This account makes it easy to see why poetry is so notoriously untranslatable, either into another language or into a paraphrase. "Untranslatable" is perhaps too severe a word, for of course there are admirable translations of some poetry, for instance the poetry of the Bible into several modern languages, of Shakespeare into

21 Philip Wheelwright, "The Semantics of Poetry," *The Kenyon Review*, II, No. 3, Summer 1940.

German, of Poe into French, of Baudelaire into English; at least the translations are good enough so that they may richly reward one who does not know the language of the original, and that without any radical distortion of meaning. Nevertheless, something is always lost. Any word in any language has its peculiar history and flavor, and no other word in any language will quite reproduce it. This is not important in science, where strenuous efforts are made to keep *out* any such qualities, but in poetry it is exceedingly important.

Now, if a good poem is sayable in no other way than its own, one understands the impatience of those who, demanding to know *what* it is that a given poem means, are told that the poem itself is the only answer. This is not to say that poetry is too fragile to touch, completely impervious to analysis, quite beyond paraphrase. No, as will be seen in the discussion on criticism, talk *about* poems can be exceedingly helpful, but it will never be quite a substitute for the poem itself.

Another way of saying this is to emphasize the ultimate inseparability of form and content in poetry. We have throughout this chapter been talking about the ideational content of literature, and so have been separating content from form, but only for purposes of analytic understanding. A. C. Bradley, who, it will be remembered, spoke of the subject of poetry as distinct from the substance, goes on to say that substance and form are so inextricably involved with each other as to form an organic union. "In poetry the meaning and the sounds are one: there is, if I may put it so, a resonant meaning, or a meaning resonance." And again:

> These heresies which would make poetry a compound of two factors—a matter common to it with the merest prose, plus a poetic form, as the one heresy says: a poetical substance plus a negligible form, as the other says—are not only untrue, they are injurious to the dignity of poetry.[22]

We must remember that whatever be the poet's ideas, these ideas insofar as they are poetic do not exist either before or even after the poem itself; they do not exist apart from the poem. The poet in expressing his ideas is arriving *at* them through the instrumentality of form; and equally, in utilizing form, he is not employing a ready-

22 "Poetry for Poetry's Sake," pp. 14, 24.

made garment for his ideas but is seeking fullness of expression. The creator may, indeed, start with certain ideas and certain forms in mind, but in the act of expression, these initial abstractions become concrete realities and they become so by becoming united.

This fact of the organic quality of poetry is the crowning reason why this form of discourse does not admit of the application of the words "true," "false," "belief," "disbelief," and "knowledge" *in the way* that factual prose does. Why not then just give them up? Why not admit that literature is noncognitive? Since, after all, there are many values in art, why insist that it have cognitive value too? These questions have been very seriously asked in our time. If it were only, as some think it is, a "matter of words," then of course the game would not be worth the candle; but it turns out to matter a great deal *what* things are called. Literature and science are very different enterprises from each other—they have interesting similarities too, but they remain very different—and so it needs to be made clear that poetry, to take this "purest" form of literature, does not contain propositions or state meanings or make assertions in the way that science does. But if one concludes from this that literature is therefore meaningless and devoid of ideational content, that it does not make *any* assertions and so cannot be either true or false, that being emotive and metaphorical and undivorceable from its own unique words it cannot therefore teach or convey knowledge, then one almost certainly, even in spite of himself, will end by disparaging literature as a humane enterprise. Since there are important ways in which we learn from literature, gain from it new insights into the ways of man and his world, it is simply false and misleading to say that literature is not cognitive. Its cognitive content, as we have seen, is typically indirect, slanting, figurative, concrete, dramatic, resistant of abstraction or translation, context-implicated, lightly asserted, and admitting not of laboratory testing but only of that sort that proceeds imaginatively within the aesthetic experience. But cognitive it is.

MUSIC AND COGNITION

Literature is of course the only *verbal* art. There is little question that its cognitive aspects are more pronounced and more important than those of any other art. Perhaps painting and sculpture, with their ability to represent and reveal and comment upon all of the visible world, stand closest to literature in ideational content, but music raises very hard problems in this respect.

Walter Pater spoke of music being "The ideal of all art, whatever, precisely because in music it is impossible to distinguish the form from the substance or matter, the subject from the expression. . . ."[23] In music there is the least possibility of a verbal "paraphrase" or a description being much more than irrelevant, and often it is an impertinence. When Samuel Johnson said that music "excites in my mind no ideas, and hinders me from contemplating my own," he did not mean to be paying music a high compliment; but many another person has particularly prized music for being a refuge from the idea-tormented seas of life.

Still, the history of aesthetics and music criticism has not gone wanting for those who find in music prophecy and revelation, truth, knowledge, and an access to a higher reality. Let us briefly examine some of the possibilities.

We will not here long dwell on music mixed with poetry and prose as in songs, recitatives, chants, and choral forms, for in such cases the presence of the words (*if* we can understand them) leaves in doubt how much the music is doing by itself. That music more or less fits and reinforces the words—or fails to do so—is clear enough, but what would the music be without the words? Then there is the case of programme music, where, as in Berlioz' *Harold in Italy* or Richard Strauss' tone poems, a regular story is told by the music—or *is* the story told by the music? No one would argue, probably, that music altogether unaided by pantomime or pictures or words could be a very effective narrative medium; but once we know the story, say from programme notes, then we can, sometimes with fair success, follow the course of events from musical clues.

But what about so-called "absolute" music, the usual string quartet or piano sonata or symphony? Is there any cognitive content here? Several quotations from eminent writers on the subject may lead our thinking.

23 *Appreciations,* quoted in E. F. Carritt, *Philosophies of Beauty* (Oxford: Oxford University Press, 1931), p. 187.

Wagner: *What music expresses, is eternal, infinite and ideal; it does not express the passion, love, or longing of such-and-such an individual on such-and-such an occasion, but passion, love or longing in itself, and this it presents in that unlimited variety of motivations, which is the exclusive and particular characteristic of music, foreign and inexpressible to any other language.*[24]

Mendelssohn: *What any music I like expresses for me is not thoughts too indefinite to clothe in words, but too definite.—If you asked me what I thought on the occasion in question, I say, the song itself precisely as it stands. And if, in this or that instance, I had in my mind a definite word or definite words, I would not utter them to a soul, because words do not mean for one person what they do for another; because the song alone can say to one, can awake in him, the same feelings it can in another—feelings, however, not to be expressed by the same words.*[25]

Susanne Langer: *Music is not the cause or the cure of feelings, but their* logical expression. . . . *The real power of music lies in the fact that it can be "true" to the life of feeling in a way that language cannot; for its significant forms have that* ambivalence of content *which words cannot have. . . . Not communication but insight is the gift of music; in very naive phrase, a knowledge of "how feelings go."*[26]

Carroll C. Pratt: *The aesthetic qualities of music are the direct counterpart in tone of the bodily reverberations involved in real emotion. . . . The ears of those who love music are filled with the form but not with the material of emotion. In this sense music is the language of emotion, and is unequalled in this regard by any other art.* Music sounds the way emotions feel.[27]

Herbert Spencer: *For this same passionate, enthusiastic temperament, which leads the musical composer to express the feelings possessed by others as well as himself in more marked cadences than they would use, also leads him to give musical utterance to feelings*

[24] "Ein Glücklicher Abend," quoted in Susanne K. Langer, *Philosophy in a New Key*, 2nd ed. (Cambridge: Harvard University Press, 1951), pp. 221-22.
[25] Quoted in John Hospers, *Meaning and Truth in the Arts* (Chapel Hill: University of North Carolina Press, 1946), p. 79. Mr. Hospers' book is one of the best treatments of the principal subjects of this chapter.
[26] *Philosophy in a New Key*, pp. 218, 234, and 244.
[27] *Music as the Language of Emotion* (Washington: Library of Congress, 1952), pp. 22, 26.

which they either do not experience or experience in but slight degrees. And thus we may in some measure understand how it happens that music not only so strongly excites our more familiar feelings, but also produces feelings we never had before—arouses dormant sentiments of which we do not know the meaning; or as Richter says—tells us of things we have not seen and shall not see.[28]

Alfred North Whitehead: *Music, ceremonial clothing, ceremonial smells, and ceremonial rhythmic visual appearances, also have symbolic truth, or symbolic falsehood. In these latter instances, the conveyance of suitable subjective form is at its height. Music provides an example when it interprets some strong sentiment, patriotic, martial, or religious, by providing the emotion which the votaries dumbly feel ought to be attached to the apprehension of national life, or of the clash of nations, or of the activities of God. Music elicits some confused feeling into distinct apprehension.*[29]

For all of the variety in these statements, there are certain very suggestive similarities. First of all, Wagner and Mendelssohn, while they disagree as to whether what music expresses is highly generalized or highly particularized, agree that the emotions of music are expressible in no other form, and so however much they are like the emotions of everyday, nonmusical life, there is something special about them. Langer and Pratt agree that music is the language of emotion, and that what this language conveys is not just the emotions themselves, but some sort of insight into the form or structure of the emotions. Spencer and Whitehead are impressed with the creative originality of the composer in providing feelings the audience would not be able to achieve by itself.

The strict *intellectual* content of music in the sense of verbally abstractable ideas is admitted on all sides to be slight or nonexistent; nevertheless, this is not to say that music is therefore only and always meaningless sound, for as J. W. N. Sullivan has tried to show in the case of Beethoven, a composer's musical creations may form part of his own spiritual development.[30] That is, he may be a person struggling to achieve an adequate religious or philosophical attitude toward himself, his fellows, and the cosmos, and he may never do it

[28] "The Origin and Function of Music," in *Literary Style and Music* (London: Watts, 1950), p. 66.
[29] *Adventures of Ideas* (New York: Macmillan, 1933), p. 319.
[30] *Beethoven: His Spiritual Development* (New York: Mentor, 1949).

or do it only haltingly and clumsily in words, but his music may seem to him somehow to be an expression of his struggle and perhaps of his victories, and may then be an expression too for others who hear it. Any gesture a person may make—a flutter of the fingers, a cry, a swaying of the body, a verbal exclamation—*any* gesture must be an expressive sign of that person and his state of being (for to say this or that *feeling* seems too restrictive); and when that gesture is recorded in whatever medium or by whatever means of notation it may conceivably awaken a somewhat similar state of being in another person. Not many philosophers choose to use "truth" as broadly as does Whitehead, when he writes of the appropriate correspondence of experienced feeling states to a situation as exemplifying truth, but many would with William James admit that "Feelings are the germ and starting point of cognition . . ." or even that there are "cognitive feelings," and some would say with Susanne Langer that there are certain aspects of the world that seem to be ineffable to verbal symbolization but expressible and communicable through the dancer's body, the architect's stones, the painter's strokes and the composer's fusion of sounds.

Chapter 10

PERCEPTION

and

REPRESENTATION

• *The* experiencing of a work of art is a perception. As a physical thing, the work of art may vary from a huge pile of granite to a few delicate sounds in the air, but in all cases alike there is *some* object capable of arousing a properly oriented person to an aesthetic experience. However, it is to be noticed that there is a difference among the several works in the (relatively) permanent form in which an art-work exists. A painting, a statue, and a building share this characteristic: all of them are tangible, visible existents. The mode of existence of music, literature, and dance is somewhat different. The composer, the poet, and the choreographer may make notations on paper, inscribing words or other signs, but these marks are not themselves the work of art—it is not the marks that are the direct object of our aesthetic regard, but something which the marks prescribe. A musical score may be regarded as directions for making music rather than as music itself. Before there is dance, the choreographer's notation must be translated into bodily movements. And—though this case is not quite so clear—poetry is not fully poetry until words have been pronounced.

The so-called "temporal arts," those which most fully exist on the occasions of their performance, have, because of their mode of existence, a somewhat less definite permanent nature than the "static arts." There is excellent reason to believe that the sounds that issued from Bach's clavier when he played his own "Prelude and Fugue in C♯ minor" were impressively different from those that proceed when Wanda Landowska or Gieseking plays the "same" piece. The *Macbeth* that an Elizabethan audience saw performed is not precisely the play we see revived on Broadway—or in the movies! Yet something—the directions, the signs on paper—stays the same, or very nearly the same. The case of prose literature, which is intended for silent reading, is still different, for here, as in the case of painting, the marks arouse the aesthetic experience without the offices of an interpreter, a player; and yet no one would say that it is the marks which he finds funny or sad.[1]

But there are further complications: the work of art is not just a physical object but an imaginative object. The statue we see is not just a shape of marble but it is a fleeing maiden and a pursuing man, and more than that, Daphne who was graciously transformed into a slender tree to escape the violence of the god Apollo. As a physical object that statue could stand right next to Hokusai's print "The Great Wave," but in other ways the works may properly be spoken of as very far apart, at least as far as Greece is from Japan. The two lines

> *Quoth the raven "Nevermore."*

and

> *Quoth the raven "Neversnore."*

are as marks and even as sounds very similar, but the act of perception in the two cases is rather shockingly different.

Perception, at least as the word will be here used, is not a simple mechanical process, the impinging of sound waves on the membranes of the ear or of light waves upon the retina of the eye. No, rather it is the whole complex act whereby the object, with its own peculiar nature as determined by its creator, calls out a more or less complete response from the percipient, a response varying both with

[1] It is not forgotten that poetry and even music may be read in this way too, though it is not so commonly nor so satisfactorily done in their cases.

the object and with the subject. Certain aspects of aesthetic perception have already been considered in some detail, especially the
ideational content of the art-work and the attitude of the would-be
appreciator, so in the present and the following chapter these elements will be largely neglected in favor of two other matters:
representation and form.

A work of art may or may not be *representational*. To say that it
is nonrepresentational or, as it is called in painting and sculpture,
"nonobjective," is to say that one does not find in the work any
representation or imitation of an object or event that might (at
least conceivably) be experienced in the outside or nonart world.
The distinction may be clearly understood from a brief consideration of dancing. A dancer may be a mimic: of his movements one
thinks, "Now he is a butterfly," or "He's a fop out for a stroll in
the park," or "He's showing Orpheus emerging from the under-
world." But another dancer, or the same dancer on a different occasion, may engender no such recognitions: one sees movement and
posture, bends and turns, strength and fragility, grace and strain,
but there is no apparent representation, the dance is not depicting
any thing or anyone or any special happening.

An intermediate stage may now be recognized between mimicry
or representation on the one side and pure nonrepresentation on the
other: the dancer may appear to us to be depicting an "abstract"
emotion, such as grief or jubilation or envy, not of this or that person or even type of person, but in its more generalized aspects. But
with this admission of an in-between, the door is almost necessarily
thrown open to several further possibilities. It seems that a work of
art is *more or less* representational; and of course its possession of
this quality is somewhat relative to the percipient. Some persons are
cleverer than others at seeing shapes in constellations, symbols in
gestures, and likenesses between painted lines and masses and figures
in the unframed world. It is partly, at least, a matter of training.
Small children do not know how to recognize objects in pictures;
some primitives cannot even tell the right side up of a snapshot of
their own home or brother.

In no other art has there been such a controversy about the legitimacy of the nonrepresentational as in painting. It is undoubtedly
true that a very great proportion of the people (at least in our cul-

ture) feel disappointed in a picture which to them "doesn't look like anything." On the other hand, there are not wanting critics who insist that the representational aspects of a painting are no source of the true aesthetic quality of the work, that they are at best neutral, but more commonly distracting and damaging.

In a famous passage in his life of Leonardo da Vinci, Vasari writes of "Mona Lisa":

> This head is an extraordinary example of how art can imitate Nature, because here we have all the details painted with great subtlety. The eyes possess that moist lustre which is constantly seen in life, and about them are those livid reds and hair which cannot be rendered without the utmost delicacy. The lids could not be more natural, for the way in which the hairs issue from the skin, here thick and there scanty, and following the pores of the skin. The nose possesses the fine delicate reddish apertures seen in life. The opening of the mouth, with its red ends, and the scarlet cheeks seem not colour but living flesh. To look closely at her throat you might imagine that the pulse was beating. Indeed, we may say that this was painted in a manner to cause the boldest artists to despair. Mona Lisa was very beautiful, and while Lionardo was drawing her portrait he engaged people to play and sing, and jesters to keep her merry, and remove that melancholy which painting usually gives to portraits. This figure of Lionardo's has such a pleasant smile that it seemed rather divine than human, and was considered marvelous, an exact copy of Nature.[2]

An exact copy of nature: in many ages, including our own, this has been widely considered to be the highest praise that can be bestowed on a picture, provided—some would add—that the artist has selected from nature something worth copying.

An old legend describes a contest between the Greek painters Zeuxis and Parrhasios. It was Zeuxis' boast that he could paint grapes which birds would peck at, so Parrhasios invited his rival to his studio and asked him to draw back a curtain which covered his new picture. When Zeuxis tried to do this, he found that the curtain was itself painted. Parrhasios was considered the victor: where Zeuxis could fool birds, Parrhasios could fool men, even another painter.

In this present age, when it is often considered a mark of sophisti-

[2] *The Lives of the Painters, Sculptors, and Architects*, trans. A. B. Hinds (New York: Dutton, 1927), Vol. II, 164.

cation in the painter to foreswear and in the appreciator to despise
copying or the making of likenesses, a few words of defense of
representative art may be appropriate. The authority of critics like
Vasari is substantiated by the testimony of great painters and great
philosophers. Aristotle, for instance, wrote:

> The instinct of imitation is implanted in man from childhood,
> one difference between him and other animals being that he is the
> most imitative of creatures; and through imitation he acquires his
> earliest learning. And, indeed, every one feels a natural pleasure in
> things imitated. There is evidence of this in the effect produced by
> works of art. Objects which in themselves we view with pain, we
> delight to contemplate when reproduced with absolute fidelity:
> such as the forms of the most ignoble beasts and of dead bodies.
> The cause of this again is, that to learn is a lively pleasure, not only
> to philosophers but to men in general; whose capacity, however,
> of learning is more limited. Thus the reason why men enjoy seeing
> a likeness is, that in contemplating it they are engaged in learning
> —they reason and infer what each object is.[3]

Rodin—to choose one artist among many who have said something similar—once wrote:

> But, after all, the only principle in art is to copy what you see.
> Dealers in aesthetics to the contrary, every other method is fatal.
> There is no recipe for improving nature.[4]

Faithful reproduction of a natural scene or a human face and
body is—contrary to some belief—no easy thing; no practicing artist,
however skillful a craftsman, will gainsay that. And all of us do tend
to take a delight in the successful accomplishment of a difficult task.

Furthermore, there does seem to be a very general human disposition—whether or not *instinctive* as Aristotle believed—to view with
satisfaction a reproduction of reality, whether it be painting, wax
statue, plaster cast taken from life, topographical map, model of a
building, or a photograph. However, it may be doubted whether the
admiration of skill and the delight in reproductions are feelings at
the very center of aesthetic appreciation. And it may be doubted
whether painting can compete or should compete with photog-

[3] *Poetics*, trans. Butcher.
[4] Quoted in *Artists on Art*, ed. Robert Goldwater and Marco Treves (New
York: Pantheon, 1945), p. 325.

REMBRANDT, Young Girl at an Open Half-Door

Courtesy of The Art Institute of Chicago
(Mr. and Mrs. Martin A. Ryerson Collection)

Above:

GIOTTO, Pietà

Arena Chapel, Padua (Photo Alinari)

Right:

EL GRECO,
Feast in the House of Simon

Courtesy of The Art Institute of Chicago
(Joseph Winterbotham Collection)

Left:

CÉZANNE,
Pines and Rocks

Collection Museum of Modern Art, New York (Lillie P. Bliss Collection)

Below left:

ROUAULT,
The Three Judges

Courtesy of The Art Institute of Chica (Gift of Mr. and Mrs. Samuel A. Mar

Below right:

CHAGALL, The Rabbi

Courtesy of The Art Institute of Chica (Joseph Winterbotham Collection)

Left:

MONDRIAN, Composition in White, Black and Red
Collection Museum of Modern Art, New York

Below:

Lever House, New York
Skidmore, Owings and Merrill, Architects

Chartres Cathedral

Left:

LACHAISE, Standing Woman
Courtesy of The Art Institute of Chicago
(Friends of American Art Gift)

Below:

MICHELANGELO, Pietà
Cast, Courtesy Metropolitan Museum of Art, New York

raphy. Henri Matisse has even said that photography fortunately relieves the painter of the necessity for exact reproduction.

In recent decades, perhaps partly because of a growing awareness on the part of painters that they cannot compete with the camera, there has been a "retreat from likeness,"[5] ranging through the various types of Expressionists and Abstractionists to the avowed "nonobjectivists."

OPPOSITION TO REPRESENTATIONALISM

The arguments fired against traditional representation (though it would be a serious mistake to imply that all art before the "modern" period was simply representational or that representationalism has expired) may be grouped under six headings:

(1) *Selectivity.* From time to time in more than one of the arts, there has been exhibited a naturalistic revolt against what have come to seem artificial, contrived, lifeless, and conventional. The naturalists have preached and practiced "setting down what is there," no matter how stark, forbidding, or commonplace; in manner too they have sometimes deliberately avoided tidiness, order, regularity, and obedience to rules. But naturalism has in time spawned its own rebels, who have endeavored to reinstate the selectivity which is at the heart of artistic creation. A remark like that of Delacroix's, "Nature is far from being always interesting from the standpoint of effect and of ensemble," could only be worth making in opposition to those who had seemed to say that nature is always interesting, that the painter has only to set up his easel at random and go to work copying whatever greets his eyes.

In the drama, too, certain excesses in the "slice of life" school called out the reminder that the artist must at the very least choose with careful discrimination what to portray, must eliminate a very great deal of dross if he is to avoid the humdrum from which art presumably rescues us.

As Goya said,

Painting, like poetry, selects in the universe whatever she deems most appropriate to her ends. She assembles in a single fantastic per-

[5] See Frances B. Blanshard, *Retreat from Likeness in the Theory of Painting* (New York: Columbia University Press, 1949).

*sonage circumstances and features which nature distributes among
many individuals. From this combination, ingeniously composed,
results that happy imitation by virtue of which the artist earns the
title of inventor and not of servile copyist.*[6]

(2) *Imagination.* The "servile copyist" has abrogated his special
human gift; he has so chained himself to nature as to deny opportunity for his creative imagination. Sir Joshua Reynolds urged the
painter to learn from the poet:

*Among the Painters and the writers on Painting, there is one
maxim universally admitted and continually inculcated. Imitate Nature, is the invariable rule; but I know none who have explained in
what manner this rule is to be understood; the consequence of
which is, that every one takes it in the most obvious sense,—that
objects are represented naturally, when they have such relief that
they seem real. It may appear strange, perhaps, to hear this sense of
the rule disputed; but it must be considered, that if the excellency
of a Painter consisted only in this kind of imitation, Painting must
lose its rank, and be no longer considered as a liberal art, and sister
to Poetry: this imitation being merely mechanical, in which the
slowest intellect is always sure to succeed best; for the Painter of
genius cannot stoop to drudgery, in which the understanding has
no part; and what pretence has the Art to claim kindred with Poetry, but by its power over the imagination? To this power the
Painter of genius directs his aim; in this sense he studies Nature,
and often arrives at his end, even by being unnatural, in the confined sense of the word.*[7]

The argument is that nature, the given, usually requires not
merely selective editing, but actual change, reassembling, improvement.

(3) *Revelation of the unseen.* Some there are who would agree
that the artist's job is that of "painting what he sees," but would
quickly and emphatically add that the artist—at least if he is a good
artist—differs from the bulk of mankind in how much and how
deeply he sees. Rodin proclaimed that the artist's "emotion reveals
to him the hidden truths beneath appearances," and this point has
been made in a hundred different ways by artists and their interpreters, but seldom better than by Richard Muller-Freienfels:

[6] Quoted in *Artists on Art,* pp. 203-204.
[7] *Ibid.,* p. 186.

Against the opinion that the essential characteristic of pictures is agreement with an actual object—with nature, as is usually said— I propose the thesis that pictures are created in order to make visible what is not visible.[8]

The author goes on to mention several ways in which this is done; one is described as follows:

In the picture certain aspects of actual objects are made visible to which generally little attention is paid, or which are not perceived at all; or the objects are presented within a different context, in different proportion, under different light and atmospheric conditions, under which they assume a completely new appearance which nobody had perceived before. . . . What makes a picture the work of a genius is not the degree to which it resembles the model, but rather what the artist has seen as "surplus value" in the model; what he has extracted from the model and projected upon the model. . . .[9]

(4) *Priority of expression.* The ideal of perfect objectivity in artistic representation is neither susceptible of being realized nor worth the striving for, it has been argued, because each man will inevitably reveal something of himself in his creations—and rightly so, for what do we want of the artist but some interpretation, some presentation of the superior temperament that is presumably his? But once the artist comes to see that creation is primarily expression and only secondarily (if that) imitation or representation, he will be actually helped to free himself. His responsibility is not to his model but to his own inward self; thus, if he can better say what he wants and needs to say by distortion, by abstraction, by dispensing with the principle of recognition altogether—why not?

To be sure, the portrait painter is often held to account by his patron; if he fails to come up with a speaking likeness, so much the worse for him. But those who have gained more than a local reputation for portraiture have asserted their own superiority to their model, whatever his status. It is said that a patron once complained to Titian that his new portrait was not a good likeness. The artist's reply was: "A hundred years from now nobody will care what you

[8] "On Visual Representation: the Meaning of Pictures and Symbols," *The Journal of Aesthetics and Art Criticism*, VII, No. 2 (December 1948), 112.
[9] *Ibid.*, 112-114.

looked like, but anybody will be proud to own a Titian." The story may be apocryphal, but it is doubtless a faithful rendering of what many artists have thought.

Henri Matisse has explained that artistic expression is not primarily a matter of mirroring the passion expressed on a human face.

The whole arrangement of my picture is expressive. The place occupied by figures or objects, the empty spaces around them, the proportions—everything plays a part. Composition is the art of arranging in a decorative manner the various elements at the painter's disposal for the expression of his feelings.

He tells how this priority of expression leads to "distortion."

To paint an autumn landscape I will not try to remember what colors suit this season, I will only be inspired by the sensation that the season gives me; the icy clearness of the sour blue sky will express the season just as well as the tonalities of the leaves.[10]

(5) *Reality beyond reality.* Phantasy art must be approximately as old as art itself. The satyrs of ancient sculpture, the gargoyles of the medieval cathedrals, the diabolic canvasses of Hieronymous Bosch, are only a few notable examples that come to mind of artistic imaginations that have portrayed what never was on sea or land. But in more recent times, a rationale has been available for the artist of phantasy. There is, the argument runs, no good reason for the painter or other artist to be restricted in his subject matter to conscious, public, rational, waking life. There is also the wealth of material contained in the unconscious, private, irrational side of life, especially as revealed in dream and illusion.

The canvas of the surrealist painter is, usually, starkly "realistic" in parts. There will perhaps be an ordinary table, an ordinary man, an ordinary office building, and an ordinary basketball; but they will be placed in quite extraordinary juxtaposition in the middle of a desert landscape: the whole will be intended to have symbolic character, strongly suggestive and evocative of moods, of hidden fears and desires. For the painter in his zealousness to be more conventionally representational is for him to be quite gratuitously cut off from these depths of life to which the artist should be peculiarly sensitive.

[10] Quoted in *Artists on Art*, pp. 410, 411.

(6) *Primacy of plastic values*. Perhaps no argument has been so strongly and persistently advanced in favor of the "retreat from likeness" that has characterized much recent painting and sculpture as that which makes the case for putting the qualities of material and form above everything else. From a Cezanne so concerned about spoiling the harmony of colors already within a picture that he left spots of uncovered canvas,[11] to a Whistler lashing out in annoyance at the sentimental public who must forever be speaking of his mother rather than the harmony of tones in his "Arrangement in Grey and Black," modern artists have tried to develop in the public their own passionate regard for plastic values themselves. Marc Chagall, whose paintings have afforded field days for critics avid for symbolic interpretation, tended himself to speak in rather severe formalistic terms:

> For me a picture is a plane surface covered with representations of objects—beasts, birds, or humans—in a certain order in which anecdotal illustrational logic has no importance. The visual effectiveness of the painted composition comes first. Every extra-structural consideration is secondary.[12]

It is not hard to understand why creative artists in all the different arts have so often been impatient with a public all too willing to praise or damn their works on the basis of very narrow expectations. Consider the feelings of a composer who, having spent a succession of sleepless nights in trying to work out a few measures of harmonic progression, hears people commenting only on the story which they hear or think they hear in the composition; of the novelist who discovers that apparently nobody has paid any attention to the intricate structure of his plot in their concern for whether the hero is seduced by Communism; of the sculptor who finds that almost nobody can think of any reason why he has a hole in his statue unless it be that he was laboring under the supposition that ordinary "real-life" cows are anatomically so arranged. It is no wonder that a Schumann will impatiently exclaim:

> Critics always wish to know what the composer himself cannot tell them—Good heavens! Will the day ever come when people will

[11] See Leo Stein, *Appreciation: Painting, Poetry and Prose* (New York: Crown, 1947), pp. 74-75.
[12] Quoted in *Artists on Art*, p. 433.

*cease to ask us what we mean by our divine compositions? Pick out
the fifths, but leave us in peace. . . .*[13]

It is no wonder that such a painter and critic as Clive Bell was led
to write, in a famous passage:

*The representative element in a work of (visual) art may or may
not be harmful; always it is irrelevant.*

*To appreciate a work of art we need bring with us nothing but
a sense of form and color and a knowledge of three-dimensional
space.*[14]

These words were written in 1913; and ever since that time they
have afforded aestheticians a text on "pure formalism." They have
done the service of a whole fleet of yeomen in eliciting amplifica-
tion, correction, and abuse; but perhaps the best simple modification of the position comes in a book which Bell himself wrote more
than twenty years later. There he says:

*In the Sistine Madonna—to take for example a picture which ev-
eryone knows—there is a human relationship between mother and
child. There is something which is not, as I formerly supposed,
purely a matter of lines and colours. It is something, however, which
can be expressed in line and colour alone. . . . It is of those sentiments which, though felt in the heart, can be externalized only in
forms, recognized only by the eye, and recorded only by an appeal
to the eye, which are, therefore, the peculiar property of the
graphic and plastic arts.*[15]

This passage furnishes a moral which can be broadened to include
all the arts, and which, then, furnishes an occasion for a reappraisal
of the role of representation.

Every work of art needs and deserves to be attended to and, if
the occasion warrants, criticized, as a unique achievement. Painters
have come to use the term "literary art" scornfully because they
have been surfeited both by charlatans who have tried to ride to
wealth and fame on the wagon of a popular subject matter (babies,
beautiful girls, fishing-holes, rock-bound coasts, etc.), and by a
public which has taken to pulling such wagons with shouts of joy.
Literary painting is art that seems to invite consideration as a form

[13] Quoted in Edward Gurney, *The Power of Sound* (London: Smith, Elder, &
Co., 1880), p. 357.
[14] *Art* (New York: Stokes, n.d.), pp. 25, 27.
[15] *Enjoying Pictures* (New York: Harcourt, Brace, 1934), pp. 79-80.

of literature and not as a form of visual art, just as programme music may invite attention to its plot to the neglect of its sounds. But a painting is surely not a good *painting* just because it is successful in reminding us of the hardships suffered at Valley Forge or arousing sexual desire or inspiring us with a yearning to visit Pago Pago. The serious painter has very often turned severely away from such themes, just because they are seductive and distracting; in their stead, he has sought out ramshackle barns or gray, eroded hillsides or austerely functional machines before which to put up his easel; or he has worked out grotesque distortions (as in, say, Picasso's women with "misplaced" eyes); or has even gone to the extreme of limiting himself to colored rectangles.[16] Sometimes painters have pretended that they were not in the least interested in the symbolic quality of their forms as composers have come to disavow their own suggestive titles or programmes. A painter, if he is any good, wants to be judged and (of course) admired on the basis of his lines and masses and colors, of the dynamic relationships among the different parts of his composition. In the same way, the sculptor cannot be content even with praise when it neglects the texture of his material, the adequacy of his modelling, or his consideration of the effects of shadows.

Workers in tones and plastic materials have often been especially resentful of what they take to be attempts to reduce their works to *verbal* accounts. Quite rightly, they insist that a mural (for instance) is something much more than even the lengthiest and most discerning analysis and description of it.

Certain topics have furnished subject matter to workers in different media. Among many others, Bach and Rubens represented the Passion of Christ. Tschaikowsky has "retold" the piteous love of Romeo and Juliet. The descent of Orpheus into Hell has been dealt with not only by dramatists and musicians but also by the great creator of dances, George Balanchine. "The Afternoon of a Faun" is a poem, a dance, a musical tone poem, and some stage sets.[17] And

16 This is not to say that Picasso, Mondrian *et al.* are merely negative in their motivations. Unquestionably they are, by their various means, seeking adequate expression.

17 See Thomas Munro's comparison of the several treatments of this theme, "Afternoon of a Faun and the Interrelations of the Arts," *Journal of Aesthetics and Art Criticism,* X (December 1951), 95-111.

yet, of course, success in one medium means nothing about success or failure in another just because the two attempts share a theme. Indeed, it is far from the case that a poem and a tone poem, a painting and a story, *mean* the same thing just because they are called by a common title or because they may be abstractly described as both about such-and-such. A painting has to be different from a non-painting, for the simple reason that no work of art is just a transparent window on a subject matter. Only a work of music employs musical tones, and they cannot be left out of account; a painting has stopped being a painting when its specific colors and lines have given way to words or a vague feeling. As Clive Bell said, whatever is in the Sistine Madonna that is not just color and line is something that can be expressed *only* by color and line. But more than that, *that* something can be expressed only by *those* colors and *those* lines. Another painter, Andrea del Sarto, for example, can also paint a Madonna, but he has something else to say, something else to invite us to see: consequently, his colors and lines are different. We go wrong if we ever suppose that there is a complete subject matter, the Madonna theme (to continue the example), which exists as it were neutrally, without any sensuous embodiment, and that the different paintings (poems, songs, etc.) about the Madonna, are simply alternative means of access to this one conception. Two paintings of a Madonna do of course have something in common; but it is entirely possible that they have less in common than do two works, one of a Madonna and one of a fir tree, both of which are by the same artist, or both of which employ a triangular composition, or both of which are done in colors of heavy saturation.

THE "GRAND MANNER"

Yet again, to say that representation is not all-important in painting, sculpture or any other art, is not to say that it is completely without importance. Though, as we have already noticed, some writers have gone so far as to aver that only the *how* and not the *what* is worth noticing, others, including artists of genius, have denied this. Consider, for a moment, the controversy over the "Grand Manner" or the "Grand Style."

Poussin maintained that painters "who elect mean subjects take refuge in them because of the weakness of their talents,"[18] whereas the best painters are careful to choose subject matter of dignity and magnificence appropriate to their abilities. Sir Joshua Reynolds agreed. The genuine painter, he told the students of the Royal Academy, forswears minutiae for loftiness and grandeur. "Invention in painting," he says,

> does not imply the invention of the subject; for that is commonly supplied by the poet or historian. With respect to choice, no subject can be proper that is not generally interesting. It ought to be either some eminent instance of heroic action, or heroic suffering. There must be something either in the action, or in the object, in which men are universally concerned, and which powerfully strikes upon the public sympathy.[19]

Strictly speaking, this means not the taking of nature literally, but the improvement of nature, the elimination of "accidental deficiencies, excrescences, and deformities of things," in order to reveal "the perfect state of nature, which the artist calls the ideal beauty."[20]

The Grand Style requires the ignoring of such mistakes as nature made in giving Alexander a small stature or St. Paul a mean body. Alexander and St. Paul are figures of great importance, well worth the attention of the sublimest painter, but they themselves must be raised to sublimity, their figures made imposing to match their military or spiritual power. Bernini comes in for sharp criticism from Reynolds for representing David when about to sling the stone as biting his lip. It is, if you will, a characteristic gesture, but it is not a noble one, and David must be represented nobly. Along the same lines, the Dutch painters doubtless exhibit ingenuity and a certain skill, but all too often they employ it on nothing higher than the interior of a Dutch home—which is insufficiently *general* to constitute the highest subject matter.

One meaning of the highly ambiguous word "realism" opposes the realist to the idealist of the Grand Style. This kind of realist insists that blemishes are not necessarily less interesting or legitimate subject matter than perfections, that "low" life is no worse to the

[18] Quoted in *Artists on Art*, p. 155.
[19] *Discourses on Art*, Discourse IV.
[20] *Ibid.*, Discourse III.

painter than "high." Millet would paint peasants in the field, Daumier, washerwomen; indeed, Reynolds' older contemporary, Hogarth, represented orgies of gin-drinking.

In the twentieth century, few require convincing that men of low economic and social status may be the heroes of drama and fiction, that primitive fertility rites may be celebrated in dance and music as in Stravinsky's *Sacre du Printemps*, or that prize fighters may be the centers of attention as in a painting by George Bellows—not only "may be" but may quite *properly* be, without discredit to the artist: such works, it would be very widely maintained in our non-aristocratic age, may be of very high rank.

And yet there are those who would go along with A. C. Bradley, generalizing what he says of poetry to apply to painting and sculpture as well. "The formalist," Bradley says,

> *goes too far, I think, if he maintains that the subject is indifferent and that all subjects are the same to poetry. And he does not prove his point by observing that a good poem might be written on a pin's head, and a bad one on the Fall of Man. That truth shows that the subject* settles *nothing, but not that it counts for nothing. The Fall of Man is really a more favourable subject than a pin's head. The Fall of Man, that is to say, offers opportunities of poetic effects wider in range and more penetrating in appeal. And the fact is that such a subject, as it exists in the general imagination, has some aesthetic value before the poet touches it.*[21]

"MODERN ART"

It may be here left an open question whether some subjects intrinsically offer opportunities of artistic "effects wider in range and more penetrating in appeal" than do others. Those who take either side of this debate might still agree that the last hundred years in the history of painting and sculpture have extended men's conception of what can be accomplished not only outside the range of noble and magnificent subject matter, but also outside the range of "realism," where now the much-bruited word signifies (however

[21] "Poetry for Poetry's Sake," in *Oxford Lectures on Poetry* (London: Macmillan, 1909), pp. 11-12. Reprinted by permission of the publisher and St. Martin's Press, Inc., New York.

vaguely) a relatively photographic representation of the visible world. This sort of realism may be given a loose but workable ostensive definition by pointing to the best-known portraits, still lifes, historical and genre paintings, and landscapes of European artists in the period from the Renaissance through the eighteenth century. Admittedly there is a great range here, but if one thinks of, say, such familiar pictures as Botticelli's "Birth of Venus," Leonardo's "Last Supper," Raphael's "School of Athens," Brueghel's "Peasant Dance," Rubens' "Descent from the Cross," van Ruysdael's "The Mill," Vermeer's "Girl with a Water Jug," and Gainsborough's "Blue Boy"; and such familiar statues as Michelangelo's "David," Bernini's "Longinus," and Houdon's "Voltaire," one can immediately add many more instances to the class taking shape.

Now the work which sorts itself into such categories as "impressionism," "cubism," "expressionism," "post-impressionism," "futurism," "surrealism," and "nonobjectivism"—all this great miscellany of styles and creeds may be, for present purposes, provisionally ranged against "realism." How? In forsaking "reality"? Not by any means necessarily. The impressionists, for instance, frequently claimed to be abandoning certain conventions of their predecessors and academic contemporaries in order to be *more* faithful to nature. They argued that there are no lines in nature and therefore should be none on the canvas; that there are no blacks in nature and therefore should be none on the palette; that their juxtapositions of raw complementary colors give far closer approximation of the way things look in bright sunlight than was possible in other techniques. The controversial "Nude Descending the Staircase" is often defended as a wonderfully accurate piece of observation, not less but more true than "static" pictures. Abstractionists have used arguments not altogether unlike those of Reynolds quoted above; saying, that is, that they are searching for the essences, not the accidents, of reality. And surrealists, as their name implies, claim to be more realistic than the old fashioned realists, carrying their penetrations below the surface into the hitherto invisible world of the unconscious.

But more "realistic" than the realists or not, these schools have this in common: that they advocate more or less drastic departures from the means of the realists in the interest, as they think, of the improvement of painting. By their means, so the claim continues, they extend the range of the painter's discoveries and revelations.

But two types of painters do specifically disavow as any part of their aim the showing or displaying of something in the natural world. One type—which has no name—though it continues to paint trees and horses and people and apples, insists that these objects as such have no significance for them but are important only as colors, shapes, movements. Finally, there are the nonobjectivists, who say that the only sure way of putting first things first is to divest the canvas of any distracting irrelevancies such as recognizable objects; then the painter and his audience can give their full attention to plastic values, to pattern, to design.

It would be fatuous to deny that some appreciators derive a genuine and even intense aesthetic satisfaction from works of plastic art without any of the satisfaction springing from a representative factor. Interestingly, the same person who will laugh or contemptuously snort at a "modern" painting or statue will be perfectly respectful toward an obelisk or the nonrepresentative design of a rug or a drape. A great deal obviously depends upon our initial expectations: if in one's experience it has been almost unvaryingly usual for paintings to display apples and people and buildings and such, then it may seem in the highest degree unnatural for a painting of similar size and shape and pigments to be only oblongs of color, and it may be difficult or impossible for one to attend to such a work aesthetically. A child who is brought up on programme music may find it hard to keep his mind on music that has no story. But it is no less certain that as one can learn to listen to and deeply enjoy absolute music, so too one can learn to appreciate nonobjective painting, and can come, at least to a considerable extent, to ignore representative aspects in other paintings in order to concentrate on the plastic values.

Neverthelesss, in a musical work in which we hear the call of the cuckoo and in a painting in which we see a mother and child, it seems gratuitous advice to insist that we should somehow suppress this recognition, noticing only the interval of the sounds, only the color and lines on the canvas. The artist in such cases, might, after all, have achieved very similar (of course not identical) formal effects without giving us a cuckoo or a mother and child. Surely our total aesthetic experience must embrace such recognitions; the seeing of a human mother and child is a very different perception from the seeing of a sow and her litter, even though it is conceivable that formal qualities should be quite close in two such cases.

It has sometimes been argued that if it is admitted that a work of art may be a genuine aesthetic object without being representative, then it must be the case that the representational element is necessarily and invariably superfluous; but such reasoning seems no more compelling than someone's insisting that since etchings may please us, the colors in oil paintings are aesthetically unimportant, or that since some poems are unrhymed, the rhyme when present deserves to be ignored. A composition in yellow, black, and white, by Piet Mondrian, may bring us an aesthetic satisfaction beyond what we had expected to find in a nonobjective work. This may teach us that there is far more in a painting than its more or less skillful rendering of familiar shapes; but if it teaches us that Rembrandt's "Windmill" differs only in its disposition of lines and colors and shapes, it teaches us too much; it teaches us what is untrue.

SUBJECT MATTER FOR REPRESENTATION

So far in our discussion of representation, too little has been said about what may be represented. It is time, now, to make amends for this neglect and to broaden our concept of "representational." It will be useful to follow the lead of Erwin Panofsky, who distinguishes three sorts of subject matter in a visual work of art.[22]

(1) Primary or natural subject matter is subdivided into (a) factual and (b) expressional. We perceive the factual subject matter of a painting when we recognize a certain configuration as a man leaning on a hoe. If we make a further interpretation and speak of his face having a tired and vacant look, we are attending to the expressional aspect.

(2) Secondary or conventional subject matter is "apprehended by realizing that a male figure with a knife represents St. Bartholomew, that a female figure with a peach in her hand is a personification of veracity, that a group of figures seated at a dinner table in a certain arrangement and in certain poses represents the Last Supper . . ."[23] In short, whenever we interpret the traditional symbols,

22 See *Meaning in the Visual Arts* (Garden City: Doubleday, 1955), chap. i.
23 *Ibid.*, pp. 28-29.

motifs, or allegories we are dealing with conventional subject matter.

(3) Intrinsic meaning or content is that about a work of art which enables us to regard it as a manifestation of the artist's personality, his times, a particular religious or political commitment, an economic class, or some other large-scale fact. This symbolic quality of art (interpretation of which Panofsky calls "iconology") may or may not be known or intended by the artist.

Now, whatever kind of subject matter a work of art does in fact have, a certain equipment is necessary on the part of the appreciator if his interpretations are to be sound and his experience informed. A child might not be able to recognize in a given painting that such-and-such a shape was a dove or that the expression on a character's face was one of holiness and piety. A Chinese might not gather that the mother with child was Mary with the infant Jesus, much less that this symbolizes an elaborate religious story and theology. These would be genuine failures of perception and appreciation: the aesthetic experience would suffer accordingly. The child might still like the painting, the Chinese might have a very deep sensitivity for its formal values; nevertheless, something rich would be neglected.

It is well worth observing that a painting might possibly lack subject matter in the first two senses and still have it in the third: indeed it may be doubted if it is possible for any artifact altogether to lack "intrinsic meaning." Any gesture of a human being is theoretically susceptible of being interpreted as "characteristic" or "symptomatic"; if the interpreter is astute enough, he will be able to see its meaning—if it be only a highly abstract or nonobjective work—in the sense that in being a product of someone at some time and place, that person and time and place are somehow symbolized by the art object.

Given these ways of symbolization or representation, we are now in a position to distinguish (though, as will be seen, not clearly *separate*) two sorts of relationship that may obtain between the art-work and its referent—that is, whatever it refers to, whatever it is about. Let us call the two "iconic" and "noniconic." Iconic representation is representation by means of likeness, resemblance, similarity. I pick up a snapshot and say, "Oh, this is Matilda." I look at a map and say, "Here is that bend in the road." I listen to a radio mimic and say, "Oh, he's taking off Senator So-and-So." In all such cases there is a quite distinct and specifiable point-for-point likeness or iconicity that enables me to know what is being represented by the sign. On the other hand, the word "cat" stands for cat without there being anything feline about the word or anything verbal about the animal.

A certain picture by Augustus John represents Dylan Thomas by looking like Dylan Thomas: one who had seen the man would be able to recognize the picture as a picture of him; one who had seen the portrait might be able to recognize its subject getting off a train. A Hindu picture of Brahman is recognized for what it is by having three heads; a pagan may be permitted to doubt that this is an actual similarity. A caduceus in a painting is iconic to the extent that we recognize a serpent, noniconic to the extent that we understand this to symbolize, conventionally, Hermes, the messenger god.

Literature is of course typically noniconic, the most obvious exceptions occurring in onomatopoeia. Music is seldom iconic, although occasionally we can pick out a bird call or the play of a fountain, the stir of a storm or the charge of a locomotive. Architecture is, apart from its sculptural adornments, noniconic: what is a building like—except another building?

And yet, may there not be iconic representation of something besides visible and audible surfaces? Can a painted canvas be *like* nothing but colored shapes? Can musical tones be like nothing but other sounds? At least two schools of psychology, the psychoanalysts (including the Jungian branch) and the Gestaltists, incline to answer that iconicity is broader than we have so far supposed. Erich Fromm, for instance, discusses what he calls "universal symbols," which are understood not by convention and not by accidental association, but by means of some deeper connection; here is a language "in which the world outside is a symbol of the world inside, a symbol for our souls and our minds."[24]

We express our moods by our facial expressions and our attitudes and feelings by movements and gestures so precise that others recognize them more accurately from our gestures than from our words. Indeed, the body is a symbol—and not an allegory—of the

[24] *The Forgotten Language: An Introduction to the Understanding of Dreams, Fairy Tales and Myths* (New York: Rinehart, 1951), p. 12

mind. Deeply and genuinely felt emotion, and even any genuinely felt thought, is expressed in our whole organism. In the case of the universal symbol, we find the same connection between mental and physical experience. Certain physical phenomena suggest by their very nature certain emotional and mental experiences, and we express emotional experiences in the language of physical experiences, that is to say, symbolically.[25]

Dreams, the psychoanalysts maintain, are symbolic not merely in showing us images of our acquaintances but even more importantly in showing us images of our fears, desires, and other feelings. The dream of a journey on a train may be latently about death and our fear of or our wish for death. And at the end of *King Lear* the weary, heartsick Duke of Kent says:

> *I have a journey, sir, shortly to go;*
> *My master calls me,—I must not say no.*

The journey as death, water as birth, majesty as fatherhood, climbing and falling as sexual stimulation—these seem to have a universality unaccountable except in terms of some underlying, intrinsic similarity between symbol and referent.

Gestalt psychologists speak of an "isomorphic" relationship between gestures and moods, facial expressions and feeling, tonal intervals and psychological states. They are impressed—in contrast with the more usual emphasis now upon the "subjectivism" and "anarchism" of the whole world of feelings—with the relative orderliness, dependability, and intelligibility of symbolic expressions of feelings. Rudolph Arnheim believes that:

> *One must assume that structural characteristics of visual form are spontaneously related to similar characteristics in human behavior. We have called this type of symbolism "isomorphic" because this is the term used by gestalt psychologists to describe identity of structure in different media. For instance, a person's mood may be structurally identical with the bodily behaviour which accompanies that mood. This isomorphic correspondence has been used to explain the fact that the "expression" of physical behaviour seems to be directly comprehensible to the onlooker. The gesture of a dancer, but also the motions of a towel on the clothes-line or the shape of a cloud, contain structural features whose kinship with similarly*

[25] *Ibid.*, p. 17.

structured mental features is immediately felt. If it is true that struc-
tural similarities transcend the difference between body and mind
and make for unified total behaviour and experience, then we
should expect the child to choose, for the pictures he makes, forms
that match his own attitudes. Thus here again the findings of gestalt
theory and work in the arts seem to confirm each other.[26]

Carroll C. Pratt has made a similar point about music, whose
aesthetic qualities, he says, "are the direct counterpart in tone of
the bodily reverberations involved in real emotion."[27] To support
his contention that by and large people agree in recognition of the
emotional form of music, he cites an experiment in which a group
of 227 students were asked to match certain adjectives with certain
compositions by Brahms, Mendelssohn, Mozart, and Tschaikowsky.
Some 91 per cent agreed with musical "experts" in calling the
Brahms "stately," better than 98 per cent in calling the Mendelssohn
"sprightly," just under 97 per cent in calling the Mozart "wistful,"
and more than 92 per cent in calling the Tschaikowsky "vigorous."[28]

Pratt's theory explaining these results is summarized in the
tantalizing formula: *"Music sounds the way emotions feel."*[29]

Although it may be doubted that the isomorphism of the Gestalt
psychologist or the intrinsic relationship between the universal symbols and their referents about which the psychoanalysts talk can
(at least as yet) be very clearly specified—for instance as to what it
is in the inward state that somehow has the same structure as does
the dancer's posture—nevertheless these theories are suggestive explanations of what nearly everybody has at least vaguely sensed:
that some important similarity exists between the aesthetic experience and the aesthetic object and furthermore between both of
these and that which stimulated the creator to express.

[26] From *Aspects of Form*, ed. Lancelot Law Whyte. Copyright 1951 by Percy
Lund Humphries & Co. Published by Farrar, Straus and Cudahy.
[27] *Music as the Language of Emotion* (Washington: Library of Congress, 1952),
p. 22. Cf. Susanne K. Langer, *Feeling and Form* (New York: Scribner, 1953), pp.
27-40 and *passim*.
[28] *Ibid.*, pp. 14-15.
[29] *Ibid.*, p. 26.

- ## Chapter 11

FORM

- O*ne* aesthetic battle is likely to last forever: that between the emphasizers and the de-emphasizers of *form*. As in the case of more violent wars, it is not by any means always clear what this one is about, but Friedrich Nietzsche has given the two camps names which have stuck. Apollonian art is the art of regularity, of precision, of decorum, of restraint, of order, of elegance, of obedience to norm, rule, and law. Dionysian art is the art of freedom, of spontaneity, of individuality, of originality, of expression, of ecstasy, of "drunkenness"—as Nietzsche liked to say. If we think of the one type being exemplified by a classical colonnaded temple, simple, geometrically symmetrical, suggesting ideal and lofty repose; and of the other type being exemplified by a jam session where everyone plays as the spirit moves, the music mounting and mounting to a sensual frenzy, we will have the extremes before us.

The history of virtually all the arts is marked by the alternation of Apollonian and Dionysian dominance.[1] Let certain norms for beauty attain to some kind of respectable status and there is sure to be a reaction in favor of free expression, the cry being: "Away with the academic, stuffy inhibitions of the *ancien regime!*" In due time, the "excesses of unrestrained, undisciplined romanticism" will

[1] Curt Sachs has elaborated a somewhat similar polarity between "Ethos" and "Pathos" in *The Commonwealth of Art* (New York: Norton, 1956), chap. vii.

be deplored and a return to the normality of classicism advocated. Think of Hellenistic sculpture replacing the Hellenic; of eighteenth-century neo-classicism trying to bury the overzealousness of the seventeenth century; of Baroque architecture asserting itself against the claims of the earlier Renaissance; of the classical ballet giving way, in part and for a time, to modern interpretive dance; of Tschaikovsky vs. Haydn, and so on.

WHAT IS FORM?

But if the Apollonian exalts form as the *sine qua non* of beauty and the Dionysian subordinates form to spontaneous expression— what *is* form? One answer proceeds by relating form to matter. The sculptor starts with a block of granite or some bars of bronze. His job is to cut away the stone, to melt and mold the metal, so that the matter is given form or shape. The painter with blobs of oil paint distributed on a palette and a white canvas on the easel before him faces the task of arranging the pigments on the canvas in some interesting and expressive order. The matter of the architect is stone, wood, metal, concrete; the matter of the poet or story-teller is words; the matter of the composer is tones and timbres; the matter of the choreographer is the bodies of dancers. In all cases such matter is formed when it is arranged and ordered with something more than haphazard relationships between the spatial or temporal parts.

So far there is no question of favoring or disfavoring form: without form there is no art, no beauty--for even a rock we stop to admire on the mountain side has a shape that commends itself to our eye. The controversy over form starts when a question is raised about whether the "natural" beauty of the material is given its just due. For instance, fashions in woodworking change: in some eras, the great emphasis is upon the carving, in others upon relatively plain, unvarnished surfaces in which the grain of the wood is readily visible. In architecture today, and in sculpture, there are somewhat parallel disputes. But what is form in one context may be matter in another. The sculptor fashions, let us say, a horse's leg, and that is now the form relative to the uncut or the rough-hewn stone; but the leg itself must be related to other legs, a body and a head: the form of the whole animal may be regarded as having the separate parts as its matter. In the same way, the lines of a poem are forms which have separate words or syllables as their matter, but the lines are matter for larger forms. A musical theme or tune is an achievement out of the single notes or chords, but the composer will usually go on to develop and relate his tune to other musical materials. On such a level as this latter, once again controversy may rage. "Yes, a perfect fugue," someone may say of a composition, "but its perfection is hollow—there's nothing to it, no beauty of subject, no tunes." An opposite criticism may go like this: "He has a gift of song, doubtless, but what does he do with his tunes? Nothing except repeat them. No organization, no development, no large structure." In a similar way, a play may be criticized for being just a string of separate scenes, each one perhaps admirable in itself, but leading nowhere; or, antithetically, another play may be commended for its well-wrought structure, its elegance of plot, but rebuked for its emptiness, its having few interesting characters or little memorable dialogue.

Sometimes form is set over against not matter but representation, the subject discussed in the previous chapter. A distinction drawn from the general theory of signs (*semiotic*) will be useful here. Within the entire context of communication, certain relationships may be singled out for special study. *Syntactics* is the name given to the investigation of the relationships which signs bear each other; for instance, such a grammatical relationship as the subject and direct object within a sentence. *Semantics* is the name given to the investigation of the relationship between signs and what they signify; for instance, the relationship of designation between a gesture of pointing and a fire being pointed at.[2]

Now it is possible to argue that the only genuinely aesthetic concern with a work of art is the syntactic one; that whether one's role be creator, appreciator, performer, or critic, his attention should be directed toward the relationships of the parts of a work *to each other*, and not at all toward the relationship of any of the

<hr />

[2] See Charles Morris, *Signs, Language and Behavior* (Englewood Cliffs, N.J.: Prentice-Hall, 1946), pp. 217-20. See also pp. 136-38, 192-96. A third kind of study is *Pragmatics*, which has to do with the relationships between sign producer and sign interpreter. This also has obvious implications for the artistic transaction, but is not directly relevant to the purposes of this chapter.

parts or the whole to something outside the work of art itself. But it is also possible to argue that artistic syntactics ought to be severely subordinated to artistic semantics; that is, that the relationships within the work are properly only means to the more important relationship between the work and something else. We have already seen that that "something else" may be the look or sound of a real brook, an historical or mythological event, a religious belief, the anguish of a bereaved husband—among other possibilities. This latter argument insists that the importance of a work of art rests in the contact it makes with the real or possible world through representation, through symbolization. The defender of syntactics, on the other hand—the *formalist* as he is generally called—characteristically mistrusts any appeal beyond the work of art itself. Leave that, he says, and you leave the aesthetic realm for politics, for religion, for philosophy, for sentimentality, for practicality. He points to the horrible example of the museum tourist who contents himself with identifying the subjects of the pictures or the music-hall interpreter who finds in every sonata a story or a scene—and thus misses the work of art in his hurry to get to its referent. He points, too, to the typical artist's almost fanatical interest in composition, in meter and rhyme, in theme and variation, in transitions, developments, structural balances, and a hundred other formal considerations. These should be our interest too, the formalist avers.

This may even require what Ortego y Gasset has called "dehumanization," an activity which, when it is not done for us by the creative artist, must be done by us in our aesthetic attention. A work of art is dehumanized when it severs its connections with reality—that is, with the world of flesh-and-blood people and their feelings and interests and ideas; and even with the physical world in which people live. The formalist continues: the work of art is an artificial construct, a world of its own, an isolate; its important relations are internal.[3] The painter who "distorts" reality may seem to the naive observer therefore a poor painter; but his distortion is purely in the interest of his composition: he needs more mass here, and so he puts in more, and if this makes the head or the arm "too big to be realistic," so much the worse for reality. Indeed, the

[3] See Henri Focillon, *The Life of Forms in Art* (New Haven: Yale University Press, 1942).

distortion, or in another case the abstraction, may be a positive gain insofar as it invites attention to the picture itself, and not to that of which it might otherwise be assumed to be a mirror image.

FORM AND MUSIC

The defenders of formalism would insist that contemplation of form isolated from reality is by no means a cold or merely intellectual activity. For instance, Clive Bell—always cited as the archformalist—has said:

> *The contemplation of pure form leads to a state of extraordinary exaltation and complete detachment from the concerns of life. . . .*[4]

Nevertheless, the form of which Bell speaks is, by his own naming, "significant form"; what is signified is not the nonaesthetic world of feelings and ideas and things, but a pure aesthetic emotion. He illustrates the purity and difficulty of aesthetic emotion by speaking of himself as a music listener:

> *I am not really musical. I do not understand music well. I find musical form exceedingly difficult to apprehend, and I am sure that the profounder subtleties of harmony and rhythm more often than not escape me. The form of a musical composition must be simple indeed if I am to grasp it honestly. . . . Yet, sometimes, at a concert, though my appreciation of the music is limited and humble, it is pure. . . . Consequently, when I am feeling bright and clear and intent, at the beginning of a concert for instance, when something that I can grasp is being played, I get from music that pure aesthetic emotion that I get from visual art. It is less intense, and the rapture is evanescent; I understand music too ill for music to transport me far into the world of pure aesthetic ecstasy. But at moments I do appreciate music as pure musical form, as sounds combined according to the laws of a mysterious necessity, as pure art with a tremendous significance of its own and no relation whatever to the significance of life; and in those moments I lose myself in that infinitely sublime state of mind to which pure visual form transports me.*[5]

He goes on to speak of his more usual state of mind at a concert, when being too tired or too inadequate to attend to pure form, he

[4] *Art* (New York: Stokes, n.d.), p. 68.
[5] *Ibid.*, pp. 30-31. Cf. E. M. Forster, "Not Listening to Music," in *Two Cheers for Democracy* (New York: Harcourt, Brace, 1951).

reads into the music the familiar emotions of "life." This, he explains, can be very pleasant—one need not be ashamed of so enjoying himself—but it is not really listening to music, it is not truly an experience of the "austere and thrilling raptures" that attend a dwelling with form itself.

Music has seemed to many students of the arts the purest, even the most ideal art—the art to whose condition, as Pater put it, all other arts aspire. Music and architecture alone of the major arts are fairly generally admitted to need no representative relationship with the human world of persons, places, and things. (Though there is, of course, programme music, we know the story more through the writer of programme notes than through the composer.)

In his defense of the purity of music, Eduard Hanslick has even debunked the common notion that it is the object of music to arouse our feelings. He denies that this is the aim either of music or of any other art. "An art aims, above all, at producing something *beautiful* which affects not our feelings, but the organ of pure contemplation, our imagination."[6]

He goes on to say:

The object of every art is to clothe in some material form an idea which has originated in the artist's imagination. In music this idea is an acoustic *one; it cannot be expressed in words and subsequently translated into sounds. The initial force of a composition is the invention of some definite theme, and not the desire to describe a given emotion by musical means.*[7]

Musical form or structure, Hanslick insists, is the music itself. When we are really listening to music, and not merely indulging our familiar feelings to musical accompaniment, we are imaginatively contemplating the forms of sound.

It does not of course follow that if a formalistic theory is sound in the case of music it is therefore sound in the case of painting or literature. However, if formalism is not ultimately defensible for music, it is *a fortiori* indefensible for the other, less "pure" arts.

Music, the most nearly self-contained of the arts, invites but few specific references to the nonmusical world. Perhaps no other art so

[6] *The Beautiful in Music* (London: Novello, 1891), p. 20.
[7] *Ibid.*, p. 73.

richly rewards him who makes a determined effort to restrict his attention to the syntax of the art. Nevertheless, there are ways, and important ways, in which music makes references beyond itself; and these must not be forgotten or minimized either in the interest of contrasting music with literature or representational painting or in order to berate the naive dependence upon music with a story.

In the first place, music has very often been closely associated with other arts to produce songs, chorales, dances, operas, and movies. In such associations the music has sometimes been predominant—as in opera, when the words are seldom wholly intelligible and often wholly unintelligible—and sometimes subordinate—as in most ballets and dramatic movies. But even in the latter case, it is always thought that music may be appropriate or inappropriate; and it is hard to see how it could be either, if it were as self-contained as purists maintain. In compositions for the ballet and other kinds of dance, music is of course closely related to types of motion, now being fast, now slow, now hopping and jumping, now gliding. It is also directional, as Albert Schweitzer has been at some pains to show in his analysis of Bach's great *Passions;* for instance, if the text indicates descent from the Cross, the music itself descends.

Purely instrumental concert music has not infrequently been avowedly descriptive. One thinks, for instance, of Debussy's *Clouds and Fetes,* of Resphigi's *Pines of Rome,* of Moussorgsky's *A Night on Bald Mountain,* of Beethoven's *Pastoral Symphony,* of Copland's *Appalachian Spring.* Now it may be true, as is often said, that a listener could scarcely evoke the appropriate visual image without at least as much help as the titles provide—paintings also sometimes require their titles as clues—but the fact remains that given such help, most sensitive listeners do gain from such music images of kinds of scenes and events.

Then there is the more clearly programmatic music, say Dukas' *The Sorcerer's Apprentice,* Richard Strauss' *Till Eulenspiegel's Merry Pranks,* Berlioz' *Fantastic Symphony;* here again the verbal programme is indispensable to the comprehension of the story, yet there are certainly senses in which the music too, does some of the telling.[8]

[8] Curt Sachs tells of a work for viol and harpsichord written in 1717 which "describes" in detail surgery for bladder stone. *The Commonwealth of Art,* p. 222.

Finally, there is a more subtle, more tenuous—perhaps in honesty one ought to say more dubious—kind of musical reference. It is hard even to name adequately, and this description of it will instantly offend tough-minded analysts: the reference we now have in mind might be said to be to "movements of the soul." It can occur in music either programmatic or absolute, descriptive or nondescriptive, associative or more purely musical. Beethoven's last quartet, *Opus 135*, affords a great example. Here is a brief analysis of the work's concluding movement by the musicologist Jonathan Schiller:

> *The* finale *is preceded by three literary labels: the famous "Muss es sein" (Must it be), "Es muss sein" (It must be) and heading both of these the still more curious designation, "Der schwerge- fasste Entschluss" (The difficult decision). The first two of these appear with musical themes as well. The movement is written in rondo-sonata form. It consists of two* Allegros *constructed from the "Es muss sein" motive (first heard in the violins when the first* Allegro *starts). The two fast sections are introduced by two* Graves *which utilize the "Muss es sein" motive (first heard at the start of the movement in viola and cello). The movement and quartet con- clude with an ingenious* Coda. *As it commences, we hear the "Es muss sein" whispered seriously three times by the first violin and the lower instruments. The mood then changes abruptly as we hear again the little march theme from the preceding* allegros, *this time played* pizzicato. *Finally, the second violin sings out the "Es muss sein" motive several times with such vigor that the other instru- ments fall in with it as the movement concludes.*[9]

A careful listening to the music will reveal the accuracy of the quoted account—as far as it goes. Of course its writer did not for a moment consider his words a substitute for the music itself. But as one listens beyond the purely technical interest in the recognition of the *allegros* and *graves* and *coda*, he may be aware of living through "the difficult decision." What decision? *That* we are not told, either by the music or by any words Beethoven penned on his score; just "the difficult decision." But a *life* decision, a decision about how to or whether to "take" life. The music may be said to put the question and to announce the answer. Is all of this

[9] From the album of the recording by the Pascal String Quartet, issued by Con- cert Hall Society, Inc.

exasperatingly vague and conjectural? Yes, perhaps. If perfect clarity and neatness are one's overriding aims, a severe formalism is easily indicated. But to many listeners music does seem to describe—no, not merely describe, but to *conduct*—journeys of the soul, in a fashion not completely different from Dante's manner in *The Divine Comedy* or Masaccio's "Expulsion from the Garden" or Bernini's "Ecstasy of St. Teresa." I don't of course mean that these various works of art are in any sense equivalents or have the same reference; I mean only that they share the characteristic of each presenting immediately, dramatically, and in such a way as to invite a contemplative involvement, an aspect of life, some things that the human being goes through. It remains of very great importance that the one work uses tones, another words, another oil paints, another marble; any neglect of the special, individual means for the presentation means *missing* the work. But adequate attention to the medium and its unique formation does not necessitate a neglect of "reference," much less a theory that matter-as-formed is all that aesthetically counts.

It is well established empirically that people differ rather markedly in the way they listen to music. There is no agreed-upon classification of the ways, even the principal ways, but one investigator speaks of four classes of listener: the intra-subjective, the character, the associative, and the objective types. The intra-subjective listener takes pleasure in the sensory surface of music, going no further than the agreeable sounds which impinge upon his ear. The character type of listener tends to augment his sensory experience by assigning to the music personality traits: what he hears is now pathetic, now gay, now tragic, now frivolous, now mystical, now delicate. The associative listener finds that music produces in him trains of images, thoughts, or memories—which he may or may not assign back to the stimulus as real qualities of the music. Finally, the objective listener, who is almost certain to be one who has been trained in musical theory, attends to the themes and their variations, to resolutions and modulations, to the harmonic make-up and the rhythmic patterns; and he judges the music in terms of strictly musical standards.[10]

[10] See Max Schoen, *The Understanding of Music* (New York: Harper, 1945), pp. 80-98. It is not suggested by anybody that any one person invariably hears in one and only one of these ways.

The close student of music, who himself may be "objective" in his hearing habits, will perhaps feel that his is the right way of listening, the other ways being functions of ignorance, and there is some justice in his position: he does doubtless hear very much that other listeners miss. If the others hear something that *he* misses, this may be a deprivation more easily corrected; it is easier to relax one's attention to form than to acquire the ability so to attend. Yet it should be recognized that an exclusive interest in form or structure may become a coldly intellectual exercise that, whatever its degree of competence, is simply nonaesthetic. The layman's sour-grapes complaint about the expert in any art has this much possible truth in it: "knowledge about" is not the same thing as participative enjoyment. But in fact most experts seem to enjoy (and *aesthetically* *enjoy*) their special arts more, not less, than their lay brothers. They do so, however, because they have learned to be more than formalists in their perception: they know how to be aware of form without losing sight of all that is formed—call it matter or content or subject or reference or whatever.

PRINCIPLES OF FORM

When asked why they approve of a work of art, some people will respond in terms of depth of insight, profundity of understanding, grasp of human nature, and the like. Others will in their response tend to speak of matters like *balance, harmony, rhythm*, and so on. And these latter qualities may appeal to some as the very essence of form.

DeWitt Parker speaks of "six principles of aesthetic form":

(1) organic unity or unity in variety
(2) theme
(3) thematic variation
(4) balance
(5) hierarchy: the principle of subordination
(6) evolution: the principle of unified development[11]

11 *The Analysis of Art* (New Haven: Yale University Press, 1926), chap. ii. For Parker, rhythm is a combination of thematic repetition and balance. His account in *The Principles of Aesthetics* (New York: Appleton-Century-Crofts, 1946), chap. v, is slightly different.

Stephen Pepper's approach to this problem, while consonant with Parker's, is interestingly based on a psychological foundation. He conceives of formal principles as means for enhancing aesthetic perception. The two dread enemies of aesthetic experience, he thinks, are monotony and confusion. The artist combats monotony by variety, confusion by unity. The repetition of a theme, for instance, unifies, whether it be a musical motif or subject (the most famous case being the four-note subject which opens and dominates Beethoven's *Fifth Symphony*), a certain kind of line (such as the verticals in Grant Wood's "American Gothic"), or a basic image (such as fire in *Prometheus Bound*). The recurrence of a theme, when it is recognized as a recurrence,[12] makes a tie. Similarly, when a weight on one side of the axis in a painting is balanced with a similar weight on the other, we feel that the two match each other, go together to make up a single whole. Or in a temporal work, when there is a close linkage of the parts, one seeming to grow "naturally" out of the preceding, the result is unification of the entirety. Again, unity is attained by rhythmic groupings. Our power of attention is limited: hence such typical arrangements as ta-ta-tum or ˘ ˘ —/ ˘ ˘ —.

Still, an artifact may be perfectly unified and also perfectly uninteresting. It is hard to surpass the unity of a single circle, but except for aspirants to mystical trance we are not likely to fix our attention for long upon such a unity. No, we need variety lest our minds wander or go to sleep. The sonata-allegro movement in a symphony is typically followed by a slow, melodic movement, and that by a lively scherzo, with another sonata-allegro for the finale. The painter touches his canvas with vermilion, but however much it pleases him, he doesn't make the whole painting in this same hue, but selects now a gray, now a cerulean blue for contrast. The architect surprises us when, expecting perfectly symmetrical towers, we find that he has placed the windows differently on the two sides. The playwright knows that even the most exciting violence grows stale, the most poignant series of pathetic incidents loses its force, unless there are contrasting moments of quiet, of humor, even

---

12 Sometimes a recurrence is so obscurely connected with its original as to defeat its purpose, just as a rhyme word may not function as a rhyme when it is too far separated from its mate.

of comparative "dullness."[13] A climax can be a climax only when it contrasts with what comes before and after. Only the novice writes perfectly regular verse, or supposes good music is simply a matter of an appealing tune.

This psychological approach to principles of form is especially valuable in tying together qualities of the work of art and qualities of the perceptual experience, for a perception itself is *formed—* or it is nothing, not a perception at all. But it is, when it is permeated by an aesthetic attitude and interest, especially highly formed. Whatever else characterizes a complete aesthetic experience, the phrase unity-in-variety seems to us as it has seemed to nearly all recent writers on this subject, inescapable.

FORM AND FUNCTION

In any aesthetic consideration of the topic of form, at least brief mention needs to be made of the recent architectural squabble over the slogan, "Form follows function." Those who employ this battle cry, whether directly in descent from the American pioneer Louis Sullivan, or working in the shadow (or light) of the Bauhaus tradition, have apparently had three chief grievances: "dishonesty" of appearance, ornamentation, and the sacrifice of efficiency to preconceived formal commitments. An appearance is held to be dishonest if it conceals its principal building material and its manner of support. Take, for instance, an office building that is erected on a steel frame: its façade may show a wall of simulated stone that may even seem to be the support of the roof. Or a college auditorium may be built in a "classic revival" style with little unusable porches placed around its sides. Or a bank, in order that it "look like a bank," may be designed uneconomically and in a fashion which makes its use inconvenient for its employees and patrons alike.

Extreme functionalism perhaps now seems to have exaggerated the necessity of "honesty," overvalued the austere appearance of bare walls and machine-like lines, and too narrowly construed the functions of working and living. As Katharine Gilbert wrote:

[13] Leslie Fiedler, for instance, insists that all great novels have and must have dull stretches.

*But if a literary aesthetic not solidly based on functional require-
ments is ghostly, a functional aesthetic unmindful of the possible
spread of human interests is thin. For what after all is function?
Activity directed to an end; and of ends man has an uncounted
number. It is a mistake to associate "functional building" with the
more obvious physical usages of man, basic as these are. A man
may need a spacious room not only to breathe in, but to think in.
Any want that genuinely stems from within is a "function"
whether it is a temperamental order for gay and fantastic decoration, or for a library full of emblem books.[14]*

Nevertheless, architectural functionalism has been a greater force
for beauty than for its absence. It has been directly responsible for
an Augean stable-cleaning of the cumbersome, the frilly, the awk-
ward, the fake, and of unhealthy reliance upon period styles;[15]
positively, it has made for a closer union of form and function than
had ever before been thought possible.

MORE MEANINGS OF "FORM"

To speak of the *form* of a work of art may be to speak of a
relatively abstract type or species, or of its highly individual arrangement and style—or of something in between. The point may
be made from literature. Consider certain decisions facing the
writer:

(1) He has in mind some characters and the outline of a plot:
shall he cast these materials into the form of a narrative poem, a short
story, or a play? The word "type" may be employed for the standard subdivisions of a given art. As a writer is primarily known for
his addiction to one of the species of literature, he is called now a
novelist, now a playwright, now an epic poet, and so on.

(2) If it is to be a play, shall he write a tragedy or a pathetic
comedy? Within a type of literature such as drama, there may come
to be conventional forms. At least in certain ages, to decide on a
tragedy may be to make very basic and definite commitments about

[14] "Seven Senses of a Room," in *Aesthetic Studies* (Durham: Duke University
Press, 1952), p. 20. See also L. A. Reid, *A Study in Aesthetics* (London: George
Allen & Unwin, 1931), p. 148, for a discussion of function as revealed in form.
[15] See Osbert Lancaster, *From Pillar to Post* (New York: Transatlantic Arts,
1938).

style, principal character, plot, intended effect on the audience, and other matters.

(3) Shall he let the acts succeed each other in chronological order, or shall he use a "flashback"? How will the events, the happenings be ordered?

(4) Shall he write in prose or verse? The following comment by Christopher Caudwell in the course of a distinction between poet and prose novelist will suggest something of the formal quality of poetry:

> *Hence poetry in its use of language continually distorts and denies the structure of reality to exalt the structure of the self. By means of rhyme, assonance or alliteration it couples together words which have no rational connection, that is, no nexus through the world of external reality. It breaks the words up into lines of arbitrary length, cutting across their logical construction. It breaks down their associations, derived from the world of external reality, by means of inversion and every variety of artificial stressing and counterpoint.*[16]

(5) If in verse, what length of line and what meter shall he employ? To decide on poetry is ultimately to decide on a pattern to the verse: unrhymed iambic pentameter, sprung rhythm, or whatever. The poet and critic John Crowe Ransom has somewhere said that the poet starts with two "definites," a meter and something he wants to say; but in the process of composition, each makes sacrifices to the other.

(6) How will he handle, among other things, the crucial "recognition scene" that may be the climax of the work? How begin, how end? So far each of the decisions has been a choice between ready-made alternatives, where "tradition" has for all but a comparatively few innovators made initial selections. But finally, there come all the choices that make a given work distinctive. There are many dramas, many tragedies with any one of the standard forms of plot progression, many poems of each of the regularly catalogued meter and rhyme schemes, but there is only one *Hamlet*, only one *Phèdre*. An individual work may be shown to be a member of various classes, but ultimately it is itself: it has its *own* form.

Without undue stretching, the elastic word "form" may be ap-

[16] *Illusion and Reality* (New York: Macmillan, 1948), pp. 199-200.

plied to each of these decisions—among others. An individual form might be called "style," except that this word too is ambiguous, now occurring in such a phrase as "in the style of Louis XIV," now in Buffon's famous expression "The style is the man." But in the latter meaning, "style" stands for all the distinctive markings of a work of art, all the results of the decisions that make it what it is.

Whatever the unique style of a work, it may vary between the poles of the Apollonian and the Dionysian. That is, its pattern and structure may be relatively neat, rational, clear, evident; or, in its subordination to the requirements of spontaneous and perhaps passionate expression, untidy, changeable, vague, even indeterminate.

Form *and* Substance, Form *and* Content, Form *and* Function, Form *or* Representation—all such formulations betray a separation of the abstract feature *form* from some other abstract feature. But if there is one sure sign that a work of art is disunified, unrealized, generally unsuccessful, it is that its form can be subtracted or abstracted without much loss. For certain critical purposes we can diagram the statement and development of the themes in a Brahms overture, the most prominent shapes in an Orozco mural, the structural supports of a Christopher Wren building; but ultimately form must be reconsidered in its intimate fusion with the formed. The proper interest of the pure formalist is in logic and mathematics, the sciences of abstract form *par excellence*. No work of art is just form, though no formless thing can pretend to be a work of art.

THE ARTIST AS A FORMER OF PERCEPTION

In creating, the artist perceives; through his creation he enables and shapes our perception. Sometimes it will seem to the artist that he is just delivering up the reality he finds ready-made; sometimes he may even speak of tearing the form of something out of its somewhat encumbered setting. But always *forming* is invention. There is no such thing as a simple rendering or copying nature, for the sufficient reason that nature is always ambiguous, always overabundant in meanings and shapes and forms. The artist must select, must choose, must reject; and this means that he must impose forms on whatever is the initial amorphous object of perception.

As Rudolph Arnheim has well shown, photographs sometimes strike us as especially unsatisfactory representations precisely because they are too unselective; they yield much of the same ambiguity that characterizes their subject; they are hard to look at, hard to understand, in not having been filtered through the forming mind of an artist:

> If a person actually approaches a human body or a tree with no other motive than to copy "it"—and it is doubtful that before the nineteenth century anyone has actually tried to, although almost everyone asserted that this was all he was doing—he will be caught by accidental suggestions of shape and color found through piecemeal observation. The result will be one of those ugly wraiths of reality that do not belong to either science or art. The scientific or technological drawing is made to transmit perceptual characteristics in order to give information about corresponding physical traits of the things depicted. The artist uses the same perceptual characteristics for the different purpose of permitting the beholder to experience the expressive qualities of a pattern of visual forces.[17]

Thus the form that enables the artist to perceive and to create turns out to be something much larger than a pleasing arrangement of lines or tones. There is no representation without form; there is no significance without form; there is no expression without form; there is no aesthetic experience without a form that achieves variety within unity.

[17] *Art and Visual Perception* (Berkeley and Los Angeles: University of California Press, 1954), p. 123.

• Chapter 12

ART

and

MORALITY

• *Oscar Wilde* wrote during the heyday of art-for-art's-sake: "There is no such thing as a moral or an immoral book. Books are well written or badly written. That is all." With this he epigrammatically summarized a revolution against Victorianism. Not only in England and America, but even in France in the early part of the nineteenth century there was, by present-day standards, such an excess of scruples and prohibitions on artistic practice as to seem to us alternately ridiculous and disgusting. If in England it was *comme il faut* always to say "limb" in place of the vulgarism "leg" (even to the "limb" of a table!), on the French stage any mention of a handkerchief was considered an indelicate reminder that noses are sometimes blown. Nor was there any shortage of earnest critics to plead with the artists for an increased devotion to Honor, Piety, Goodness, and for a world in which Virtue is always rewarded and Vice is sternly punished. Of course, not all artists bowed to the moralizing demands, but enough did to make it no wonder that there came a time of Montparnassian bohemianism and hyper-aesthetical amoralism.

No age is all one way or all another, and in our own time there are to be found both John Ruskins and Oscar Wildes, but the great majority of practicing artists, critics, and aestheticians would doubtless find a middle ground between the extremes of making art strictly subservient to the narrowest conception of the prevailing moral code, and of making art altogether independent of any ethical principles. Nearly all would agree that morality is in some sense relevant to art, but in *what* sense? It may aid the attainment of a sane position in this controversial field to review the tactics of some of the principal antagonists throughout history.

Perhaps the first thing to notice is that there has been no straight line of "progress"—whatever direction one takes this to be—over the course of the centuries, whether one has in mind artistic practice or critical judgment. Everyone knows something of medieval restrictions on artistic subject matter, of the Puritans' closing of the theaters in seventeenth-century England, and of the Victorianism already alluded to, but it is sometimes forgotten that the fifth-century B.C. Athenians, the fifteenth-century Englishmen and Frenchmen, and the Elizabethans produced art-works that "shock" many people of our advanced time; that most museums dare not show statues that have been typical in certain Asiatic traditions; that in certain respects there have been more severe restrictions on artists during the last hundred years than perhaps in any like period in history.

Is art immoral? Never? Always? Sometimes? What does it mean for art to be—or not to be—immoral? Accusers of art may for convenience be divided into three camps: (1) the Politicians and Religionists, (2) the Puritans, and (3) a left-over miscellaneous group of Moralists.

POLITICAL AND RELIGIOUS OFFENSES

As in so many matters, Plato can get us off to a good start.[1] In the *Republic*, it will be remembered, Socrates is shown developing a theory for the state, the state in which justice will obtain, and therefore such subordinate virtues as rationality, military strength, efficiency, and temperance as well. In considering the proper education of the ruling or guardian class, Socrates encounters the prob-

[1] See *The Republic*, Books II and III.

lem of whether these select youth will be permitted to read any literature they happen across, or even indeed whether they ought to be encouraged to read the classics. His answer is No. After all, the youth are going to be influenced by what they read; if they are to be influenced in the right way, their books must be of the right kind. And for an example of how books can be deplorably wrong, Socrates argued, one need go to no less classic works than the Homeric epics themselves—in some ways, almost the Bible of the Greeks. It is well known that the Olympian gods are said by Homer to have practiced theft, deception, and hypocrisy; to have been on occasion drunken and lecherous; to have been subject to jealousy, envy, violent anger, and other irrational passions. But the gods are at the same time held up to the youth as supernatural models for men, the perfect or near-perfect beings. Here is a contradiction, then, and a serious one: We worship the gods and try to emulate them, without at all approving their actions—as those actions are narrated by Homer. Homer must therefore have been lying. And no matter how charming his lies, they are still lies and must be expunged. Indeed, it is precisely because literature such as the *Iliad* and the *Odyssey* has great power over men's minds that any of its possible evil effects must be carefully guarded against. Hence, the youth will be permitted to read Homer, but Homer expurgated, in the interest of their soul's health and the state's justice.

Nor was poetry alone to come under Socrates' disapproving scrutiny. Music, he taught, has a most powerful effect on men's feelings and therefore upon their actions. Certain musical modes, he said, are known to have a debilitating, enervating effect, and therefore are most ill-advised for the citizenry of a nation that must be ever vigilant. Consequently, the musicians will be required to employ only those modes which have beneficial, stirring, martial effects.

That Plato's kind of fear of art, the "wrong" kind of art, is not merely a theoretician's pipe dream is easily proven by a glance at the censorship record of virtually every government of every age. The rulers of states have been, now more, now less, impressed with the powers of artists, and few have discounted them. For instance, Russian artists have been under surveillance by a regularly-consti- tuted censorship for many decades, by both the Czarist and the

Soviet governments; such great novelists as Dostoevsky and Turgenev were made to suffer under the censors' powers for political
indiscretions that appear to us distinctly minor, while in more recent
times the best of Russian composers—Prokofiev, Shostakovitch,
Khatchaturian—have upon occasion been severely reprimanded for
compositions declared "bourgeois" in spirit. Nor has government
concern over artists' activities been confined to disapproval of offending works: it has also made known its wishes, by the promise of
both threats and rewards, for future creations. Under the English
and French monarchies, for instance, many a playwright has known
that his only hope for crown sponsorship or for a pension lay in in-
corporation within his plays of attacks on the king's enemies and
blandishments directed toward royal policy and whim. And only
an overdose of partiality in reading the past and present would
permit one to believe that such restrictions were the monopoly of
totalitarian regimes. If, in general, democratic regimes have been
more inclined to respect the freedom of the artist, there have not
been wanting unofficial agencies within the state for protecting the
citizenry against "dangerous" political, economic, and other social
doctrines lurking in the painter's brush and the writer's pen. In the
United States the government has sometimes used its power of regu-
lating imports and mails to protect itself against artifacts pronounced undesirable in some way; and more recently it has made
extensive use of investigating committees of legislatures to disap-
prove of a Post Office mural that someone found to satirize capitalism, or to lend weight to the blacklisting of certain actors and
writers for television and radio. Private vigilante groups have, in
the interests of both financial profit and patriotism, compiled such
blacklists for the guidance of the public and the sponsors, and have
been otherwise active in publicizing and warning against "subversion" in the movies and other arts.

One would make a serious mistake if he supposed that all opposition to works of art and artists has proceeded from the side of the
ruling party or class or caste. In our day particularly, a very heavy
attack has been waged by revolutionaries and other radicals upon
artists whom they have found guilty of crimes of both commission
and omission. For instance, Granville Hicks in *The Great Tradition*
divided American writers, not only of our own time but throughout

the nineteenth century, into the sheep—who, whether dimly or clearly, saw the necessity of class warfare—and the goats—who either actively supported the capitalistic economy or failed to expose its evils. Throughout the thirties it was popular among Marxist and other leftist critics to decry "escapism" in art, their argument being that the painter who chooses to show a row of poplars on a green hillside rather than a tumble-down shack of a sharecropper or a big-city slum, or the novelist who elects to write a love story of the magnolia-scented South instead of a story of sweatshop labor, is just as surely supporting the *status quo* by his "opiate" art as is he who comes right out and denigrates the communist agitator or whitewashes the racist or the exploiter.

Thus, just as rulers have sometimes required of artists their active support, so have opposition groups, though of course usually with less power to support their decrees, cried out, "Those who are not with us are against us!" Some, following the lead of Thorstein Veblen, have directed their sharpest barbs against those "modern artists" who by their very "obscurantism" have sought to preserve the invidious distinction between an aristocratic leisure class, which flaunts its idleness by a useless learning and a propensity for puzzles, and the working class, which is too busy to bother with such sophistication. Experimental artists have also frequently come under fire from those who suspect an inevitable correlation between artistic radicalism and politico-economic radicalism; but ironically, nowhere has so-called "modern art" been more severely frowned upon than in the Soviet Union, which typically has insisted upon traditionally representative painting and sculpture, movies and novels that end happily and with perfect poetic justice, and music that is amply and simply melodic, preferably deriving from the work-chants and the peasant songs of the people.

Perhaps all religious institutions in all ages have taken stands for and against trends and particular works of art. Often the Church has taken upon itself authority to specify in advance the proper content of art. Thus the Second Council of Nicea in 787 A.D. laid it down that

> *The substance of religious scenes is not left to the initiative of artists; it derives from the principles laid down by the Catholic*

*Church and religious tradition. . . . The art alone (sic) belongs
to the painter; its organization and arrangement belongs to the
clergy.*[2]

In our own time disapproval has been expressed by such means as
listing books which the faithful are forbidden to read; exposing
movies as improper or heretical; and, of course, in nations in which
there is a national church, by close collaboration between church
and state in all matters of censorship. Church bookstores have been
known to refuse to stock or order books under its ban, and of
course denunciations and commendations of works have been heard
from most pulpits.

PURITANISM

When leaders of churches and states and industries and political
parties have denounced art and used their powers to diminish its
influence or even to suppress it altogether, they have nearly always
been selective, saying that art is bad insofar as it criticizes law or
tradition or authority, insofar as it blocks the progress of reform,
insofar as it is blasphemous or subversive or escapist. But it is possible
to oppose art on moral grounds not selectively but altogether, and to
say that art is bad insofar as it is art. For the evil of art, say these
extremists, lies not in the fact that it sometimes goes wrong, but in
the fact that it is a slough in the pilgrim's path. Poetry, painting,
music, dance—all are alike in this one all-important respect: they
are celebrations of the *now*. They invite even the most earnest
seeker to put aside his search and to enjoy the present, to dwell in
the delights of sound and sight, with no care for what lies beyond.
For him who is doing God's work and the world's work, there can
be no relaxation of vigilance. His concern is with tomorrow and the
day after, with the salvation of souls and the reordering of institutions and societies; and when a work of art beckons, inviting the
wayfarer to refresh himself in self-sufficient beauty—no matter how
innocent—it beckons away from work to be done.

One may wonder whether this category of objectors is more than

[2] Quoted in John Dewey, *Art as Experience* (New York: Minton, Balch, 1934),
p. 329.

a logical possibility. Are there really people who take this position? The easiest answer is to point to real Puritans and their denunciations of painting and ornament, music and verse, stories and plays: to the point of erecting the most forbiddingly austere churches, devoid of stained glass and murals and draperies on the altar and long graceful tapers—but sometimes in spite of themselves achieving a kind of severely classical beauty; to the point of denuding the service of chants or songs or organ music; to the point of depriving the worshippers of any personal ornamentation over their somber black clothing. The story is well known and need not be elaborated, but it may be regarded as only a curious page of history, hardly relevant to the status of art today.

It is probably true that this type of Puritanism is not a major force in today's world, but it may well be that there are traces of a Puritanical attitude in not a few minds, among them minds that would indignantly deny any affinity with Puritanism. One thinks of "dedicated" people of many kinds—reformers, serious students, scientists, organizers, and promoters—who betray in themselves an impatience with what they regard as the essential triviality of beauty. Art doesn't *get* you anywhere, doesn't cut ice, doesn't bake bread. Does it afford pleasure and delight? Yes, doubtless, but so do many drugs. The land of art is the land of the lotus-eaters, tempting, but not a proper abode for one with ideals.

Yet when one encounters the word "Puritan" he is likely to think not of this wholesale rejection of art for its sensuous ornamentation of the present, but of a selective rejection of that art which is objectionably sensual or coarse. As has already been said, there is a very wide difference among ages and societies as to what has been considered sensually objectionable. There have been and are societies in which drunken, orgiastic dances have been not only permitted but required by religious custom, and there are other societies in which dancing has been considered inherently sinful. The story has been circulated that when a number of years ago a production of Aristophanes' *Lysistrata* was raided by the Los Angeles police, a warrant was issued for the arrest of the author. Only a few years ago all respectable publishers would typographically protect their readers with "d—n" and "h—l," and theatrical producers would ring down the curtain when the lovers' hands had but chastely touched. Thomas Bowdler has given his name to the expurgation of the works of Shakespeare and other eminent authors, and nearer our own time the energies of Anthony Comstock and the Watch and Ward Society were thrown into the war for purity. Currently there are of course some city-wide bans on the sale of certain books and magazines. Some librarians refuse to keep or keep only in locked cupboards such works as Rabelais' *Gargantua and Pantagruel*, Balzac's *Droll Stories*, and the complete *Arabian Nights*. Such movies as *La Ronde*, *The Moon is Blue*, and *Baby Doll* have stirred up public controversy or even court battles because of alleged improprieties, obscenities, and salaciousness.

A particularly famous case centered around the prohibition against importing James Joyce's *Ulysses* into the United States. The book was said to offend on both of the major counts within the presently discussed category: the use of tabooed words and the description of intimacies. It may be seriously argued that the objection to the printing of obscene words is not a moral but an aesthetic one—a matter of taste and delicacy—but "pornography" is a matter of morals, it being often held that art may so dangerously inflame the sexual passions as to promote socially forbidden practices. D. H. Lawrence suffered under censorship, not only for *Lady Chatterley's Lover*, but also for his paintings, which were at one time confiscated by the police and actually locked up in the jail.

OTHER MORAL OBJECTIONS TO ART

Although when art has been pronounced morally objectionable, the grounds have most commonly been political, economic, religious, or sexual—there are many possibilities. Today one hears a good deal about the possible effects on juvenile delinquency of films featuring violence and crime. Ibsen's *A Doll's House* was attacked and banned because it seemed to some to constitute a threat to the sanctity of marriage and the home. Goethe's *The Sorrows of Young Werther* has been widely deplored as setting off a wave of suicides among melancholic romantics. W. K. Wimsatt makes out a charge against Shakespeare's *Antony and Cleopatra* as immoral, even though artistically great:

What is celebrated in Antony and Cleopatra *is the passionate sur-render of an illicit love, the victory of this love over practical, political and moral concerns, and the final superiority of the suicide lovers over circumstance.*[3]

The variety of such charges is much too great to bear examination here. Instead it will be interesting to dwell for a time with one of the most famous attacks, not on all art, but on much art, an attack from a moral position: that of Leo Tolstoy in *What Is Art?*

After developing his theory that art, strictly as art, is the better as it is better able to communicate the feelings of its creator, Tolstoy moves on to ask whether therefore it is good for all feelings to be transmitted. Is there not aesthetically effective art whose content is morally objectionable? Art must finally be judged according to a moral, or as Tolstoy puts it, a religious standard, the best standard available to us:

The religious perception of our time, in its widest and most practical application, is the consciousness that our well-being, both material and spiritual, individual and collective, temporal and eternal, lies in the growth of brotherhood among all men—in their loving harmony with one another.[4]

Only that art can be judged good according to this standard which promotes the sense of brotherhood, serving to unite men, not merely those of a certain nation or creed or class, but all men. Such art will be truly Christian art, not in any narrow doctrinal sense, but in a universal sense. This may happen in two ways:

Christian art is only such as tends to unite all without exception, either by evoking in them the perception that each man and all men stand in like relation toward God and toward their neighbour, or by evoking in them identical feelings, which may even be the very simplest, provided only that they are not repugnant to Christianity and are natural to every one without exception.[5]

It turns out, according to Tolstoy, that by this test a very great deal of what is considered the best plastic, musical, and literary art

---

[3] "Poetry and Morals: A Relation Reargued," in *The Poetic Icon* (Lexington: University of Kentucky Press, 1954), p. 96. Note that Mr. Wimsatt himself calls the statement here quoted "crudely one-sided."

[4] *What Is Art?* (New York: E. R. Dumont, 1899), pp. 482-83.

[5] *Ibid.*, pp. 486-87.

of the ages, and what is the best on purely aesthetic norms, turns out to be morally iniquitous, either by a deficiency in its ideational content or by some snobbishness or provinciality in its manner, so as to suggest that it is not intended for everybody but only for a certain elite.

Such, in literary art, are all novels and poems which transmit church or patriotic feelings, and also exclusive feelings pertaining only to the class of the idle rich; such as aristocratic honor, satiety, spleen, pessimism, and refined and vicious feelings flowing from sex-love—quite incomprehensible to the great majority of mankind.

In painting we must similarly place in the class of bad art all the church, patriotic, and exclusive pictures; all the pictures representing the amusements and allurements of a rich and idle life; all the so-called symbolic pictures, in which the very meaning of the symbol is comprehensible only to the people of a certain circle; and, above all, pictures with voluptuous subjects—all that odious female nudity which fills all the exhibitions and galleries. And to this class belongs almost all the chamber and opera music of our times, —beginning especially from Beethoven (Schumann, Berlioz, Liszt, Wagner), by its subject-nature devoted to the expression of feelings accessible only to people who have developed in themselves an unhealthy, nervous irritation evoked by this exclusive, artificial, and complex music.[6]

Tolstoy does not fail to assign his own works, *War and Peace, Anna Karenina*, and all the rest, excepting only two little stories, to the class of art "deserving not to be encouraged but to be driven out, denied, and despised, as being art not uniting but dividing people."

ASSESSMENT OF THE CHARGES

Having before us some of the more important meanings of "immoral" when that word is leveled against art works, it will be well to pause now to examine the charges.

One line of defense, of course, is that of the "amoralist" school: to say that art is neither immoral nor moral, but is morally neutral, morally indifferent, morally irrelevant. That is, so far as something

[6] *Ibid.*, p. 495.

is aesthetic, to that extent it is nonmoral, the two categories being mutually exclusive; and to ask about the moral effects of a work of art is always to ask the wrong question, for the concern of the critic should be wholly with the work's beauty or lack of beauty. Thus J. E. Spingarn says, "To say that poetry is moral or immoral is as meaningless as to say that an equilateral triangle is moral and an isosceles triangle immoral."[7] But, as has already been noticed, this line of argument, though it is easy to understand as a pendulum swing away from an excessively moralistic criticism, seems seriously exaggerated. It would be very odd indeed if works of art had no effect at all on the social conduct of the people who have to do with them, leaving even their most sensitive and deeply-moved appreciators exactly as they had been in all but the quite isolated realm of the aesthetic. And in fact this seems not only antecedently improbable, but false, according to observations everybody can make, both of himself and of others. Now it is possible to argue that though art *does* have moral effects, it *ought not* to have, and that it is one's duty to guard against such; but such a moral judgment (which, in a sense, it is) seems quite gratuitous, and in any case constitutes advice which could be followed only by those who take art, not too seriously, but hardly seriously at all.

Now, if art does have moral effects, is there any guarantee that these effects will always be good, so that art so far as it is relevant to morality is always positively moral and never immoral? It seems dubious that anything should be capable of having beneficial moral effects and at the same time be inherently incapable of having bad moral effects; and art seems in this respect to be no exception. Still, to admit this is not to admit all the specific charges against art's immorality.

In the first place, it appears likely that most of those who have seen in art-works a great danger to established institutions or a great instrument of social reform (so that neglect of this potentiality constitutes a moral delinquency on the part of the artist), have quite seriously exaggerated the power of art in any society yet known. It is not at all inconceivable that there should arise a society in which the novelists and the painters and the architects constituted such

---

[7] Quoted in H. L. Mencken, *Prejudices, First Series* (New York: Knopf, 1919), p. 11.

a tremendous influence over the entire citizenry that politicians, ecclesiastical authorities, and financial leaders should tremble before them, but it is hardly necessary to do more than to entertain such an idea in order to see how extraordinary a revolution this would require. Plato, to be sure, was thinking of a very different kind of a state and of very remarkable youth to be trained as its leaders, so he may well have had a better reason for his high estimate of the effect of literature and music than could anyone describing an actual state; but even so it is very hard for us to imagine a situation in which the introduction of a certain musical mode could make or break a war. The music of the Scottish bagpipers has been called the "fightingest" music in the world, and it is entirely possible that it and other sorts of music as well do, under proper circumstances, conduce to bravery and daring and group solidarity in battle; but it seems simply impossible that allowing soldiers on leave to hear quite unmartial music should necessarily undermine their fighting morale.

In the two years prior to December, 1941, there was considerable debate in the United States about involvement in the war between the Axis and the Allies, and there were some who deplored the attitude of suspicion, scepticism, and distrust they found to characterize American youth, saying that it was the direct result of the post-World War I novels of such authors as Hemingway, Dos Passos, Céline, and Cummings. These authors, it was said, however sincere their own disillusionment had been, had now to bear the heavy responsibility for undermining the morale of the new generation. But it was quickly pointed out that these novels had been read by only a very small proportion of the youth, and that it was highly unlikely that this group was powerful enough to have such an influence. It is always easy for sophisticates to exaggerate the influence on the mass of people of works, theoretical or aesthetic, which, however important they were in shaping the opinions of the intellectual minority, can have had at best only a very indirect effect on the majority. Besides, there came to be more and more doubt that American youth were so sour on war.

But the moral effect of art-works is limited not only by the relatively small number of people any work is likely to touch, but also by at least two other factors. First of all, as will be shown at greater length subsequently, works designed to be aesthetic objects do tend to be self-contained, conducing much more to appreciation than to further action. Secondly, to the extent that art-works do have an influence on moral conduct, it is an influence which is in comparison with many other influences seldom impressively strong. When one considers all of the social agencies—home, church, school, clubs, business, unions, government, mass media, etc.—which often quite directly aim at shaping moral beliefs and behavior, one can well ask, with a meaning somewhat different from Shakespeare's, "How with this rage can beauty hold a plea?" It seems very likely that when a painting or a literary work or a ballet does seem decisive in the world of action, conducing, let us say, to immorality, it is because the influence of art has combined with and supported and augmented the influences of other agencies. DeWitt Parker has sagely asked how it could be expected that the virtue of a person capable of being seduced by a statue or a poem should be strong enough to withstand the ruder buffetings of day-to-day living.

Nevertheless, this is not equivalent to denying that it is possible for a work of art to lend weight to a program of subversion or reform or change, to affect elections and wars and church attendance, to help people be satisfied or dissatisfied with their lot and station, to alter somewhat their attitudes toward eating and drinking, family life and sexual conduct, races and economic groups, education and amusement—or anything else in the universe. Indeed, it must be affirmed that art does sometimes effect such changes, whether with or without the intentions of the artist. It cannot also be denied that art does sometimes serve the escapist and withdrawal tendencies of individuals, affording them a make-believe substitute for the rawer textures of life. And finally, it must be admitted, as Tolstoy insists, that art often serves as a divisive force among men, not only by pitting nation against nation, religion against religion, class against class, but also, indirectly, by fostering snobbism, dividing off an "elite" from a "mob." Whether any one of these charges is well founded in any given case must of course be decided with respect to that case. To make the admission that it is possible for an epic poem to promote a certain blasphemy and even to promote delinquency by racy stories about the gods is not at all the same thing as saying that Homer's *Iliad* therefore stands convicted. To say that a painting may encourage discontentment with capitalism is not to say that Diego Rivera's original mural in Rockefeller Center would have had this effect. Nor is the admission that music may alter attitudes to admit that Shostakovich's *Fourth Symphony* is shot through with bourgeois qualities. It is much clearer that art may be escapist than that Virginia Woolf's *To the Lighthouse* is blameworthy for not concerning itself with the class struggle. One of the great problems, of course, is about the validity of the standard by which a moral judgment is made. *Uncle Tom's Cabin* undoubtedly seemed to some an immoral travesty of a natural institution.

But another big problem is this: what, in the case of some agreed-upon instance of immorality in a work of art, ought to be done about it? There are three general possibilities: (1) to use some method of suppression or censorship, whether by bringing economic or political pressure upon the creator, or by altering the objectionable work, or by withholding it from public consumption; (2) without any suppression, to criticize the work with the intention of minimizing or canceling out its pernicious effects; (3) to do nothing about it. The topic of censorship is a very complex one, legally, philosophically, and in many other ways, and certainly not to be satisfactorily dealt with by any brief statement; but *for* a brief statement, the following seems sound: Works of art ought to be censored or suppressed only when they can be shown to constitute a "clear and present danger"—to borrow Justice Holmes' famous phrase—to the public welfare. Some will be discontent with this formulation, insisting that censorship is never justified; but in its way this seems just as excessive as an insistence that there should be no restrictions to freedom of speech. There are instances in which restrictions on freedom of speech are highly desirable for everyone, but such instances seem to be, in a reasonably stable community, altogether rare; they should be expected to be so, and very great care ought to be exercised whenever the curbing of freedom looks justified. So too, it seems irrational to deny that there may be cases where a work of art stands to cause serious injury to a community and so should be suppressed. But it should always be kept in mind that censorship by its very nature is an evil, and where the harm believed to result from the work is dubious or not great in extent, the censorship ought not to be applied. Why

censorship is in itself evil will not be argued here except by suggesting that its employment may have very deleterious effects on the
future of art. The terrible example of Nazi Germany, where a tight
governmental censorship virtually killed artistic creativity in that
nation for more than a dozen years, should not be easily forgotten.
For the larger case against restrictions on freedom, the reader may
be referred to John Stuart Mill's *On Liberty*. Nearly everything
said there may be without distortion applied to freedom of artistic
productivity and distribution.

The policy of infrequent and highly discriminating employment
of censorship powers is well indicated by the decision of Judge
Woolsey in lifting the ban against importation into the United
States of Joyce's *Ulysses*. It will be instructive to quote amply from
this important document. After saying that he had very carefully
read this famous novel in the light of the insistence of its opponents
that it was obscene, Judge Woolsey wrote:

> *In writing "Ulysses," Joyce sought to make a serious experiment*
> *in a new, if not wholly novel, literary genre. He takes persons of*
> *the lower middle class living in Dublin in 1904 and seeks not only*
> *to describe what they did on a certain day early in June of that*
> *year as they went about the City bent on their usual occupations,*
> *but also to tell what many of them thought about the while.*
>
> *Joyce has attempted—it seems to me, with astonishing success—*
> *to show how the screen of consciousness with its ever-shifting*
> *kaleidoscopic impressions carries, as it were on a plastic palimpsest,*
> *not only what is in the focus of each man's observation of the*
> *actual things about him, but also in a penumbral zone residua of*
> *past impressions, some recent and some drawn up by association*
> *from the domain of the subconsciousness. . . .*
>
> *   *   *   *
>
> *If Joyce did not attempt to be honest in developing the technique*
> *which he has adopted in "Ulysses" the result would be psychologi-*
> *cally misleading and thus unfaithful to his chosen tehnique. Such*
> *an attitude would be artistically inexcusable.*
>
> *It is because Joyce has been loyal to his technique and has not*
> *funked its necessary implications, but has honestly attempted to*
> *tell fully what his characters think about, that he has been so often*
> *misunderstood and misrepresented. For his attempt sincerely and*
> *honestly to realize his objective has required him incidentally to*

*use certain words which are generally considered dirty words and
has led at times to what many think is a too poignant preoccupa-
tion with sex in the thoughts of his characters.*

*The words which are criticized as dirty are old Saxon words
known to almost all men and, I venture, to many women, and are
such words as would be naturally and habitually used, I believe, by
the types of folk whose life, physical and mental, Joyce is seeking
to describe. In respect of the recurrent emergence of the theme of
sex in the minds of his characters, it must always be remembered
that his locale was Celtic and his season Spring.*

*Whether or not one enjoys such a technique as Joyce uses is a
matter of taste on which disagreement or argument is futile, but
to subject that technique to the standards of some other technique
seems to me to be a little short of absurd.*

*Accordingly, I hold that "Ulysses" is a sincere and honest book
and I think that the criticisms of it are entirely disposed of by its
rationale.*[8]

Judge Woolsey goes on to say that the book seems in no sense
to exploit its "dirt" nor to act on the average man as an aphrodisiac.
And that consequently it cannot be called "obscene" where that
word has been legally defined by the courts as meaning "Tending
to stir the sex impulses or to lead to sexually impure and lustful
thoughts."

This kind of a decision not to ban a book, but to allow it legally
to circulate (as of course it had already been rather widely circulated illegally) does not in any sense militate against the second of
the courses of action mentioned above with respect to a work suspected of conducing to immoral ends, namely criticism. It seems
altogether healthy and right that any critic should be permitted and
even encouraged to argue against any work on moral grounds, if
he finds such grounds genuinely relevant. If Shakespeare was guilty
of anti-Semitism in *The Merchant of Venice,* then it is certainly
legitimate to point this out and to deplore it. If Ibsen was quite
unfair to democracy in *An Enemy of the People,* then the play's
artistic qualities should not mask an exposure of this deficiency.
When such criticism is made, it may be opposed by others, and
decisions can be made in the light of such public debate.

[8] U.S. District Court, Dec. 6, 1933, Hon. John M. Woolsey. Opinion A 11-59,
reprinted as a preface to Modern Library edition of *Ulysses.*

ART AS MORALLY GOOD

If art can be morally reprehensible in the several ways mentioned, then in those same ways it can be morally commendable:
for instance, by promoting feelings of human brotherhood as Tolstoy find Dickens' *Tale of Two Cities*, George Eliot's *Adam Bede*,
Dostoevsky's *Memoirs from the House of the Dead*, Millet's "Man
with the Hoe," and Chopin's "Nocturne in E-flat Major" to do.
Surely the architect, and with even greater potential the city-
planner, can do a great deal to weld people who are only geo-
graphically adjacent into the much different entity that is a community. Surely the theater can at times function as it did in the most
glorious days of Athens as (far more than an amusement center) a
focus, a genuinely religious focus, for community life. The po-
tentialities of radio and television along these lines are gaspingly
great: the tens of millions of Americans who listen to the New York
Symphony Orchestra's Sunday afternoon concert are sharing an
experience, a fact that somehow runs counter to the many divisive
forces within the nation. And art may be community-promoting on
a larger scale, even, than the national. Probably no one today would
be so sanguine as to maintain that world peace could spring from a
free sharing of the artistic products of all cultures any more than it
could from any other single factor—student exchange, international sports competition, United Nations Assembly, Point-Four
programs, etc.—but there is a sense in which the art of a people often
serves especially well to *picture*, as we say, their character, their
way. Thus art serves the immensely important purposes of that
communication which is at the core of community.

The aesthetic surface of the world is important too in making a
people aware of itself. David Prall has said it well:

> *If we are to be happy in a world as it really lies before us and about
> us in its actual appearance, that appearance can not remain un-
> satisfactory to contemplate, that is, aesthetically unsatisfactory—
> condemned in the bare honesty of recording aesthetic judgments.
> If poverty and disease bore a pleasant aspect to discriminating per-
> ception, if injustice were aesthetically and directly satisfying to
> experience, and to dwell upon, what would there be to condemn
> it in any rational creature's eyes? For it is only in the embodiment*

in concrete aesthetic data of such abstractions as injustice and suf-
fering and poverty, only their appearing in the world as unmistak-
ably marked for aversion in a direct aesthetic view, that makes
them unsatisfactory and ugly and bad. Thus it is finally aesthetic
criteria that allow us to make those ethical and moral evaluations
that we agree upon sooner or later; and it is aesthetic discernment
that is required both to see the evils of the world and to picture a
better one. . . .[9]

Closely related to this important function is the much-celebrated capacity of art to "afford insight" of a moral kind. This is a point which must be treated with circumspection, for so intricate is its subtlety that there are constant temptations to cut the knot instead of untie it, or just to throw the whole thing away as a muddle.

A start may be made through mention of the so-called "cathartic" effect of art, a topic started, of course, by Aristotle when he asserted that tragedy not only arouses pity and terror but by arousing them in the way it does serves to purge the audience of these emotions.[10] It is a tenable interpretation of this famous assertion that emotions were regarded by Aristotle as diseases or as agents of disease, so that certain aesthetic experiences may function in a way analogous to homeopathic medicine. We pity the noble protagonist for the awful distance we see him fall; we are made fearful because we perceive that we are not altogether unlike him in his "tragic flaw." Now, pity and fear as they normally dwell within us are not helps but hindrances to the happiness that Aristotle believed to be synony- mous with the fully adequate functioning of the human self; but through the imaginative identifications evoked by drama, we are enabled to "handle" our emotions, get rid of them perhaps, or as we would be more likely to say today, to incorporate them within the whole personality, to integrate them, if you will; in becoming thus "saner," the art appreciator is the better enabled, as Plato failed to see, to be an adequately political animal.

I. A. Richards has in recent times made somewhat similar claims for art, holding that aesthetic experiences are the most impressive examples of a "balanced poise" of impulses and attitudes that would

---

[9] *Aesthetic Judgment* (New York: Crowell, 1929), p. 349.
[10] This is the most discussed passage in the whole history of aesthetics; it will be returned to in the Appendix on Tragedy and Comedy.

normally clamor and war. Through art, Richards goes on to claim—extravagantly, many believe—modern man is enabled to attain to that wholeness of personality which men have often sought through the agencies of religion.

Now *if* art experiences, not necessarily always but at least sometimes, do contribute to healthiness of personality, better balance, a finer adjustment of emotions and attitudes, there can be no question that art therein contributes very significantly indeed to moral relations, for it can no longer be doubted (if it ever was) that moral goodness and rightness are very intimately associated with psychological health. But whether (and if so to what degree) art does tend to have such effects perhaps cannot be decisively determined at present, though there are certainly distinguished observers among psychologists, aestheticians, and art critics who testify to the reality of such a tendency.

In any case, this matter of emotional health is only a part of the problem about moral insight, and not the whole of it. Most of those who have ascribed to the arts an insightfulness that is relevant to moral conduct have had in mind either the understanding of some principle[11] or the liberation of the imagination. The former has been dealt with during the discussion on the cognitive components of art, but briefly the point is that whether by fairly abstract statement or by concrete embodiment, the artist—the literary artist particularly, of course—may adumbrate an insight into the nature of duty or sin or love (among other possibilities). An example lies in George Meredith's sonnet:

> *Thus piteously Love closed what he begat:*
> *The union of this ever-diverse pair!*
> *These two were rapid falcons in a snare,*
> *Condemned to do the flitting of the bat.*
> *Lovers beneath the singing sky of May,*
> *They wandered once; clear as the dew on flowers:*
> *But they fed not on the advancing hours:*
> *Their hearts held cravings for the buried day.*
> *Then each applied to each that fatal knife,*
> *Deep questioning, which probes to endless dole.*

[11] For instance, Ezra Pound: "It's all rubbish to pretend that art isn't didactic. A revelation is always didactic." Letter of July 9, 1922, in *The Letters of Ezra Pound*, ed. D. D. Paige (New York: Harcourt, Brace, 1950), p. 180.

Ah, what a dusty answer gets the soul
When hot for certainties in this our life!
In tragic hints here see what evermore
Moves dark as yonder midnight ocean's force,
Thundering like ramping hosts of warrior horse,
To throw that faint thin line upon the shore.

It can scarcely be doubted that, reading this, a person at least entertains the ideas presented, and he may find in them an expression of something he had himself been searching to clarify; if so, this expression might then come to be a guide in his own life. Or one might from Euripides' *Hippolytus* gain a dawning recognition, not so much from any explicit statement as from observing the slow march of doom, of the danger of a certain pride-in-virtue, and from this recognition be led to change one's own conduct.

But it may be that literature and to some extent other arts are more important for their encouragement of imaginative identification and sympathy with others than for any principles formulated, explicitly or implicitly. No one has made this point better than Shelley:

A man, to be greatly good, must imagine intensely and comprehensively; he must put himself in the place of another and of many
others; the pains and pleasures of his species must become his own.
The great instrument of moral good is the imagination; and poetry
administers to the effect by action upon the cause. . . . Poetry
strengthens the faculty which is the organ of the moral nature of
man, in the same manner as exercise strengthens a limb. A poet
therefore would do ill to embody his own conceptions of right and
wrong, which are usually those of his place and time, in his poetical
creations, which participate in neither.[12]

This, as Shelley says, does not make poetry the same as moral philosophy; moral philosophy is discursively systematic and abstract, while poetry tends to be dramatic and concrete, but both are important. A statement of Shelley's in the Preface to his tragedy, *The Cenci*, is apropos:

The person who would treat such a subject [as the Cenci] must
increase the ideal, and diminish the actual horror of the events, so

[12] "A Defence of Poetry."

that the pleasure which arises from the poetry which exists in these tempestuous sufferings and crimes may mitigate the pain of the contemplation of the moral deformity from which they spring. There must also be nothing attempted to make the exhibition subservient to what is vulgarly termed a moral purpose. The highest moral purpose aimed at in the highest species of the drama, is the teaching the human heart, through its sympathies and antipathies, the knowledge of itself; in proportion to the possession of which knowledge, every human being is wise, just, sincere, tolerant and kind. If dogmas can do more, it is well: but a drama is no fit place for the enforcement of them.

One may doubtless be imaginative but fail morally for want of principles to guide his conduct; one may also fail though he have the very best principles at his command, if he lacks the imagination necessary to their discriminating application. John Dewey has gone so far as to claim:

The sum total of the effect of all reflective treatises on morals is insignificant in comparison with the influence of architecture, novel, drama, on life, becoming important when "intellectual" products formulate the tendencies of these arts and provide them with an intellectual base.[13]

And the way in which the arts are morally most important is in stirring and exercising the imagination, prodding us to go beyond the provinces of our immediate environment, beyond the limits of stereotyped explanations and conventional judgments, beyond the taken-for-granted. Perhaps the principal reason that artists have been feared by authoritarians is not so much because of their specific criticisms and proposals, but because of their tendency to sponsor the activities of criticizing and proposing; but in any society claiming to be democratic, there can be no such thing as too much creative imagination in a citizenry, and therefore the artist, at least the good artist, ought to be recognized as making a contribution to the social weal whether or not he is himself and in his art especially concerned with so-called "social problems."

Ultimately the moral life is no more a matter of formula and rule than the aesthetic life. It is not very hard to teach a person to paint a picture or even to compose a song, but it is impossible to teach

[13] *Art as Experience*, p. 345.

anyone to paint a good picture or to compose a good song, for the teaching can go only so far in the way of providing skill and technique and suggesting possibilities. At some point the producer himself must take over and see what he can create with the tools he has been provided. All this is truistic. It is perhaps not so generally recognized that moral goodness is also impossible to produce by training or teaching, though it is possible and even comparatively easy to teach a moral code. An individual's moral progress is marked by his increasing ability to "take the role of the other," genuinely to perceive another person's interests and motivations. And here of course is where the artist may help. Not through literature alone, but in dance, sculpture, painting, music, and architecture too, are we helped to extend our consciousness of ways other than those we have known firsthand. The sublimity realized in the nave of a great cathedral constitutes an extension of our consciousness in ways that may easily have moral significance, as for instance in our dealings with persons we would describe as "religious." Our empathic perceptions of a carved Chinese Buddha may communicate to us a more intimate understanding of a certain repose that we had hitherto half-known, an understanding likely to be relevant to our dealings with live people. But we may also learn through such experiences something about how it is and what it takes to be thus imaginative, and we may be enabled thereby to be more flexible, more subtle, more penetrating, more sensitive, and more deeply sympathetic in our dealings with other persons. Every person, every situation is unique; and only great imaginative power can cope with uniqueness. Not only in the understanding of other people and why they do what they do, but also in the understanding of oneself, is art a help; and again both in the sense of actual revelations about our own motivations as we see these reflected in the motivations of fictional characters, and in the sense of conducing to the practice of *trying* to understand ourselves. Ultimately, taking ourselves for granted is just as morally crass as taking other people for granted.

But if it is now bluntly asked whether this constitutes a claim that he who through extensive experience has acquired a high capacity for appreciation of art-works is therefore a person of very great moral discernment and fine character, the answer must certainly be: not necessarily. Perhaps no one knows very much about the process of becoming morally good, but nearly everyone who has thought about it knows that it is an immensely complicated matter. Childhood training has something to do with it, health has something to do with; so does being loved, living in a friendly society—and many many other things. Therefore, a person can be aesthetically imaginative and still something of a scoundrel. But to the extent that being morally good means something more than avoiding certain overtly sinful acts, there is required a free and live imagination. To the development of that, art may help.[14]

MORALITY AS AN AECONOMY OF VALUES

Clive Bell has written:

To justify ethically any human activity, we must enquire—"Is this a means to good states of mind?" In the case of art our answer will be prompt and emphatic. Art is not only a means to good states of mind, but, perhaps, the most direct and potent that we possess. Nothing is more direct, because nothing affects the mind more immediately; nothing is more potent, because there is no state of mind more excellent or more intense than the state of aesthetic contemplation. This being so, to seek any other moral justification for art, to seek in art a means to anything less than good states of mind, is an act of wrong-headedness to be committed only by a fool or a man of genius.[15]

[14] Compare D. G. James' summary of his discussion of this problem: "The imagination is not a moral affair but it has great importance for morality. First, by its penetration or attempted penetration to what transcends morality, it keeps morality under constant criticism, and saves it from the humourless solemnity, the pessimism, and the legalism, which are only too natural to it. In seeking to represent to itself a state which is beyond good and evil it may indeed be but dreaming, only 'imagining things'; but the dream can exert power and keep before morality a recognition of its ultimate helplessness. Secondly, the self-perception which a strong imagination affords is vital to the moral life; without it we quickly become lost in the quagmires of self-ignorance and of humbug. And equally, the keen perception of the life of others, which marks the imaginative life, dissolves from them, as Coleridge says, the film of familiarity and selfish solicitude with which an unimaginative life quickly wraps them round. Such perception both of the self and of others is not indeed sought for moral ends; yet it becomes a factor of incalculable importance in the moral life, a vital condition of tenure of a moral ideal which seeks to maintain itself in vitality. These are the 'gifts' of the imagination to morality." *Scepticism and Poetry* (London: George Allen & Unwin, 1937), pp. 136-37.
[15] *Art* (New York: Stokes, n.d.), p. 114.

Now one may strongly disagree with Bell that art never has any moral justification other than in being a means to "good states of mind"—we have already suggested that at least sometimes art has other values—but still find in this statement a tonic reminder that the chief values of works of art are *aesthetic*. If Santayana has said, "Art being a part of life, the criticism of art is a part of morals,"[16] it must be recognized that he is using the word "morals" in an unusually large sense, namely as having to do with *all* the values of life. It is commoner to reserve "moral" for application to those values that concern the rights and duties of rational beings in their relationships to other such beings, and, to a lesser extent, to other animals and things. For instance, it is not normally thought to be a moral question whether a person should choose for dinner lamb curry or creamed chicken, nor whether one should play chess or listen to some music. Nevertheless, such are *value* considerations, and we do require some name for a human being's concern with all values—his concern to live the best life possible to him, where the best life will be one embracing, among many other values, a variety of sensual delights, such as perhaps gratifying one's hunger with a well-prepared lamb curry. We will speak of this over-all concern for the best life as the "Aeconomy of Values," using the archaic spelling to avoid confusion with the Economy of the production and exchange of material goods and services. Now, in the Aeconomy of Values, aesthetic value is certainly of importance, even of great importance, since, as Bell has said, the best art affords us direct access to exceptionally good states of mind. Or, as Santayana has put it, "Beauty gives men the best hint of ultimate good which their experience as yet can offer."[17]

In saying that the principal value of most works of art is aesthetic rather than moral, we have intended to place the emphasis upon

[16] *Reason in Art* (New York: Scribner, 1906), p. 178. John Dewey has declared art "more moral than moralities. For the latter either are, or tend to become, consecrations of the *status quo*, reflections of custom, re-enforcements of the established order. The moral prophets of humanity have always been poets even though they spoke in free verse or by parable. Were art an acknowledged power in human association and not treated as the pleasuring of an idle moment or as a means of ostentatious display, and were morals understood to be identical with every aspect of value that is shared in experience, the 'problem' of the relation of art and morals would not exist." *Art as Experience*, p. 348.

[17] *Reason in Art*, p. 172.

those experienced values which arise in the transaction between an art-work and the aesthetically-oriented perceiver, rather than upon the long-range values of making men kinder and more understanding in their dealings with each other.

The deficiency of that Puritanical objection to art which deplores the distraction of the appreciator from his duty is that it tries to make moral values the *whole* of the Aeconomy of Values, rather than just a part, though of course an exceedingly important part. The Puritan fails to see that play, and idle but interesting conversation with a friend, and sleep, and a swim on a summer's day, and the hearing of a good joke—and very much else—are all components in a good life too. One with a taste for paradox might put it: It is not one's duty to do only one's duty. And ultimately there seems something mean and crabbed about a life devoid of or deficient in aesthetic values.

This is not to say that everyone ought to be greatly taken up with the fine arts, nor that anyone ought to be an aesthete—indeed, "aesthete" may now be defined as one who exaggerates the importance of the values of art in the total Aeconomy of Values. For one thing, it should not be forgotten that works of art have no monopoly on aesthetic values. Indeed it may be that works of art are only the necessary spectacles for those amongst us who are a little myopic aesthetically: if a person were sufficiently perceptive and keen, he would see beauty anywhere he looked. In the experiment with peyote, reported in *Doors of Perception*, Aldous Huxley says that in his state of hyperaesthesia he was so taken with the myriad colors and textures of a simple flower that he was indifferent to and even almost disgusted with the paintings his eye fell upon. But apart from mystical trances and peyote-induced states, there is perhaps no mortal whose life can be altogether satisfactory on the aesthetic side without access to music and poetry and paintings and other art, though of course one may have such access and still not be realizing the special values thus available.

Whitehead has called great art "the arrangement of the environment so as to provide for the soul vivid, but transient, values."[18] Such great art as we possess we may well be thankful for, but it is not enough that we avail ourselves of the opportunity of enjoying

[18] *Science and the Modern World* (New York: Macmillan, 1925), p. 290.

the beauty that is already with us. If our group Aeconomy of Values is to be optimal it becomes important to do what we can to facilitate the increase of beauty. This implies that a society needs to be concerned with its present and future artists and with its present and future works of great art, in Whitehead's use of the term. Would anyone seriously argue that because New York and London have wonderful art galleries, libraries, and concert halls, those cities are therefore aesthetically ideal? Only those who are entirely with- drawn from reality fail to realize that our cities and towns (and much that is in between) are in very large measure architecturally drab and ugly, the few fine buildings and parks standing out like patches of newly-cleaned wallpaper. And *if* a few of the very largest cities are relatively satisfactory in the opportunities af- forded for enjoyment of ballet, live music, legitimate theatre, and original paintings and sculptures, the vast majority of communities are exceedingly unsatisfactory. There are some who think that this is inevitable, but actually it is not. The small towns that do have their own art galleries, their summer stock companies, their own concert programs, conclusively prove the possibility of such. The beautiful highways that are increasingly to be enjoyed make us wonder at our toleration of inefficient, billboard-cluttered roads. But examples can be cited in easy profusion. The great point is that the quest for beauty is in larger measure than our society has yet discovered or admitted a matter of social policy and public de- cision, of politics and economics, of community and national plan- ning and education.

Chapter 13

AESTHETIC
TASTE

and

VALUATION

• *To the* ancient saw, "There's no disputing taste," it has been perversely answered, "What else is there to dispute?" But the often-quoted maxim presumably does not deny that men *do* debate their preferences; what it does deny is the possibility that such disagreement should be rationally adjudicated. You like something and perhaps I do too; but perhaps I don't, and if I don't—well, there we are. You may persuade or cajole me until I change my mind, or if you have a certain power you may compel me to change my mind or to say that I do, but what you cannot do is to show that reason requires me to surrender my position.

Yet if one listens carefully to the man who insists that everything is relative, that it's all a matter of opinion and personal preference, one may be rewarded by hearing this person say one or both of the following things: "That's absurd: no one in his right mind could say that Edgar Guest is better than Shakespeare," or "Well, I know so little about sculpture that I'm in no position to judge; my opinion wouldn't be worth anything." It is hard to say which is the commonest of common-sense opinions: that taste is relative, that some things are certainly better (or more beautiful) than others, or that only if one knows a fair amount about a given subject is he "entitled" to an evaluative opinion. Probably most people are sufficiently inconsistent to believe all three, though not perhaps at exactly the same time. The tactics of social intercourse have something to do with it. It is very modest to say, "Really I don't know enough to judge. . . ." In an argument, if you're out to win you may want to dogmatize: "Without any doubt, this is better than that." If you are willing to settle for a draw just to put your cocksure opponent in his place, you may say, "Well, that's *your* opinion, but one man's meat. . . ."

To express one's taste is to make an evaluation. To make an evaluation is to criticize. But criticism is broader than evaluation.

There are four relationships that one can have to a work of art while remaining within the aesthetic domain (outside it, one may be destroyer, seller, buyer, wrapper, and so on): its creator, its appreciator, its performer or executor, or its critic. To begin with a very commodious definition: the critic is he who verbalizes about works of art.[1] However, two possible misconceptions must be guarded against, right from the start. So many harsh things are so often said about critics and criticism, it may be inaccurately assumed that to speak of the critic as verbalizing is to disparage his function, meaning by implication the familiar charge that whereas the artist "does something," the critic only "talks." Such is not intended here. Here "verbalizing" means only "expressing or asserting in words." Indeed, what follows may be read as a defense and justification of criticism. The second possible misconception, though it is a naive one, is to suppose that "criticism" in this context has the same meaning as it does in such usages as "Don't always be criticizing!" or "He's too critical"; that is, where to criticize is the same as to find fault with, where the critic is assumed to be a captious caviler. For our purposes criticism may be destruc-

---

[1] The critic is not to be confused with the aesthetician, whose relationship to the work of art is less direct. The aesthetician may be said to be to the critic (but also to the creator, appreciator, and performer) what the critic is to the work of art—at least approximately.

tive or constructive, complimentary, fault-finding, or neutral.

Nor is it here assumed that criticism is a strictly professional function. There are of course regular, established, career-critics, but the amateur and novice may also be a critic; indeed he is almost certain to be one because hardly anyone can help discussing art. Nevertheless, it will be useful to begin our investigation of criticism by looking not at the casual criticism of someone strolling through an art gallery or comparing notes with a friend during an intermission, but with criticism seriously pondered, formed, and publicly urged.

TYPES OF CRITICS

A first type of critic is the art *historian*. His is the task of providing the historical "background" or "setting" for a work of art. He justifies his work by claiming explanatory power for historical facts: we cannot really understand the music of Bach without knowing Vivaldi's influence; Virgil's *Aeneid* is not adequately intelligible to anyone ignorant of Roman history; a grasp of Medieval Catholic theology is indispensable for him who approaches the French Gothic cathedral. These examples suggest two general sorts of history relevant to aesthetic appreciation. There is the history of art, or *an* art, proper—as in the tracing of influences of one artist on another or the development of some particular form of art, such as the novel or landscape painting, or the emergence of a certain prevailing style. And there is the intellectual and social history of a people, which may be shown to be reflected in artistic products— as when the economy of a nation, its form of government, religious trends, or reigning philosophical ideas are pointed to as determining causes. Here is a passage from a popular history of Art which illustrates both these types of history:

> *During the early seventeenth century, the southern Netherlands was still under Spanish domination. Among the richest and most industrious of the Spanish possessions, Flanders remained within the fold of the Catholic Church, though it required the bloody persecutions of the Duke of Alva to stem the tide of the Reformation in those provinces. Also, an aristocracy continued to play an important role there; like the Church, it patronized the arts and so helped to form the character of Flemish painting. That character*

was embodied in the world of Peter Paul Rubens. . . .
    Rich in color, which is inherited from Venice, his paintings, re-gardless of subject, have vigor and a robust, sensuous, physical character.
    The Descent from the Cross, painted not long after his return from Italy, is highly dramatic. . . . The figures sway backward and forward, partly because of their roles in the incident, but more because of the Baroque love of movement.[2]

Some historians of art have been content to propose only in general terms that art is influenced by political, economic, and other events, but others have worked out more particular formulas for expressing this influence. The most famous of these in recent times is the Marxian theory of economic determinism, but perhaps the best known dogmatic sociological critic is the nineteenth-century positivist, Hippolyte Taine, who laid it down as a rule that "In order to comprehend a work of art, an artist or a group of artists, we must clearly comprehend the general social and intellectual condition of the times to which they belong. Herein is to be found the final explanation; herein resides the primitive cause determining all that follows it."[3] A work of art, he argued, can be as comprehensively understood, and in a strictly causal way, as a shrub or a tree. And it is the job of the critic, as it is the job of the botanist, to investigate such factors as climate, genetic traits,[4] and milieu. In short, criticism is not only historical, but scientifically historical, capable of an exhaustive finality in its explanations.

    Probably most students of art today would own to the importance of the historian's contribution—and ours is a day of such notable practitioners of historical criticism as Bernard Berenson, Erwin Panofsky, Alfred Einstein, and René Wellek—but few, including many of the historians themselves, would fail to set rather severe limits to the explanatory power of history. One serious limitation within which the historian works is that his "historical background"

[2] Everard M. Upjohn, Paul S. Wingert, and Jane Gaston Mahler, *History of World Art* (New York: Oxford, 1949), pp. 255-56.
[3] *The Philosophy of Art*, trans. John Durand (1873). Cited in Katharine Gilbert and Helmut Kuhn, *A History of Esthetics* (New York: Macmillan, 1939), p. 479.
[4] Race was to Taine an important determinant. Others have, of course, similarly argued. For a concrete instance, see *The Poetry of the Celtic Races*, by Taine's contemporary, Ernest Renan.

is the common background of artists ranging from the greatest to the worst (on any standard whatever). Historical criticism typically does more to show what Mozart and Oskar Schiltz (completely and deservedly forgotten today) shared than what distinguished them. It is this point that Sainte-Beuve makes in his famous criticism of Taine:

> *Now Mr. Taine has done nothing but try to study, methodically, the profound differences which race,* milieu, *periods of time, cause in the composition of minds, in the form and the bent of talents. But, it will be said, he does not succeed sufficiently; it is in vain that he gives us an admirable description of the race in its general features and fundamental lines; in vain that he draws and throws up, in his powerful pictures, the revolutions of time and the moral atmosphere that prevails at certain epochs of history; in vain that he disentangles, with address, the complication of incidents and particular adventures in which the life of an individual is engaged and as it were engeared. Still something escapes him; and what escapes is the most living part of the man—that which brings it about that of twenty men, or a hundred, or a thousand, subjected apparently to the same internal or external conditions, no two are alike, and that one only of all possesses original excellence.*[5]

Still, there is another type of historical critic against whom this criticism cannot be leveled. He is the *biographical* critic, the one who attempts to explain an artist by the artist's life. Again, biographers range from the eclectic to the "single-factor" theorists—that is, those who attempt to explain an artist's productions in terms of some one sort of event, characteristic, or relationship. Especially prominent today is psychoanalytical biography, of which the classic instance is Freud's study of Leonardo da Vinci. This much-debated essay is at the very least a brilliant speculation, and it does give a plausible explanation of Leonardo's characteristics. However, it is perhaps significant that this work is more useful toward an understanding of Leonardo's tendency to leave works unfinished than it is toward understanding his genius for composition; that is, it throws light on a general personality trait (which is in turn most certainly reflected in his work) and this, though it is important, is scarcely the whole job of criticism.

[5] Quoted in George Saintsbury, *Loci Critici* (Boston: Ginn, 1903), p. 417.

A first cousin to the historical critic is he who may be called the *textual* critic, where, lacking a word, "text" is used to mean the body, not only of a literary work but of an art work in any medium at all. A few examples will suffice to clarify this function. Working with X-ray equipment, a technician may discover that an earlier version of a painting has been in part obliterated by the now visible surface, or that such and such a figure has been added or altered by a later hand. A musicologist may uncover a manuscript score of Bach which indicates that certain notes in a standard edition are copyist's errors. It may be learned that of two similar statues one is a copy and the other the original. Ruins may be unearthed that allow the reconstruction of an ancient temple. Evidence may be compiled for the theory that a certain passage in the *Book of Job* has been interpolated by a writer living later than the writer of the bulk of the work. Or someone might uncover seemingly authentic stage directions for the first presentation of *Macbeth*.

In short, the textual critic's job is to reveal the work of art as it was produced by its creator and to identify alterations, additions, subtractions, and copies.[6] The textual critic sometimes makes discoveries that are valuable both to other types of critics—for instance, suggesting new interpretations—and to the consuming public. But it hardly need be pointed out that when the textual critic's work is done, there still remains nearly the whole job of criticism.

A third type of critic takes his chief function to be *analytical explication*.[7] Though he depends upon the textual critic to furnish him an authentic work of art and upon the historical critic and biographer for important background data, his job is—as he frequently insists—with the work of art itself as an artifact and as a meaning. He may even rebuke the scholarly historian for becoming so engrossed in the milieu of the artist as to lose sight of "the main thing." "Come," he says, "let us get back to the work of art. What does it say? How is it put together? What does it mean? What mood does it convey?"

---

[6] It is not here assumed that the original is necessarily better than later versions. Just as a translator may have a better style than the translatee, so a disciple may surpass his master, or a copier the original maker.

[7] In Biblical scholarship, a familiar distinction is that between "lower," or textual, criticism and "higher" criticism, which is concerned with the origins, the nature, and the meanings of the text.

His principal interest may be in the form and structure of the work, especially if his field be music or the visual arts. He may say, for instance, of Giorgione's "Madonna, with St. Francis and St. Liberal":

The general compositional plan is the traditional pyramidal organization of the main constituent units arranged in bilateral symmetry. . . . . An organized network of internal compositional rhythms of color, light, line, space, mass, pattern, and decorative motifs is powerfully active throughout the picture; and these rhythms contribute variety, subtlety, and a highly distinctive identity to the general pyramidal plan to which they are subordinated.[8]

Or he may say, as one critic does of the Mozart *D minor Quartet*:

The first movement is an Allegro in square time and in recognizable sonata form. The first subject is stated at once by the first violin, and repeated an octave higher. The harmonic progressions follow the classical alternation of the tonic and the dominant, but soon the Mozartean plaintive harmonies of the augmented sixth appear, with their inevitable resolutions into the octave. Simultaneously with chromaticization of the harmonic texture, the rhythmic pattern is quickened in the second section of the exposition. There are bold modulations in the development, transitions to remote keys, at one juncture connecting E-flat Minor and A Minor by a sudden chromatic move.[9]

Formal criticism is of course sometimes encountered in the case of literature too, as when a novel's plot may be shown to follow a graphic model, or when a poem's meter and rhythm are under discussion as in the following analysis of Yeats' poem "That the Night Come."

The prevailing metrical form of the poem is iambic trimeter. (The poem rhymes: a-b-c-b-a-c-d-e-f-e-d-f.). . . . The normal line is composed of three iambic feet, that is, three divisions containing an unaccented and an accented syllable in that order. But the fol-

[8] Albert C. Barnes, *The Art in Painting*, 3rd ed. (New York: Harcourt, Brace, 1937), p. 420.
[9] From Nicolas Slonimsky's analysis on the album of the Columbia Masterworks recording.

*lowing lines have variations: 6, 8, 9, 10, 12. It will be observed that
in the first section of the poem, that is, the first five lines, there
are no variations.*[10]

Instead of or in addition to concentrating upon structural elements of the work of art, the analytic critic may concern himself
with the ideas, or more broadly, the meaning of the work. Here are
some samples:

First, a description of Delacroix' "Liberty Leading the People":

*The canvas is dominated by the fiery allegorical figure of Liberty,
here seen as the spirit of the French people whom she leads on-
ward to triumph. No relaxed Mediterranean Goddess here, instead
a virile, energetic reincarnation of the spirit of 1789. Her muscular
arms are strong enough to hold with ease both a bayoneted rifle
and the tricolored banner of the Republic. Though bare-breasted
she betrays no sign of softness or sensuality, and her powerful
limbs stride over the street barricades as she leads her followers
forward through the oncoming barrage. Though an allegorical
figure, she is treated by the artist as a living personality, clothed in
the garments of a daughter of the French people. Only the Phryg-
ian cap (modeled after that worn by liberated slaves in Rome and
adopted as a symbol of liberty by the first French Republic) and
the almost classic profile, serene in the face of danger, indicate her
symbolic significance. She does not hover over the action on wings
as so many other artists depicted her; instead, with her feet on the
ground, she is in the midst of action.*[11]

Here is Coleridge analyzing some lines of Wordsworth:

> *Thou best philosopher, who yet dost keep
> Thy heritage! Thou eye among the blind,
> That, deaf and silent, read'st the eternal deep,
> Haunted for ever by the Eternal Mind,—
> Mighty Prophet! Seer blest!
> On whom those truths do rest,
> Which we are toiling all our lives to find!
> Thou, over whom thy immortality
> Broods like the day, a master o'er the slave,
> A presence that is not to be put by!*

[10] Cleanth Brooks, Jr., John Thibaut Purser, and Robert Penn Warren, *An Approach to Literature*, rev. ed. (New York: Appleton-Century-Crofts, 1939), p. 470.
[11] William Fleming, *Arts and Ideas* (New York: Holt, 1955), p. 640.

Now here, not to stop at the daring spirit of metaphor which connects the epithets "deaf and silent," with the apostrophized eye: *or (if we are to refer it to the preceding word, philosopher) the faulty and equivocal syntax of the passage; and without examining the propriety of making a "master* brood *o'er a slave," or the* day brood *at all; we will merely ask, what does all this mean? In what sense is a child of that age a* philosopher? *In what sense does he* read *"the eternal deep"? In what sense is he declared to be "forever haunted" by the Supreme Being? or so inspired as to deserve the splendid titles of a* mighty prophet, a *blessed seer? By reflection? by knowledge? by conscious intuition? or by any form or modification of consciousness? These would be tidings indeed....*[12]

About the final two movements of Beethoven's *Eroica Symphony*, Roy Dickinson Welsh writes:

The clearly perceptible content of these movements are spiritual universals which may be defined as heroic striving, grief, joy, exaltation, or in Wagner's words, Action, Tragedy, Serenity, Love. Expressed in these terms the content is apparent to the perceptive ear and mature mind from a hearing of the music unaided by any association with Napoleon's career.[13]

It is to be noticed that the analytic critic may deal as much—or *more*—with feelings as with more strictly intellectual components; indeed feelings may be the whole of his concern. But when the attention of the critic shifts to his own subjective reactions, scarcely claiming that his own feeling and imagistic reaction is even typical, he may be designated an impressionistic type of critic:

I allowed myself, as I sometimes do, to wander out of myself. The conceit came to me of a copious grove of singing birds, and in their midst a simple harmonic duo, two human souls, steadily asserting their own pensiveness, joyousness.[14]

Next in this rapid survey of types of critical practice, we may come to the very broad classification of explicitly evaluative—or, as

[12] *Biographia Literaria,* chap. xxii.
[13] "Supplementary Essay," in Theodore Meyer Greene, *The Arts and the Art of Criticism* (Princeton: Princeton University Press, 1947), p. 591.
[14] Walt Whitman, writing of Beethoven's *Septet,* quoted in E. M. Forster, "The Raison d'Etre of Criticism in the Arts," in *Two Cheers for Democracy* (New York: Harcourt, Brace, 1951).

it has traditionally been called, *judicial*—criticism. What comes under judgment may be a single work—even a single phrase or word, a single chord, a single brush stroke; or it may be the entire output of an artist or a school or a century. The standards by which the judgment is arrived at may remain tacit (even to the point of being unknown to the critic himself) or they may be quite explicitly stated and applied. The judgment may be adverse or favorable, or both. It may or may not proceed by comparison with another work or another type of work. It may be severely aesthetic or it may invoke moral norms. And many other subdivisions are possible. But here are some samples, chosen to suggest the variety of judicial criticism:

Of Balanchine's ballet *Theme and Variations*, George Amberg has written:

> *It is an abstract composition and there is no factual content or literal meaning of any kind. There is, however, an alternation of action and reaction, derived from movement tensions, which makes the visual drama more exciting than any story. . . . The profusion of intricate and startling detail is subordinated to a master plan, gradually revealed as one dynamic phrase infallibly follows another to the rousing terminating climax.*[15]

Here is Longinus on Homer:

> *So in the* Odyssey *one may liken Homer to the setting sun; the grandeur remains without the intensity. For no longer does he preserve the sustained energy of the great* Iliad *lays, the consistent sublimity which never sinks into flatness, the flood of moving incidents in quick succession, the versatile rapidity and actuality, brimful of images drawn from real life. It is rather as though the Ocean had shrunk into its lair and lay becalmed within its own confines. Henceforth we see the ebbing tide of Homer's greatness, as he wanders in the incredible regions of romance.*[16]

Samuel Johnson wrote of the seventeenth-century "metaphysical" school of poetry in this way:

[15] *Ballet* (New York: Duell, Sloan & Pearce, and New American Library, 1949), p. 149.
[16] *On the Sublime*, trans. W. Hamilton Fyfe (Cambridge: Harvard University Press, 1932), *IX.*

From this account of their compositions, it will be readily inferred
that they were not successful in representing or moving the affec-
tions. As they were wholly employed on something unexpected
and surprising, they had no regard to that uniformity of sentiment
which enables us to conceive and to excite the pains and the pleas-
ures of other minds; they never inquired what, on any occasion,
they should have said or done, but wrote rather as beholders
than partakers of human nature. . . . Their wish was only to say
what they hoped had never been said before.
Nor was the sublime more within their reach than the pathetic; for
they never attempted that comprehension and expanse of thought
which at once fills the whole mind, and of which the first effect is
sudden astonishment, and the second rational admiration. Sublimity
is produced by aggregation, and littleness by dispersion. Great
thoughts are always general, and consist in positions not limited by
exceptions, and in descriptions not descending to minuteness. . . .
Those writers who lay on the watch for novelty could have little
hope for greatness, for the great things cannot have escaped former
observation. Their attempts were always analytic; they broke every
image into fragments; and could no more represent, by their slender
conceits and laboured particularities, the prospects of nature or the
scenes of life, than he who dissects a sunbeam with a prism can
exhibit the wide effulgence of a summer noon.[17]

Vasari writes on Michelangelo's "Judgment Day":

The whole work is finely and harmoniously executed, so that it
looks as if it had been done in one day, and no illuminator could
have equalled its execution. . . . Every human emotion is repre-
sented and marvellously expressed. The proud, envious, avaricious,
luxurious, and others, may be recognized by an intelligent observer
from their attitudes and treatment. . . . A man of judgment who
understands painting will see the tremendous power of art in the
thoughts and emotions of the figures, never displayed by any other
artist. . . . Happy indeed is he who has seen this stupendous marvel
of our century.[18]

George Bernard Shaw (who, if he had written no drama at all,
would still be remembered as an important music critic) wrote of

[17] "Abraham Cowley," in *Lives of the British Poets.*
[18] *The Lives of the Painters, Sculptors, and Architects,* trans. A. B. Hinds (New
York: Dutton, 1927), Vol. IV, 143-44.

Beethoven that of course he had many qualities, the most disturbing and distinctive of which was:

> ... *his power of unsettling us and imposing his giant moods on us. Berlioz was very angry with an old French composer who expressed the discomfort Beethoven gave him by saying "J'aime la musique qui me berce," "I like music that lulls me." Beethoven's is music that wakes you up; and the one mood in which you shrink from it is the mood in which you want to be let alone.*[19]

One type of judicial critic deserves a special category, the reviewer. The reviewer is a journalist, writing against a deadline, writing of art that is *news*, frequently trying to serve as a guide to his readers, telling, that is, whether in his opinion this movie, that play, so-and-so's performance of Mozart, the current exhibit at the gallery, tonight's dance recital, the much ballyhooed new novel, or the opera which "by popular request" will be repeated on Channel 7 is worth one's time, trouble, or money. Reviewer-critics are often spoken of with scorn and even loathing by artists and performers, but their power is sometimes awesome. The drama and music critics of two or three New York newspapers can by their verdicts virtually assign a play or a performer to oblivion or to success. A large number of persons will buy tickets only if their favorite reviewer gives them the sign. This is very much less the case, for a variety of reasons, with films and books.

It would be quite false to suggest that reviews are read solely for the purpose of guidance. Just as spectators at a basketball game frequently enjoy reading an account by a sports writer of what they themselves have the night before seen, so too do concert-goers enjoy comparing notes with the *Times* expert. Often, too, the review serves as a substitute for what it reviews. Especially are oral book reviews valued as time-savers. Or, again, the review may be read for its wit; thus a Robert Benchley review of a play now otherwise forgotten may still be enjoyed.

From the play review prized for its cleverness it is an easy step to the last kind of criticism which will here be taken into account: it is what may be called the "literary essay," if that rather vague name may be assigned to such famous pieces as Sainte-Beuve's

---

[19] "Beethoven's Centenary," reprinted in *George Bernard Shaw: Selected Prose*, ed. Diarmuid Russell (New York: Dodd, Mead, 1952), p. 203.

"What Is a Classic?," De Quincey's "The Literature of Knowledge and the Literature of Power," Walt Whitman's "Democratic Vistas," and the critical prefaces of Henry James and Joseph Conrad. Two qualities in particular may be assigned to this species: the literary essay is itself or makes pretensions to be a work of some literary merit; and it is on some relatively large literary or other artistic issue, rather than being about a single artist, a single work of art. Here is a small sample drawn from Walter Pater:

> *The charm, therefore, of what is classical, in art or literature, is that of the well-known tale, to which we can, nevertheless, listen over and over again, because it is told so well. To the absolute beauty of its artistic form, is added the accidental, tranquil, charm of familiarity. There are times, indeed, at which these charms fail to work on our spirits at all, because they fail to excite us. "Romanticism," says Stendhal, "is the art of presenting to people the literary works which, in the actual state of their habits and beliefs, are capable of giving them the greatest possible pleasure; classicism, on the contrary, of presenting them with that which gave the greatest possible pleasure to their grandfathers." But then, beneath all changes of habits and beliefs, our love of that mere abstract proportion—of music—which what is classical in literature possesses, still maintains itself in the best of us, and what pleased our grandparents may at least tranquillise us. The "classic" comes to us out of the cool and quiet of other times, as the measure of what a long experience has shown will at least never displease us. And in the classical literature of Greece and Rome, as in the classics of the last century, the essentially classical element is that quality of order in beauty, which they possess, indeed, in a pre-eminent degree, and which impresses some minds to the exclusion of everything else in them.[20]*

In the scope of its subject matter, the literary essay is close kin to aesthetics, which takes the further step into the abstract and general.

THE USES OF CRITICISM

Having now looked at a number of different activities that may deserve the name "criticism," we may go on to ask about the *raison d'etre* of criticism, whether historical, textual, analytic, judicial, or

[20] "Postscript," in *Appreciations* (New York: Macmillan, n.d.).

general and literary. Critics have been much abused, particularly by artists who, when they cry out in pain and anger from beneath the critical lash, may be supposed to be something less than dispassionate; but it is fashionable in some quarters for amateurs of the arts to speak disparagingly of the critic as a parasite or a drone, one who because he lacks creative ability himself turns to this seemingly derived, secondary function. "Why," the indignant artist or his protector may cry out, "why, if you dislike my work, don't you improve on it yourself?"[21] But the critic has available to him an answer: "One can tell a rotten egg without being able to lay a fresh one!"

In the ranks of critics, however, there is more internecine warfare than a unified defense against the enemy of all criticism. To the scholarly historian, the analyst may seem a trifling fellow engaged in a picayune business; to the textual technician, the judicial critic may seem a mere wallower in the troughs of opinion; to the reviewer, the elegant essayist may seem "long-haired," remote, effete; and so on.

There are trends in criticism as in the arts. An age of great historical emphasis may beget a reaction from the more analytically inclined. A passion for statistical science may engender a splenetic scorn directed against the old-fashioned belle-lettrist. Yet without being a mere appeaser, one may discover a certain legitimacy and significance in each of the several sorts of criticism; indeed, it will be argued that the best criticism is sufficiently flexible and catholic to function now in one mode, now in another.

It is doubtful whether criticism helps the practicing artist very much, once he is past his student and apprentice period. At least it is hard to find much testimony from artists on the value of criticism. C. Day-Lewis has remarked that the artist is less likely to be annoyed or gladdened by criticism than he is to be puzzled by its irrelevance: by the time the criticism appears, he has gone on to something else, has a new artistic problem to cope with, and cannot easily get back into that which is over and done with. However, in "The Making of a Poem," Stephen Spender says, "In common with other creative writers I pretend that I am not, and I am, exceedingly affected by unsympathetic criticism. . . ."

[21] Familiar too is the admonition of Cezanne, "Don't be a critic, paint."

E. M. Forster thinks that a critic may influence the artist, but usually only in a minor way, as in pointing out to him some mannerism or habit of which he had not been aware. Forster says that in his own instance he has been told that he uses too many "buts," and now he tries to be more moderate in the employment of this academic conjunction. Poussin felt more strongly the benefits of criticism, and once wrote in a letter that the reproof and even slander directed against his paintings "has brought me not a little profit, for it has prevented a vanity that might have blinded me and has made me proceed cautiously in my work—a practice I wish to adhere to all my life. Well, even if those who find fault with me cannot teach me to do better, they will be the cause of my finding the means myself. . . ."[22]

Perhaps artists themselves have tended both to exaggerate the harm the critics do (as in the famous instance of Shelley's eulogy of Keats as having been the mortal victim of vicious critical attacks) and minimize the good. However, even if this is not so, or if, to put the case extremely, critics never influence artistic practice at all, criticism is scarcely thereby condemned, for criticism is ordinarily directed not at the artist but at the appreciator. In general, criticism stands or falls as it succeeds or fails (1) to be intrinsically interesting, and (2) to be illuminating about the work of art it has as its object.

To judge criticism—as some do—from the practice of "criticasters" rather than from that of its most distinguished practitioners is like judging the art of painting from the contents of an academy ash can. Only he who has read the criticism of writers like Donald Tovey, Meyer Schapiro, R. P. Blackmur, Erwin Panofsky, Desmond McCarthy, and Edmund Wilson (to snatch at a few contemporary examples) can be acquainted with the concrete case for

[22] Letter of April 7, 1647, quoted in *Artists on Art*, ed. Robert Goldwater and Marco Treves (New York: Pantheon, 1945), p. 151. Perhaps criticism has more effect on performers than on other creative artists. The distinguished actor Alec Guiness claims that it is not unusual for actors to change a performance after reading criticism. He says too, "I would never think of tackling a classical role without at some time browsing through Coleridge, Lamb, Hazlitt, Montague, Lewes, and Shaw in the hope, if not of inspiration, then at least of stimulation." Quoted in Christopher Fry, *An Experience of Critics* (New York: Oxford, 1952), Prologue. This volume is well worth reading for provocative statements by Mr. Fry and several London play reviewers.

criticism. Prose literature itself would be seriously deprived if there were subtracted from its body the critical writings of such masterful authors as Anatole France, Coleridge, Goethe, Hazlitt, Matthew Arnold, Sir Philip Sidney, George Brandes, Henry James, and Virginia Woolf. And without the critical interpretations of Giotto's iconography, of the structural function of the flying buttress in Gothic cathedrals, of the psychological assumptions of surrealism and stream-of-consciousness, of the harmonic innovations of Wagner and the allusions of Hart Crane—without, that is, the help of experts in getting at the significance and form of works of art, a very great many persons would be denied much of the satisfaction they derive from their associations with these works. But why, it will be asked, should a work of art *need* interpretation; if it is truly art (in the best sense) will it not speak directly, without the need of any intermediaries, to the appreciator? The point of view expressed in these questions is a rather common one. Persons who would not hesitate to ask at a service station for the way to the concert hall sometimes think it is illegitimate to seek help in finding their way through the music they hear there; and if the music is not thoroughly comprehensible to them, unaided (and perhaps on first hearing!), they may blame the composer for writing and the conductor for playing such music. Perhaps it is ideal when we are fully capable of understanding a work without outside help, but probably no one ever developed such a capacity, except in the case of the very simplest art, without the help of critics. And the fact is that there is hardly anyone who does not stand to improve his relationship to works of art through the interpretations of those who have taken more than ordinary pains to examine the work, its background, its maker, its relationship to other works, and other such matters.

The greatest value of the critic, then, lies in his contribution to our aesthetic satisfaction, whether in his own achievement or in other works of art. Sometimes he helps us appreciate particular objects which unaided we might have misunderstood or ignored; sometimes he shows us the significance of movements in art, and thus forestalls or removes a prejudice that might interfere with our appreciation; sometimes he helps us understand artistic intentions, so that at least we do not blame the artist for not succeeding in doing what he had not the least wish to do. And sometimes, of course, the critic works negatively, teaching us to *de*preciate a certain work or kind of work; but even this kind of criticism is not in its production or enjoyment rooted exclusively in sadism. De- structive criticism, does, to be sure, tend to deprive us of aesthetic enjoyments—for instance, if we become convinced by a critic that neither Norman Rockwell nor Grandma Moses is America's great- est painter, we may thereafter feel a slighter satisfaction in their works—but this deprivation may be amply compensated by a sharpening of our appreciation of, say, Ben Shahn and Georgia O'Keefe.

To be sure, if one's attitude toward the critic is slavish, the result will be more likely to be an abnegation of one's own critical and appreciative powers, and a substitution of the critic's judgment for any spontaneous reaction of one's own. But in the more fortunate case, criticism is not only a source of delight in itself but a means to greater aesthetic delight in the works of art that it is directed toward. H. L. Mencken has compared good criticism to a catalytic agent. He says that the critic's business is

> *to provoke the reaction between the work of art and the spectator. The spectator, untutored, stands unmoved; he sees the work of art, but it fails to make any intelligible impression on him; if he were spontaneously sensitive to it, there would be no need for criticism. But now comes the critic with his catalysis. He makes the work of art live for the spectator; he makes the spectator live for the work of art. Out of the process comes understanding, appreciation, intel- ligent enjoyment—and that is precisely what the artist tried to produce.*[23]

MARKS OF THE GOOD CRITIC

Like the value of art itself, the value of criticism cannot be as- sessed apart from the needs, interests, and disposition of the persons whom it reaches. Consequently, just as there is nothing in all the world, whether an artifact or a natural object, that might not be beautiful—we do not say merely "called beautiful"—to someone some time, so too there is no critical work so poor that it might not

[23] "Criticism of Criticism of Criticism," in *Prejudices, First Series* (New York: Knopf, 1919), pp. 20-21.

be helpful to someone some time, nor any so good that it could gain universal approbation. Nevertheless, if we can assume that there are two demands we normally make of critical writing, that it be intrinsically interesting and that it contribute to our aesthetic appreciation either by helping us become more sensitive and discriminating persons or by putting us into closer touch with actual art-works, then it is possible to list some general characteristics of the "good critic." It need hardly be added that men will differ in their more specific appraisal of critics, even if they adopt these criteria.

(1) A critic ought to be himself an art-lover. Only one who feels a strong affection for at least one of the arts is likely to have anything important to say about art.

(2) A critic ought to be, to an unusually high degree, sensitive to an art. Only if he has a special facility for getting inside an art-work, reacting strongly to it, being aware of small differences, will he qualify.

(3) A critic ought to have a strong power of analysis. Only if he can show how a work is organized, what are some of the significant relations between its parts, is he likely to be helpful to his audience.

(4) A critic ought to have the ability to employ aesthetic principles in his evaluation, citing reasons for his judgments. Only if he can go beyond a registration of liking and disliking into a consideration of the causes of failure and success, will he be likely to improve appreciation.

(5) A critic ought to have a wide experience in his chosen field. Only if he can work in terms of comparisons and contrasts and give good indication of the fact that he is judging with a sense of what has been and can be done in somewhat similar ways, will he be able to broaden the orientation of his audience.

(6) A critic ought to be able to communicate his judgments in a clear and interesting manner. Only if he can get his ideas across to somebody, no matter how skillful his own interpretation and how sensitive his own appreciation, will he deserve approbation as a critic.[24]

---

[24] Compare similar discussions in Bernard C. Heyl, *New Bearings in Esthetics and Art Criticism* (New Haven: Yale University Press, 1943), pp. 92-93; D. W. Gotshalk, *Art and the Social Order* (Chicago: University of Chicago Press, 1947), pp. 177-79; and Greene, *The Arts and the Art of Criticism*, pp. 369-73.

CRITICAL RELATIVISM

The discussion so far of kinds of criticism and their value might provoke one who has been taught the relativity of all value to some such objection as this:

Isn't all of this a disguised absolutism? Doesn't the whole case for criticism rest upon the unjustified assumption that some art is really and universally better than other art? Isn't the critic, whoever he be and whatever his claim to "expertness" and "authority," just expressing his personal opinion, to which, of course, he is entitled so long as he does not claim that it is anything more than that; a purely personal opinion, not necessarily valid for anyone except himself?

The case for "critical relativism" may be argued along two important lines: (1) by citing apparently unresolvable disagreements among different ages, different "authorities" and different cultures; (2) by showing the "subjectivity" of all value.

(1) An amusing anthology of depreciations of famous artists by famous artists would include the following: El Greco said of Michelangelo that he was a good man but that he did not know how to paint. Goethe had a low opinion of *The Divine Comedy*. T. S. Eliot has argued that *Hamlet* is a failure. Whistler remarked of a painting by Cezanne that it might have been done by a ten-year-old —who ought to have been spanked. Berlioz could not abide the music of Rossini. And so on.

At least as much disagreement can be found among reputable critics of any age. For instance, the poetry of Walt Whitman is praised as the highest product of nineteenth-century America, or dismissed as the worthless effusions of a completely undisciplined mind—depending on which critic you pick up. Is Picasso the most gifted painter of the twentieth century or a confused and unimportant artist? He has been called both. Is Bartok to take his place in the front rank of composers or be assigned to oblivion? Both futures have been predicted for him.

The stock of virtually every artist of note has risen in one age only to fall in another. Johann Sebastian Bach seemed to those who directly succeeded him (including his sons) a fuddy-duddy, hopelessly old-fashioned and therefore presumably destined to be forgotten. In high repute among his contemporaries, John Donne fell into ill repute and neglect among critics and the reading public, until he was "rediscovered" in the twentieth century. Sophocles' *Oedipus the King*, which has seemed to the critics of many ages (including our own) one of the greatest if not the single greatest of all tragic dramas, was accorded only a second prize in the original Athenian competition. (The play ranked above it, which has not come down to us, *might* of course seem to us also the superior work, but such is unlikely.) And indeed, there are almost endless examples not only of the artists we prize most highly having been roughly handled by their own generation but of artists we consider contemptible or at least negligible having been praised to the skies by their contemporaries. Take for instance the case of Ludwig Spohr (1784-1859), who in the middle of the nineteenth century was an exceedingly popular composer, so much so that in 1850 his music accounted for almost ten per cent of the program of the New York Philharmonic orchestra. Today his name is known only to musicologists.[25] And even where some masterpiece has been highly regarded by many ages, it often turns out that *what* was especially esteemed in it varied radically from time to time.[26]

Furthermore, one need hardly be a professional anthropologist to realize that what is accepted in one place as beautiful may appear to the people of another place hideously grotesque, ugly, or simply dull and uninteresting. A love song of Siam may seem as repellent to Western ears as—well, as Schubert lieder to Siamese ears. But sometimes it seems that taste varies almost as much within a culture, at least a complex culture, as between cultures. What is there for the reader of *Wild West* and the reader of *Partisan Review* to say to each other? How can the avid fan of hillbilly music and the devotee of Gustav Mahler even compare notes?

(2) Such disagreement, some will say, is not only actually but theoretically ultimate: there is literally no saying, or at least no

25 See John H. Mueller and Kate Hevner, "Trends in Musical Taste," Indiana University Publications Humanities Series, No. 8 (1942), p. 44 and *passim*.

26 On this point see particularly George Boas, "The Mona Lisa in the History of Taste," in *Wingless Pegasus* (Baltimore: Johns Hopkins Press, 1950), Appendix II. See also Stephen Pepper, *The Work of Art* (Bloomington: Indiana University Press, 1955), chap. v.

proving, that one is right and the other wrong, no matter how strong one's feelings are on the subject. For it *is* a matter of feeling, not of logic or of fact. A person likes what he likes, and *that* is a fact; and what he calls good or beautiful is really good and beautiful —for *him*, but not necessarily for anybody else, because the assignment of the quality *goodness* or *beauty* (or any other "value") is simply (though often misleadingly) a recording of a personal taste or preference.

Most persons will admit this quite readily in such cases as one's favorite color in automobiles or taste of chewing gum. And though we note the differences, we scarcely think this is a matter of another person's being wrong or stupid or insensitive—no, just different. Taste is always somebody's taste, and somebody's taste is nothing more than the pattern, the tendency of somebody's likings and dislikings, preferences and aversions, as surely in architecture and opera as in gum and automobiles. If some tastes seem to us "better" or "more highly developed" or "crude" or "barbaric" or "exquisite" or "bad," these words register nothing but—once again—our feeling reaction, our preferences, our taste in tastes. "He has good taste" is just a disguised way of saying, "His tastes and mine are similar."

If taste were other than subjective feeling, there would, after all, be some objective, measurable conditions by which we could determine the presence of values like "beauty," but there are none. Oh yes, we say of a Bach invention that its counterpoint is technically perfect or of Leonardo's "The Last Supper" that it is a superb example of radial composition, but who is to say whether exact counterpoint and radial composition are worth achieving? They are if you like them and they aren't if you don't. Artistic rules and standards are themselves nothing more than expressions of likes and dislikes. They are mere rationalizations of preferences which are, as preferences must be, emotional and thus subjective, personal, finally inscrutable. And with that we are back to where we began: There is no disputing taste.

In examining the case for relativism or subjectivism—the two words will for the present be used interchangeably—it may be noticed in the beginning that just as laymen often *admittedly* mean nothing more by "It's good" than "I like it," so professional critics of the arts have not infrequently laid it down as a rule that criticism is just autobiography—Oscar Wilde called it "the only civilized form of autobiography." In a famous passage, Anatole France writes:

> *As I understand it . . . criticism is, like philosophy and history, a sort of romance designed for those who have sagacious and curious minds, and every romance is, rightly taken, an autobiography. The good critic is he who relates the adventures of his own soul among masterpieces. . . . To be quite frank, the critic ought to say: "Gentlemen, I am going to speak about myself apropos of Shakespeare, apropos of Racine, or of Pascal, or of Goethe."*[27]

But if there is such impressionistic criticism in both theory and practice, there is much more that at least claims to be otherwise, to make a distinction between simple liking and approbation. E. M. Forster has put it this way:

> *Appreciation ought to be enough. But unless we learn by example and by failure and by comparison, appreciation will not bite. We shall tend to slip about on the surface of masterpieces, exclaiming with joy, but never penetrating. "Oh I do like Bach," cries one appreciator and the other cries, "Do you? I don't. I like Chopin." Exit in opposite directions chanting Bach and Chopin respectively, and hearing less the composers than their own voices. . . . The objection to untrained appreciation is not its naivete but its tendency to lead to the appreciation of no one but oneself. Against such fatuity the critical spirit is a valuable corrective."*[28]

Whether criticism goes beyond bare recording of appreciation, of liking and not liking, it is not to be doubted that judicial criticism (and it will be this type that mainly occupies us from this point forward) uses among its primary data the positive and negative affective reactions to a work of art. Almost universally, our hope with respect to a work of art is that we shall like it. One thinks of contrary cases. A playwright might secretly hope not to like a rival's production. A sadistic critic might look forward to a new opportunity for displaying his talents for vituperation. But in such instances, other values than the aesthetic are predominant. Nearly

---

[27] Reprinted by permission of Dodd, Mead & Co. from *On Life and Letters*, by Anatole France, pp. vii-viii. Copyright, 1924, by Dodd, Mead & Co.
[28] *Two Cheers for Democracy*, pp. 107-108.

always when our aesthetic attitude is uppermost, not-liking is a disappointment: there is a failure somewhere. Yet this is not to say that not-liking is equivalent to complete disapproval, for we may confess that the fault is in ourselves or that while we do not like we do admire or respect a given work. But when we do say this, as for instance when a work "reveals an impressive skill" or "is the product of a highly developed technique" or "exhibits an ingenious organization" or "is good for the kind of thing it is," we feel that, even so, the fact of our not-liking, in spite of these qualifications, is very important. Then too, however much we prize knowledge about art, we recognize that unless knowledge is instrumental to liking it is regrettably and even pathetically hollow. If someone "knows a great deal about music but doesn't really like it"—that's too bad.

But the recording of likes and dislikes is not such a simple, and perhaps not even quite such a "subjective" matter as it might at first appear, for the report may be about the past and the future as well as the present, and it may be about others and not merely about oneself. Let us look at a few of the possibilities.

Sometimes we have occasion to remember and report our former likings. When I was a child, I liked a certain lithograph that hung in my room, called "The Lone Wolf." This of course does not mean that I like it now, as I do not, except for its value in stirring reminiscences. Quite different is the case when I report my liking or disliking for an art-work directly or very recently before me, as when standing in front of a painting in the Museum of Modern Art I may express my reactions to a companion, or when I say whether I liked the short story I read yesterday. Then there are the times when I am trying to predict whether I will like something in the future. It is worthy of note that not everything that I like now will continue to be liked by me, and there are even some things about which I predict that my liking will fade. For instance, I might say during the intermission of a musical comedy, "I'm enjoying it very much. However, it's not something I'd want to see again." Then there are times when though we do not presently like a certain work, we may expect to come to like it; I for instance recall having that expectation when I first read a novel of Thomas Mann, realizing that I was too young to get out of it what I suspected was there. And of course there are many times when we feel that something we presently like very much will continue to be a source of delight for us, unendingly.

It may be protested at this point that such predictions are notoriously conjectural and liable to error. This is true, but it is to be noted that our memories are, too, and it may be that even our recording of present feelings is not quite the matter of certainty it is often assumed to be. This requires a little elaboration.

First of all, there is the possibility of deceit. Mr. A. may say to Mr. B., "Oh, I like that Brancusi statue very much," and Mr. B. may say to himself, "I'll bet he doesn't." He may suspect Mr. A. of just trying to be agreeable or of trying to impress his audience with his advanced tastes or of something else that would account for a false report. It is always *possible* that somebody else's expression of liking, no matter how immediate and strong, may be false and should therefore be disbelieved. But there is a less obvious point contained in the following miniature conversation:

> *I like it.*
> *Do you really?*
> *Well, perhaps I don't. I'm not sure.*

It is a commonplace that whatever else may be uncertain, every person is and can always be certain about one thing, and that is his own feelings. However, like some other commonplaces, this one is far from indubitable. To be sure, every occurrence of a feeling is a fact; that is, just that particular feeling did upon that occasion arise. But in this as in all other phenomena, there's many a slip between the cup and the lip, many a misinterpretation between the experiencing of a feeling and the naming or describing of that feeling. If perhaps there are some experiences that impress us as *pure* pleasure or *pure* displeasure, surely these are rare as compared with those which are part one and part the other (among other characteristics). Furthermore, it appears that in many cases of ambivalence, it is difficult or impossible to judge whether positive or negative affectivity predominates. Another consideration making for difficulty in achieving certainty in even immediate evaluations is this: even if one is quite decidedly in a state of satisfaction or pleasure, it is not always easy to account for this. If you accuse me of contradicting myself because now I speak slightingly of a play I praised yesterday, perhaps I will reply, "Oh, but I was in such an extraordinarily good mood then that anything would have pleased me; it wasn't really that I liked the play, even then, but that I was so pleased by the good news that for a moment it seemed to me that I liked the play." That is, there is a difference between being pleased and being sure that *that* object accounts for my pleasure.

Thus, though it must be admitted that a prediction of future pleasure is always somewhat risky, we can now see that this characteristic in itself does not distinguish predictions from memories or even from immediate reports. But it needs to be said also that a prediction about a future liking is not just a shot in the dark, a mere unguided guess. One of the most important ways in which we mature is in learning the difference between relatively enduring or recurring and relatively ephemeral satisfactions. This is not to imply that there is necessarily anything wrong with that which pleases only momentarily or only once, but there is a special richness in that experience which is not only immediately gratifying in itself but also bears the marks of that which will continue to be gratifying, perhaps even increasingly so, as time goes on. Take the difference, for instance, between hearing two pieces of music, one a pretty but "superficial" popular love song of the moon-June variety, the other a Vivaldi concerto. One likes both of them, let us say, but likes the Vivaldi as an old friend whose companionship will continue to be valued and not as a club-car acquaintance who may get off at the next station.

So far, then, it has been urged that to the extent that an expression of approval of a work of art is an expression of liking on the part of the expresser, the liking may be not only present but also the remembered past or the anticipated future. It now needs to be added that somtimes the critic talks not merely (perhaps not even at all) about his own liking, but about the liking of others. If a friend asks me whether the show at the neighborhood theater is a good one, I might reply that though I hadn't much liked it, he very well might, because he is more interested in historical romances than I am. A professional critic may occasionally predict a great popular success for a work of art which he himself thoroughly dislikes.[29] A librarian

[29] Obviously the success of the entrepreneur in the arts depends upon his ability to predict what his potential audience will and will not like, his own taste quite apart.

might, though she is not herself a devotee of *The Rover Boys and the Secret Cave*, recommend it to an eleven-year-old client; her expression might even quite honestly be put into the words: "Here's a good book."

Whenever any one of us makes a prediction about another person's reaction to a work of art (where such sentences as "Don't miss it!" and, more commonly, "It's excellent!" are taken to be implicit predictions that you to whom the remark is addressed will in fact enjoy the work thus recommended) there is always some conditional that is intended, though not always expressly mentioned. Thus, I don't ever mean to predict that you will like such and such a recording *no matter what*—even if when you hear it, it is badly scratched, or you have a severe headache, or you have made up your mind to prove me wrong. No, I *assume* certain favorable circumstances, physically and in your attitude—on that is my prediction based. (Of course, I still may be wrong; but *any* prediction, no matter how scientific, *may* be wrong.) Sometimes the conditional may be quite elaborate. To approach this point, let us look at the aesthetic "ought."

The literary critic, F. L. Lucas, has written:

> *When Crabb Robinson owned to Wordsworth that he found it embarrassing to read aloud in company those justly famous lines:*
> *I've measured it from side to side,*
> *'Tis three feet long and two feet wide,*
> *Wordsworth curtly replied, 'They ought to be liked.' We smile. The reply is clearly ridiculous. But I believe that all such remarks about works of art are always ridiculous; that one can never rationally say (as people persistently do, with that familiar air of mingled sorrow and superiority), 'But you ought to like it.'*[30]

This puts the question: is it clearly ridiculous to say of something that it ought to be liked? Here it will be argued that though it is sometimes, it is not always, ridiculous. Let us start by exposing the case that does seem ridiculous: it is that in which a person is narrowly and dogmatically assuming that whatever he himself or (more usually) he in common with a certain group of people likes will necessarily be liked by all "right-minded" people. Such a view is highly provincial in its typical failure to take account of differ-

---

[30] *Literature and Psychology* (London: Cassell, 1951), p. 185.

ences in taste among individuals and cultures. Perhaps we call to mind a conservative gentleman who, though he knows there are persons who do not smoke his brand of cigars, do not like brandy after dinner, belong to another political party, read a different newspaper, and do not belong to a club at all, knows also that such persons are barbarians and scarcely worth bothering with.

It is easy to say that this caricature fits *all* those who use an "ought" about works of art, but suppose now a person who says to a friend, "I realize that in fact you *don't* like the poetry of Gerard Manley Hopkins, but I think you ought to. I mean that you are capable of liking it; that if you took certain measures to increase your understanding of and your sensitivity to this work, you would probably end by liking it; that if you did come to like it, you would be unusually gratified by this change in your taste, perhaps regarding it as a development; and, therefore that you would be well advised to give this poetry a fair trial."

There are several points to be noted about what this argument does *not* do. It does not automatically justify *any* taste of the individual employing the "ought"; for instance, probably most persons who would argue in this way would also willingly admit about some of their preferences that they are "idiosyncratic" or "personal." The argument is not intended to apply indiscriminately to everyone; for instance, it would be recognized that since this poetry is fairly difficult to understand, it is not the case that persons of below-average intelligence "ought" to like it. Furthermore, the argument is in every instance a matter of "probably" and not of "certainly." There is always the chance that the other person is not capable of this liking; that even if he tried, he would not succeed in liking the work; that even if he did, the change would not appear to him important; and that it would not be worth his effort.

Nevertheless, this constant possibility of making a mistake when one uses "ought" as indicated does not mean that its use is purely arbitrary. On the contrary, it is not hard to think of a variety of observations through which one would increase the probability of his judgment's being sound, observations both of the person to whom the recommendation is made, and of the means toward appreciation.[31]

[31] Cf. Pepper, *The Work of Art*, p. 44.

By those who take an extremely relativistic view on this vexing problem, it is sometimes quite unfairly assumed that everybody all of the time regards his own present level of taste as the highest; but this seems patently false. In fact, most persons are, in some fields at least, relatively modest about their preferences. This is signified by the very fact that it is so common to find people avowedly trying to "improve" their taste—admitting, say, that although they do not presently much enjoy abstract painting such as that of Joan Miro, they consider the fault their own and are trying to read up on the subject to see if they can find out what they've been missing.

{ It is also sometimes said that whereas tastes change, they don't really develop—as that word means *advance* or in some way *improve;* we just speak of those changes as development which are in the direction of our own preferences at a given time. But nearly everyone who thinks back on the history of his own changes of taste in any particular artistic field will probably be able to distinguish mere "changes" from "developments"—a development being, let us say, the kind of change in which one seems to increase his appreciative capacity, realize more of his potentiality for a deep aesthetic response.}Thus, a person might feel that though he presently enjoys playing his Handel records more than his Brahms, whereas three months ago it was the other way around, this change doesn't signify anything important. But the same person may remember the time when he "discovered" Brahms, almost suddenly attaining an appreciation of music that before had been quite unavailable to him, a time perhaps when he began to regard himself as one who could now see something in "classical music" that theretofore had appeared only noisy and "longhaired" and dull. Such he might justifiably regard as a development, not just a change.

It is not even impossible that one should recognize in his own case a kind of deterioration of taste. Darwin testified to an atrophy of certain of his powers of appreciation because of the extraordinary concentration of his interests and work in biology, and in a similar way a man or woman caught up in the busy whirl of practical duties might with perfect candor admit that whereas at one time he had been a discriminating and acute reader, he had gradually suffered a diminution of such powers.

What is the point of noticing that a person may look forward
to "improving" his taste, almost always considers that some but not
all the changes in taste he has experienced have been "developments," and may even think of himself as having lost ground in taste
and discrimination? It is just this: the popular assumption that when
anyone uses "ought" in making an aesthetic judgment, he is necessarily reflecting arrogance about his present set of preferences, is
false.

It is no less false—and just as usual—to say that since persons do in
fact differ in their aesthetic preferences, perhaps so much so that
neither can persuade the other to change, there is no reasonable way
of assessing their respective preferences, no disputing their tastes,
nothing to do but notice the difference and perhaps pronounce
something about "relativity." It is certainly very common for a
person to feel about his friend that he ought to like Bach more and
Franz Lehar less. This feeling *may* be nothing more than a self-
satisfaction, a feeling that in this as in all other respects his friend
would be better in becoming more and more like himself. But may
it not be supposed without implausibility that there may be some
more reasonable basis for the feeling? For instance, he may notice
that his friend gives evidence of deriving rather rich satisfactions
from the theater, being discriminating in the sense that he has fairly
definite standards in mind for judging theatrical success, standards
based upon a considerable experience of varying types of drama,
that he is a careful and keen perceiver of dramatic effects and of
relations between parts of a play. Though he often criticizes a
play sharply and tells of his lack of satisfaction in it, on the other
hand, when a play pleases him, the pleasure seems deep, strong, and
relatively durable. Now, this same friend may seem quite different
in his musical experience. Here he may seem relatively unattentive,
little aware of subtle differences of interpretation, only very
moderately enthusiastic about what he likes best, and able to do
little more than to register "impressionistic" likings and dislikings.
Consequently his preference of Strindberg to Barrie may seem not
altogether on the same footing as his preference of Lehar to Bach.
And our hypothetic man might therefore say to his friend that he
ought to like Bach better, not merely because in this change he
would better approximate his own taste, but because in doing what

would be necessary to effect such a change, he would in all likelihood be deepening his own satisfactions in music. It is not a fore-
gone *necessity* that he who prefers Bach to Lehar is one who "gets
more out of music" than does he whose preferences are the other
way around, but it does seem (on the basis of informal observations) as if there is an impressively high correlation. (Admittedly
there is a danger in begging the question: one may use "a liking for
Bach" as the infallible indication of "getting much out of music.")

Thus there seem to be two ways in which someone's taste (one's
own or another's) may be reasonably assessed: (1) in relation to the
actual appreciative level of another person, and (2) in relation to his
own potential appreciative level. Mr. A. may have "poor taste"
in that compared with many other persons he seems not to "get very
much out of" this or that art. Or he may have "poor taste" in that
he seems to be operating much below his own potentiality for appreciation.

It must be admitted that the assessment of level of appreciation is
very far removed (at least as yet) from the exactness of a science,
but this is not to say that it is wholly arbitrary or chaotic. A hundred years ago psychologists had no instruments for measuring I.Q.,
but people were not wholly in the dark as to the relative intelligence
of people they knew, even though many mistakes were made, even
more, probably, than are made today. Nearly every one of us would
be willing to risk a classification of his friends according to, for
instance, relative level of music appreciation. We would admit that
we might be wrong in some cases—now overrating a certain glibness
as a reliable sign of deep aesthetic reaction, now underrating the shy
person, and so on, but we would feel that there were some fairly
good evidences available to us for our rating. And in the cases of
those who ranked low, we would, I think, feel justified in saying
to them, "You *ought* to. . . ."

A good deal has been said, both here and elsewhere, about disagreement among critics. It is always good fun to pit Berenson
against Venturi, Eliot against Richards, one association of sculptors
against the other. But perhaps we are inclined to exaggerate what
this proves. Though there are differences in critical opinion, sometimes these differences are not necessarily cases of disagreement.
One critic may examine a given artist's strengths, another his

weaknesses, without there being any disagreement whatsoever: the difference is one of focus and emphasis. Gotshalk has cited, in behalf of his assertion that every artist has defects, the judgment of Joseph Wood Krutch: "Fielding lacked at least one-half of all the 'finer feelings'; the structures of Goldsmith's one novel would shame a kindergarten; Jane Austen regarded the failure to possess an inherited income as placing a man outside the pale of humanity; Dickens had the sentimentality of a nursemaid; Theodore Dreiser cannot write the English language." And "Accordingly, two able critics may give the most divergent judgments on the work of an artist without actually being inaccurate, irrelevant, unintelligible, or even biased beyond excusable limits."[32]

Furthermore, it must be admitted in all fairness that there is far greater agreement among critics than some people like to admit. The agreements are less spectacular than the disagreements, just as the instances of virtuous behavior are less often in the newspaper than the crimes, but they are not clearly less significant. Although close students of the opera may sharply disagree as to which is the greater, *Don Giovanni* or *Die Meistersinger,* there is an exceptionally good chance that they will both put both rather high on their list. Indeed, in all of the major arts, one can without great trouble draw up a list of either artists or art-works on which there will be an impressive convergence of judgment among the best recognized critics. Although press agents can always manage to carve out of a review at least one complimentary phrase (if they have to cut out a "not" to do it!), newspaper reviewers are frequently nearly unanimous in their condemnation or the commendation of a new play.

Even where there are disagreements about the same things, these disagreements can often be accounted for in a way other than just saying "You see, everybody to his own taste." For instance there is probably much more agreement about the beauty of Vivaldi's *The Four Seasons* and the triviality of Tschaikowsky's *First Symphony* among men who have studied music professionally, than there would be among an unselected sample of the population. It happens with revealing frequency that the person who "can see nothing in" the writings of James Joyce has taken but very little time to read

[32] "The Half-truth of the Whole Truth," *The Nation,* CXLIV (January 2, 1937), p. 21, quoted in Gotshalk, *Art and the Social Order,* p. 178.

him. The disparager of Frank Lloyd Wright or LeCorbusier typically turns out to be someone who knows little about architecture beyond some gossip about leaky roofs. And very often indeed a professional critic's "blind spot"—as when a man of good training and normally good judgment comes up with some highly "eccentric" evaluation—can often be fairly well explained in terms of a prejudice that is fortuitous.

All of which is not to say that there are, after all, absolute values which attach to works of art, but only that men of considerable training and experience *tend* to come together in their judgments, especially if we keep constant the time and the place.

PRINCIPAL CRITICAL TERMS

It will perhaps be useful at this point if something is said by way of tenable distinctions among some of the most widely used terms of critical praise and condemnation.

Ages differ, of course, in the way they praise the works they do praise. If in the Middle Ages and the eighteenth century a work was likely to be censured for being erratic or divergent, the Renaissance and the nineteenth century prized originality.[33] In the twentieth century we are fond of words like "mature," "neurotic," "compelling," and "insightful."

But instead of dwelling on such difference among ages, let us turn to this phase of the problem: what may we wish to mean by "beautiful," "sublime," "great," and their opposites? Without explanation the words are most certainly ambiguous. Of course, even with definitions their use is most likely to be vague.

A definition for "beautiful" and for "ugly" has already been proposed. That will be called beautiful which has in eminent degree the disposition to arouse, sustain, and reward the kind of attentiveness we call "aesthetic." Popularly, "ugly" is the antonym of "beautiful," but it must be noticed that we are unlikely to designate anything as ugly unless it in fact does call out in us a certain aesthetic response. For instance we might call a gargoyle ugly, or a twisted mass of broken machinery that happened to catch and hold our eye, or such

[33] At least this is as true as most statements about "ages"—all of which vary far more than any generalization can take into account.

a face as that of Rodin's "The Old Courtesan"; but in all these cases the response is aesthetic, not nonaesthetic. "Ugly" seems to indicate a certain kind of negativeness, a sort of antipathy, or aversion—but aversion right along with fascination. A work of art is ugly when, though it attracts and even sustains aesthetic interest, it punishes rather than rewards that attentiveness: it signifies that the elements of painful aversion are too strong. We can accommodate quite a lot of pain within a work of art that we still call "beautiful," as, for instance, Goya's famous picture of a man being shot by a firing squad, or such plays as Hauptmann's *The Weavers*, O'Neill's *The Hairy Ape*, or Gorki's *The Lower Depths*; or, I will venture to say, Beethoven's *Grosse Fuge*. But if the pain is such as to overbalance the satisfactions and make the aesthetic experience a principally negative one, then we legitimately speak of the ugliness of the art-work.

Perhaps it is worse for a work of art to be *drab* or *dull* than to be ugly, for these words signify that aesthetic attentiveness, though it has been initially aroused (and this is not necessarily at all difficult—when the curtain rises we are all prepared to attend receptively) has not been sustained. They signify "let-down," disappointment. After all, interest in a work of art is a *sine qua non*.

The word "sublime" has long been distinguished by aestheticians from "beautiful." From Longinus to Edmund Burke and Immanuel Kant, sublimity of aesthetic effect or aesthetic object has been associated with that which by its immensity, its overpowering power, and its magnificence induces a certain awesomeness into our imaginative perception. Here is Burke, for instance:

> *Whatever is fitted in any sort to excite the ideas of pain, and danger, that is to say, whatever is in any sort terrible, or is conversant about terrible objects, or operates in a manner analogous to terror, is a source of the* sublime; *that is it is productive of the strongest emotion which the mind is capable of feeling.*[34]

The beautiful, by contrast, he described as comparatively small, smooth, and delicate.

Kant distinguished two types of sublimity, the mathematical and

[34] *A Philosophical Enquiry Into the Origin of our Ideas on the Sublime and Beautiful,* 5th ed. (1767), I, vii.

the dynamic, the first being a matter of size, the second, of fear-fulness.[35]

Without entering into the details of such arguments or the minute differences among the theories, we may subscribe to the general distinction and find the word "sublime" sometimes useful for describing aesthetic matters that are large, powerful, or magnificent.

Finally, a few words may be said about the category of *greatness*. There would perhaps be a pretty general agreement among critics that a work of art may be "perfect" without being "great," perfection but not greatness being consonant with minor effects, small endeavors, restricted compass. It might therefore be said of a cameo that it was exquisite or even perfect; scarcely that it was great. That which is considered trivial, superficial, light, or transient is *ipso facto* refused greatness; yet something may be less than great without thereby standing condemned: we may say of it that it is unpretentious and yet very fine. Greatness as a quality is perhaps advisedly restricted in its assignment to those works which to an eminent degree possess beauty of a profound and seemingly lasting sort. This is in agreement with Theodore Greene's illuminating account, which is sampled in the following:

> *A work of art will be judged to possess profundity or greatness in proportion as it seems to the observer (his philosophy of life being what it is) to mediate a profound experience by expressing, via artistic form, some profound interpretation of its subject-matter.*
>
> *The profundity of any artistic interpretation and evaluation must, in turn, be regarded as a function of the "depth" and the "breadth" we predicate of the artist's normative insight. The depth of his insight is proportionate to the adequacy with which he comprehends the nature and human import of any subject-matter, however limited, from any point of view, however restricted. Its breadth is proportionate to the scope of the subject-matter surveyed and to the catholicity of the agent's normative outlook. The greatness of a work of art can be determined only by reference to both of these complementary criteria.[36]*

[35] See *The Critique of Judgment*, sections 25-28.
[36] *The Arts and the Art of Criticism*, pp. 463-64.

PERSUASION

Any decent list of the principal human characteristics would include the longing to have others share our opinions and especially our valuations. It is unusual to discover a man who, when he has read a book that delights him, bothers not at all to recommend it to someone else, remaining quite content in his own unshared prize.

Some students of ethics claim that to say of an institution, an action, an object, "It is good," is to issue an invitation to a hearer to share one's approval.[37] Probably if predicating value of something signified nothing more than the fact of our own liking, we often wouldn't bother to utter the evaluation. We speak out because of our liking (or, of course, disliking) *and* because we like company in our judgments, ethical, aesthetic, or some other kind.

How effective is the persuasion contained in a simple utterance, "It is beautiful" or "It is excellent," will of course depend on a great many factors. Spoken over the radio by the President of the United States or the Prime Minister of Great Britain, such words would make any book or record an overnight best-seller. Spoken by one of our acquaintances who is notorious for always gushing, the words might be ignored, or have a negative effect. Generally, one has to extend himself beyond such a simple recommendation to have much effect.

Today, in many arts in many lands, persuasion is a function exercised chiefly not by critics, professional or amateur, but by advertisers, publicists, and propagandists. A new book, a new musical recording, a new Broadway play or Hollywood film—these are works of art that involve not only the investment of talent and energy by an artist, but the investment of money, usually by someone whose interests go beyond that of wanting someone to share his own feelings of approbation. Consequently, it is increasingly felt that an organized campaign of persuasion is a natural part of the investment. A skillful advertising agency can guarantee a publisher a large sale for a book—one may almost say *any* book—for a price. The question may be raised, of course, whether this type of persuasion is really directed at evaluation or only at buying; but the an-

[37] See C. L. Stevenson, *Ethics and Language* (New Haven: Yale University Press, 1944).

swer must be that people are undoubtedly strongly influenced not only to buy but to like a product that is extravagantly and effec- tively praised by experts.

Sometimes governments become publicists, and, if they will stop at nothing, they can be most effective of all. F. L. Lucas says that a certain poet by the name of Kolchev, once called the greatest poet of the Soviet Union, enjoyed the honor of having the following poem translated into one hundred and sixty-seven languages:

> When Budyenny smiles,
>   The ice breaks on the Don;
> When Budyenny smiles,
>   The maple bloom is on.
>
> When Voroshilov smiles,
>   The sun begins to shine;
> When Voroshilov smiles,
>   Then spring falls into line.
>
> When Stalin smiles,
>   What might a poet dare?
> When Stalin smiles
>   It is beyond compare.

The success of this work (if the report is true) would seem to justify a boast made by a Moscow literary organizer to Arthur Koestler: "We build up the reputation of writers whom we think useful; we destroy writers whom we consider harmful; aesthetic considerations are petit-bourgeois prejudice."[38]

THE JUDGMENT OF POSTERITY

One of the commonest beliefs about art evaluation is that, given sufficient time, art-works tend to get sorted out and assigned by general consent to their "proper" station. The following distinct but similar views are deserving of some attention:

> In art there operates a kind of law of "survival of the fittest," so that trivial works become in time very obscure or even lost, while the better works are the permanent possession of mankind.

[38] Quoted in Lucas, Literature and Psychology, p. 296.

Although it is common for great art-works to be neglected and inferior works to be esteemed at or near the time of their production, posterity corrects all this and attains a stable evaluation: fine works, given time, become and remain popular.

It is impossible to achieve anything more than a hit-or-miss evaluation of art-works until they have been subjected to the "test of time" and until we can see them in "proper perspective."

Each of these pieces of popular wisdom may be suspected of being very incompletely wise, and popular more because of an uncritical acceptance of easy answers than because of any special merit in the views.

Against the first belief it may be successfully argued, first of all, that there seems very good reason to believe that there are lost to us great works of art. Today there is extant only a small fraction of the art-work of fifth-century Athens, for instance. We know that there was at one time a great (at least in size) statue of Athena in the Parthenon, that there were hundreds of now lost tragedies and comedies which were performed in the theater, including prize-winners and dozens by Euripides, Sophocles, and Aeschylus. We know almost nothing about the music which was popular at that time and place—or rather, though we know something *about* it, we know none of the music itself. The list could be extended to great length, but the point is clear: some of the works that have been lost in the course of centuries are such that they probably would be highly esteemed today if they could be recovered: they were lost not because they did not deserve to survive, but for other reasons.

Furthermore, hardly anyone could intelligently maintain that all the works which have survived for a long time are especially meritorious. Only the most slavish antiquarian could believe that *all* the statuary of ancient Egypt now in museums, *all* the extant hymns of the Rig Veda, *all* the still-standing buildings of the Renaissance are artistic triumphs. Indeed, there are many paintings hanging in museums in various parts of the world whose age seems the sole reason for their being exhibited.

As to the belief that posterity corrects the initial opinion of an artist's contemporaries, it is of course to be admitted that many of the artists we today proclaim as great masters were inadequately recognized in their own day: Schubert, Vermeer, Keats, Lucretius,

J. S. Bach, Van Gogh, Bartok, to name a few. But what exactly can be concluded from this fact? That we today have arrived at a definitive appraisal of these artists? Against that is the fact that an artist may be first neglected, then acclaimed, neglected again—and so on. To take a reputation that has had its ups and downs in a short period of time, F. Scott Fitzgerald, the American novelist, after considerable popularity fell for a time into disrepute, made a strong comeback a few years ago, and perhaps is presently again declining. Henri Peyre has written: "Our estimate of Browning and Wagner has been subtly revised downward in the last two decades. Which is the 'infallible' verdict of Time, that of 1940 or that of 1920?"[39] Similarly Anatole France has wittily opposed the argument for the judgment of posterity:

> *I believe that posterity is not infallible in its conclusions. And the reason I have for believing it is that I myself, that all of us, that we human beings are posterity, in regard to a long procession of works with which we are but ill acquainted. . . . The posterity of the Greeks and Latins has preserved little, and in the little that it has preserved there are some execrable works, which are none the less immortal.*[40]

Finally, we meet the argument that it is truly impossible to form an adequate appraisal of works that are close to us in time (it may be said that here, if ever, we encounter a timidity altogether too often associated with academe). It is perhaps true that opinions about recent works tend to fluctuate somewhat more than those about works of the past, and it is certainly true that one cannot predict with entire confidence what lies in store tomorrow for today's *succès d'estime*. But the more important truth remains: that there is no theoretical reason why critical justice cannot be done to contemporary productions. If we are more likely to be led astray by factors that posterity will shrug off as irrelevant (that such and such a composer flirted with Nazism, that such and such a novelist was a courageous fighter in the underground, that such and such an architect has made a million dollars) we are also likely to be alive to elements genuinely within the work of art that will be obscure to later generations. In any case, we cannot and will not wait for the

39 *Writers and Their Critics* (Ithaca: Cornell University Press, 1944), p. 247.
40 "On the Quai Malaquais," in *On Life and Letters*, I, pp. 94-95.

judgments of the distant future; for decisions, some of them practical (shall I buy a ticket?), need to be made now.

RELATIVISM RECONSIDERED

After criticism and persuasion have done their work, when all is
said and done, there remains this simple truth: Nothing is beautiful to *me* except that which affords *me* a positive aesthetic gratification. I may be too easily satisfied and so fail to develop my capacity
for "difficult beauty." I may be crass and hard-hearted and inexperienced and thus reject out-of-hand what would delight me
if I had more sensitivity or more breadth of experience. I may have
a weak eye or a poor ear and thus fail in the discriminations and perceptions on which some works of art depend. I may be left cold
by what the greatest experts praise or delighted by what they agree
in condemning. But the fact remains that beauty in an object is
always beauty for someone, since it is a capacity of the object for
rewarding someone's aesthetic attentiveness, and people are different, both in their physiological equipment (including "brains")
and in their psychological conditioning. In our day it need hardly
be insisted upon that what each of us *is* depends to a very great
extent on what each of us has been through. Each of us has been
born, and each of us knows he must die. Each has played and
worked, been punished and rewarded, loved and hated. Most have
been cold and hungry as well as warm and well-fed; each has seen
and felt the seasons turn and the days and nights. Much we share,
not only we of the twentieth century, but we of all the centuries
that have been. And these sharings are important; on them are
dependent the durability of the works we prize as classics and
masterpieces. But each of us is also unique. No one has experienced
exactly what I have experienced; no one is exactly what I am; therefore, the *Fifth Symphony* and *Hamlet* and "The Last Supper" are
things different to me than to anyone else. If I join others in being
bored or repelled by them, again my reasons cannot be quite the
same; if I judge them differently from anybody else, that is only
because I must, being different myself.[41]

[41] This is not a return to "There's no disputing taste." The truth is perhaps expressed by Max Beerbohm's deliberate inanity: "For people who like that sort of
thing, that is the sort of thing they like."

Consequently, my relation (or anyone else's) with a work of art is never simply a matter of what the creative artist intended, nor simply a matter of what a critic discovered or decided. It *is* a matter of what the work is and can become to *me*—but that is not simple.

Insist too much on my individuality and the necessary irrelevance of any different person's judgment, and I rob myself of what might be good help in gaining additional aesthetic values. Insist too much on "the one and only right" and I sacrifice and deny the uniqueness of my aesthetic experience. Fortunately, the choice need not be between perversity and dishonesty.

• *Chapter 14*

The

WORTH

of

BEAUTY

• *Jf it* was remarked during the discussion of how art has been castigated, confined, and censored, that religions—religious institutions—have been sometimes anti-art, and more frequently antipathetic to art regarded as blasphemous or heretical or worldly or sensual, yet the last word has not been said on the relation between two of men's dearest values, the religious and the aesthetic. Nor is this subject exhausted by making due obeisance to the impressive achievements that may be named under the heading "Sacred Art," even though in the Christian tradition alone are to be found hundreds of men's supremest creations of beauty.

Still more central to this relationship is the affinity first between the attitudes, moods, and realizations of the religious worshipper and of the aesthetic appreciator; and second between the creative impulses of artists and of prophetic holy men. Indeed, there are likenesses also between theology and art criticism that even further strengthen the ties between the religious and the aesthetic.

RELIGION AND ART

Students of religion differ profoundly in the importance they attach to religious ritual, but it is not necessary to go along with those extremists who say that ritual is the very core and essence of all religion in order to remark on its ubiquity and its strength. Now a rite is above all an act, a collective gesture whereby religious communicants celebrate a holy occasion or dedicate themselves to their highest calling. It may, of course, be but perfunctorily enacted— as what may not, including paying our respects to declared beauty? —but if participation in a rite is full and whole, the quality of experience achieved is indeed similar to that of the rapt contemplator of beauty in nature or art. In fact, in religious dances, in religious drama, in the chanting or singing of hymns and liturgies, it is impossible to separate the specifically religious and aesthetic strands. And even where religious observance is not collective but singular, where the individual worships alone—and has not Whitehead said that religion is what a man does with his aloneness?—there remains a likeness to the attitudes and realizations of the aesthetic appreciator. In his contemplation of both holiness and beauty, man escapes the practicalities of everyday existence, the getting and spending, the conflicts of wills, the drive for egoistic advancement, in order to dwell unselfconsciously in an exalted reality, however illusory such an object might appear to a purely rational scrutiny. Or if "escapes" is too strong a word, let it be said that at the least in successful contemplation, one sublimates—makes sublime—the drosser matter of his everyday life.

George Herbert has created a work of art which itself shows something of the affinity between the aesthetic and the religious domains:

The Quidditie

My God, a verse is not a crown,
No point of honour, or gay suit,
No hawk, or banquet, or renown,
Nor a good sword, nor yet a lute:
It cannot vault, or dance, or play;
It never was in France or Spain;
Nor can it entertain the day

With my great stable or demain:
It is no office, art, or news,
Nor the Exchange, or busie Hall;
But it is that which while I use
I am with thee, and most take all.

Although all men may be worshippers and appreciators, it is given
to only a few to be importantly creative in the religious and artistic
ways. Now, among the creative holy men, it is no less worthy of
remark how often they have perceived and conceived their gods,
their ultimate destinations, their most completely ideal realities in
the form of beauty, than it is worthy of our attention how often
great artists have reserved their finest energies for religious subjects.
A god has of course been often and variously described as frightful
in demeanor and manner, but perhaps not less often as of a beauty
that transcends earthly attainment. Divine beauty, it has been said,
shines forth with a splendor wholly dazzling to human eyes, but for
him who has learned to contemplate it, supernal beauty brings
unique rewards. Whether this ultimate beauty is conceived as an
attribute of God, of a heavenly sphere, of the highest mode of being,
or as the absolute, it has repeatedly been set forth as no meaner ideal
than Truth or Goodness.

The creative person in religion, like his counterpart in art, is
endeavoring to do two principal things: to express, in a way more
satisfying to his own needs than any previous formulation has been,
a vision, a conception, an ideal; and to make this achievement per-
suasively and eloquently available to others for the more adequate
fulfillment of their somewhat similar needs. And in religion as in
art, such expression and such communication require symbols. It
is not enough to look on beauty bare, or as Plato put it, "beauty
absolute, separate, simple, and everlasting"; it is not enough to be-
hold God. It is also required, if one is to be a creator, to articulate
the vision. And though the prophet may first and last deplore his
inadequacy and proclaim the ineffability of the object of his worship, he will yet try to say the unsayable, to make visible both to
himself and to those who heed him what is thus forever elusive. He
will fail if he be too bound up with evoking an image in others to
satisfy his own demands, just as he will fail if he be satisfied with
a merely personal, narrowly idiosyncratic expression. Like the

artist, his success must be both expressive and communicative, and the two are finally inseparable.

In neither religion nor art is the sublimity of the subject matter or intention sufficient to guarantee nobility of result. There are preachers who demean the lofty object of their concern just as there are artists who uglify the perceivable world. Nor is there any guaranteed success when piety and beauty are summoned to dwell in the same artifact; indeed a visit to a "Religious Art Dealer," a quick sampling of an ordinary hymnal, or a tour of selected local church and temple buildings may even make one temporarily sceptical of such a combination. And on the other side, it is no news that some crucifixes (to take one example) have been found blasphemous by ecclesiastical authorities. Jacques Maritain, after insisting that in order for art to qualify as sacred, it is by no means necessary that some special subject matter or technique be employed, goes on to suggest that the wedding of artistry and religious emotion "can be achieved only by not being directly pursued."[1]

Of course the artistic and the religious can be brought together, whether successfully or unsuccessfully, only when they are already apart; and in a day when religion sometimes seems housed within a few buildings and confined to a single day of the week, and when art may seem to be an affair of museums and concerts, it is easy to forget how very much more widely diffused religion and art have been in other days, and how much they interpenetrated each other. And yet the question, "Is this religion or art?" when asked about the Parthenon, the Taj Mahal, the Bhagavad Gita, or a choric dance among the Pueblo Indians, can only be answered by noticing that it requires a feat of severe and somewhat arbitrary abstraction to separate these characteristics in such phenomena. Mythical attempts to explain ourselves and our world, the dramatic representation of our worst fears and our best hopes, the presentation in stone and metal and wood of gods and apotheosized men, the erection of buildings which are appropriate coverings of holy ground and fit inspirations of men's worship—all such creations, whether primitive or civilized, exotic or familiar, are inextricable fusions of the religious and the aesthetic.

[1] "Some Reflections upon Religious Art," in *Art and Scholasticism*, trans. J. F. Scanlan (London: Sheed & Ward, 1949), p. 114.

Sometimes men have endeavored to reduce religion to art, or art to religion. In times of great zeal, secular art has been condemned and proscribed, and sometimes even "religious" art itself has been curbed on the belief that art is by its very nature worldly and irreligious, and the love of it a manifestation of impious idolatry. Fanatics have said that God alone is beautiful, a fact which in their minds implies that all merely human creation is an abomination. Nor have there been wanting men who find that religion is disappearing, its values to be absorbed (without loss and with a great gain in purity) by the arts. But this is to neglect the differences between these two kinds of value and fact. For all of their coming together, religion and art are not identical nor is either one an altogether adequate substitute for the other.

Whether the essence of religion be thought to lie in the holiness of its object or in the devotion and reverence of communicants, holiness is not the same as beauty, and reverence is not the same as the aesthetic attitude. The Moslem salaaming toward Mecca, the Christian kneeling at the altar, the Jew chanting his response to the cantor—none of these or other exemplars of religious celebrants are manifesting that special combination of sensuousness, consciousness of form, and appreciative openness to the very quality of the object that have been found to characterize aesthetic moments. No, the religious and aesthetic experiences are not identical and neither is one merely a species of the other, but perhaps at their best, they are alike great affirmations of life, being among the most intense realizations of which man is capable and thus assurances that life need not be lacking in greatness. Mozart's *G minor Quintet* approaches religiousness, not in being specificall) for a sacred occasion, but in being a sounding reminder and reassurance of the ability of its composer and those of us who can follow his lead to live beyond our usual selves, to transcend our mundane somnolence, to come alive.

ART IN AND FOR LIFE

The great aesthetic objects and the activities that produce them are more often undervalued than overvalued, yet the aesthete is no less in error than the philistine. Art is something, and something important, but it is not everything, not of sole worth; and he who neglects politics and friendship, science and play, philosophy and sensuality for an exclusive reveling in aesthetic delights not only lives narrowly but does art itself a disservice. Although there is nothing effete about love of music or painting or poetry, there are some persons whose preciousness of art cultivation gives art a bad name, and tempts the undiscriminating to blur the distinction between art cultists and more balanced devotees.

As with the other principal types of value, the aesthetic demands a place, but not the whole place, in the good life. What that place will be properly and necessarily varies from person to person, perhaps from nation to nation and from age to age. Probably no people have ever been so intently practical or so bestially unimaginative as to be aesthetically uncreative and unappreciative. Cave dwellers have found time from their hunting forays to decorate their walls, starving Indians have found means to model painstakingly their clay jars or weave their woolen rugs; in every pioneer society there are the singers of songs and those who in secret rhyme their hearts' words. Yet not every age is a Renaissance, not every city a Periclean Athens. Although no person above the state of the Yahoo is quite empty of the capability for aesthetic joy, men doubtless differ greatly both in their potentiality and in the relative degree of development of this potentiality, a fact which, like many another, we know better from the revelations of artists than from any other source.

Yet for all of the odiousness of the "arty" aesthete and the fact of individual and cultural differences, there remains a proper commendation of the aesthetic dimension of life. It is not necessary to swell the common cry against our own age and its presumed depravity of taste (with the usual despairing gestures toward comic books, soap operas, and hillbilly wails) in order to praise the life that includes a healthy portion of appreciation of beauty. Yet since it is altogether too easy to overload a final encomium, let ours be restricted to a few words about art (for most of us the chief dependable instrument of rich aesthetic satisfactions) and its enrichment of our sensuousness, its forming of our efforts at expression, and—more generally—its contribution to life-enhancement.

Whether or not the arts are important factors in the survival of the race,[2] they are undeniably that not inconsequential thing, the great educators of our senses. Born, all of us, with ears and eyes, we must learn the uses of them; and whether we go very much beyond their employment for the sake of identifications and the recognition of only the more urgent signs in our environment depends in most cases upon our experience in the arts. Though we do not learn, ever, to see real sunlight in real trees the way Renoir shows it to us in his pictures, we advance, with his help, some steps out of our native caves. Though nature gives us no such sounds as we hear in Schubert's music, yet in the gaining ability to hear what that music is, we can but be glad thus to have gone beyond mere practical and conventional listening. Art is the best instrument of happiness, Santayana has said, "for it alters the material conditions of sentience so that sentience becomes at once more delightful and more significant."[3]

Yet art's sensuous surface *is* only its surface. The works for which we reserve our highest praise involve our whole selves and all our faculties, perceptual, emotional, volitional, intellectual—or however otherwise they may be classified. The great wonder about any masterpiece is just this: how it could say so well what it does say, how it could say what we needed and wanted to say, how it could shape and form these urgent stammerings of our own selves. Doubtless we can truly like only that art which is relevant to our own condition, but who could know the scope of relevance before reading the *Book of Ruth,* or seeing Cezanne's pine trees? For here again art at its best not merely delights us but delights us by showing, teaching, and disciplining us. As Susanne Langer has said so well:

> *A work of art is intrinsically expressive; it is designed to abstract and present forms for perception—forms of life and feeling, activity, suffering, selfhood—whereby we conceive these realities, which otherwise we can but blindly undergo.*[4]

To say finally of great art that it not only provides us moments of high joy, but also affords us a touchstone with which to separate

---

[2] As Ernst Grosse has argued in *The Beginnings of Art* (New York: D. Appleton, 1897), pp. 312-13.

[3] *Reason in Art* (New York: Scribner, 1906), p. 229.

[4] *Feeling and Form* (New York: Scribner, 1953), pp. 395-96.

the gold and dross in the rest of life, is not to say anything specifically different from what has already been said; but perhaps the notion of art as "a great yea-saying to the human condition,"[5] as Abraham Kaplan has put it, or in Berenson's words, the great force for "life enhancement," deserves the final emphasis, so accustomed are most of us to regarding this side of life as fleeting, and in being fleeting, trivial. It would seem to some ironic to have to admit that among the finest and (might it even be said?) most real experiences of life are those which are often thought to lie *outside* life, to contrast with actual life in being visionary, being illusory, being mere vapors of the fancy. But the irony disappears as soon as man's imagination is given the blessings of legitimacy so that no longer is everything else made to contrast invidiously with "good, solid practicality." Living in and with the artistic masterpieces of the ages is not suspended animation but intensified animation; the cultivation of our aesthetic capacities, creative and appreciative, is not withdrawal from life, but a plunge into life. Man's fate is not wholly composed of struggle and confusion; there are the times too of order and culmination: such are aesthetic realizations, the times when man's quest for beauty is fulfilled.

[5] Abraham Kaplan, "Obscenity as an Esthetic Category," *Law and Contemporary Problems* (Autumn, 1955), p. 559. He goes on immediately to say that "In mastering its medium and imposing form on its materials, art creates a microcosm in which everything is significant and everything is of value, the perfection of what experience in the macrocosm might be made to provide."

TRAGEDY

and

COMEDY

• *Among* the innumerable ways in which one might write an illuminating history of the arts there is that of tracing the meanings which creative artists and critics have assigned to the classificatory concepts "Tragedy" and "Comedy." If to the fifth-century Greek these words represented the two principal types of drama, they have come to be applied not only to all branches of literature, but to music, dance, and the visual arts as well. "Tragic" now qualifies an overture or a symphony, a novel or a dance; "Comic" is used to describe a statue or a poem, a bassoon cadenza or a pantomime. Perhaps only in the language of architecture do these words have no currency—excepting of course as used to describe an inadvertency.

Academically, the problem of tragedy is often approached as an exercise in literary taxonomy: equipped with a touchstone, the student assays the specimens spread before him. But where is he to get his touchstone? To start with there is the current, rather general use of the terms "tragedy" and "tragic." In the daily newspaper every fatal accident, every regrettable deprivation, every calamitous loss of property or limb is a tragedy. The tragic is that about which we frown, shake our heads, say "Too bad"; it is the pitiful and the greatly deplorable.[1]

In any classification process it is useful to have before us some certified examples. One way in which we are likely to proceed when trying to decide whether *Death of a Salesman* or *Mourning Becomes Electra* is a tragedy is by remembering some "undeniable" tragedies: *Macbeth*, *Agamemnon*, *Phèdre*. But this is, of course, a very inexact enterprise unless we frame the characteristics whereby these prime examples themselves are tragic. They differ in certain obvious ways, not only in story and character, but in style and manner; perhaps not all of the ways in which they are similar are necessarily important. Therefore, we are driven to try to find or to frame a definition.

Aristotle's is by far the most famous:

> *Tragedy, then, is an imitation of an action that is serious, complete, and of a certain magnitude; in language embellished with each kind of artistic ornament, the several kinds being found in separate parts of the play; in the form of action, not of narrative; through pity and fear effecting the proper purgation of these emotions.*[2]

Brief glosses may be offered on some of the words in this passage:

Imitation—For Aristotle all poetry—perhaps he would have said all art—is mimetic or imitative.

Serious—Common usage in all times has taken seriousness as a principal distinguishing characteristic between the tragic and comic.

Magnitude—As sublimity has often been thought not to apply to what is dainty or small in size or scope, so Aristotle and many others have insisted that nothing can be tragic unless it is on a large scale, presumably in the size of both the art-work itself and that which it represents.

Play—Aristotle was discussing here tragic *drama;* he, in common with the usage of his time, did not apply the term to other types of literature.

---

[1] Even Schopenhauer came close to this generality in saying, "The representation of a great misfortune is alone essential to tragedy." *The World as Will and Idea*, trans. Haldane-Kemp, Vol. I, Bk. III, section 51.

[2] *Poetics*, trans. Butcher, 1449b.

Pity and Fear—Aristotle insisted on both. We pity him on whom the calamity not altogether deservedly falls. And we fear lest we, who are after all not entirely unlike the protagonist, should suffer a like fate.

Purgation—Here is John Milton's interpretation of this famous word and its context:

> *Tragedy, as it was anciently composed, hath been ever held the gravest, moralest, and most profitable of all other poems: therefore said by Aristotle to be of power, by raising pity and fear, or terror, to purge the mind of those and such-like passions,—that is, to temper and reduce them to just measure with a kind of delight, stirred up by reading or seeing those passions well imitated.*[3]

Aristotle was, of course, writing in the wake of the supremely great period of Athenian tragedy. He was in no sense pretending to invent or propose some new literary form; rather he and those with whom he was immediately communicating had in mind certain specimens that were already clearly and undeniably labeled "tragedy"—it was his job to try to discover wherein these dramas *were* tragedies. In one sense, then, nothing but "Greek Tragedy"—that is, works like the *Oresteia* of Aeschylus, the *Ajax* of Sophocles and *The Trojan Women* of Euripides—could qualify as tragedies in Aristotle's sense. Aristotle might well have been so puzzled by a so-called Shakespearean tragedy—puzzled for instance by its lack of a chorus and by its division into acts—that he could hardly have thought of its belonging to the same type as those works that competed for the prize of tragedy in the Athenian theater. Still, many commentators on the *Poetics* have so interpreted Aristotle's definition that the real essence of tragedy is a certain tragic *effect,* so that anything which produces this effect qualifies thereby as a tragedy. Thus it is easily possible to claim that Christopher Marlowe's *Doctor Faustus* earns the title of tragedy in spite of its difference in many ways from the works of Sophocles, because it shares with Greek tragedies the "cathartic" effect. Indeed, there seems to be no theoretical unlikelihood that nonliterary art may sometimes have a like enough effect also to be called tragic.

Still, however many the ways in which this tragic effect can be

[3] Preface to "Samson Agonistes."

produced, it should be noticed that the effect is not just something
as vague as the vernacular synonyms of "tragic": "unfortunate"
or "regrettable." For instance, it is possible for a work to produce
an effect of pity but not of fear, as in exhibiting the downfall of
a being so utterly exalted as to seem quite beyond us. Or the
catastrophe which befalls the protagonist may impress us as exactly
"what he had coming," and then our reaction is deficient in pity.
Or the protagonist may be such a paltry being to start with that
we are little moved by his fall. In these and many other cases, there
would be no tragedy in the Aristotelian sense.[4] But there is a
further essential. To qualify as a tragedy a work must not merely
arouse fear and pity, but arouse them in such a way as to "accomplish its catharsis of such emotions." For one reason or another a
work of art might leave us more fearful than it found us, and thus
fail of being an Aristotelian tragedy. Plato seems to have been
especially worried lest art have such pernicious effects; but Aristotle's emphasis was more positive: he was chiefly impressed with
the wholesome and altogether improving effect that tragedy at its
best—as well as music, epic, and perhaps other types of art—does
have.

It is interesting to read such an endorsement of Aristotle's theory
as the following, from a psychoanalyst writing in 1952:

*The progress of psychoanalytic knowledge has opened the way
for a better understanding of the cathartic effect; we are no longer
satisfied with the notion that repressed emotions lose their hold
over our mental life when an outlet for them has been found. We
believe rather that what Aristotle describes as the purging enables
the ego to reestablish the control which is threatened by dammed-
up instinctual demands. The search for outlets acts as an aid to as-
suring or reestablishing this control, and the pleasure is a double
one, in both discharge and control. The maintenance of the aesthetic illusion promises the safety to which we were aspiring and
guarantees freedom from guilt, since it is not our own fantasy we
follow. It stimulates the rise of feelings which we might otherwise
be hesitant to permit ourselves, since they lead to our own personal
conflicts. It allows in addition for intensities of reaction which,
without this protection, many individuals are unwilling to admit to*

---

[4] "Pity is aroused by unmerited misfortune, fear by the misfortune of a man like
ourselves. . . ." *Poetics,* 1453a.

themselves; with many, we know, this is due to educational pres-
sures, which under certain cultural conditions have generally de-
valued high intensity of emotional display except in regulated and
institutionalized channels: Art offers such socially approved occa-
sions. The vicarious participation in the hero's destiny is the mecha-
nism by which this effect comes about.[5]

TRAGEDY AS DEPENDENT ON A SOCIAL ATTITUDE

Although we have chosen so far to emphasize that part of
Aristotle's theory which describes the catharsis tragedy produces,
other aspects of his theory have appealed to some critics as still
more important. For instance, Joseph Wood Krutch has argued[6]
that when the cry goes up for new tragedies, tragedies in the
modern world, the impossible is demanded. We have no tragedies
today not because there are no longer such geniuses as past ages
produced, but because tragedy necessarily belongs to an age with
quite different social attitudes than are possible today, at least in the
democratic peoples. Krutch is especially concerned with the Aristotelian conception of the tragic protagonist or hero.

Aristotle wrote that the kind of personage whose fall can be
tragic is "A man who is not eminently good and just, yet whose
misfortune is brought about not by vice or depravity, but by some
error or frailty. He must be one who is highly renowned and
prosperous. . . ."[7] The protagonist must, it would seem, be of
noble and lofty station, if we are to be very much moved by what
befalls him. But now, Krutch asks, what happens when through the
development of democratic, egalitarian ideologies, and scientific
theories which enable us to understand the motivations of even the
most eminent of leaders, we lose our sense of "nobility"? It is notable
that Oedipus, Agamemnon, and Lear were kings; Hippolytus,
Orestes, and Hamlet were princes. The audiences who first saw the
plays about these heroes knew that they *were* heroes, that their
eminence was natural and right, and that they had a world to lose, a
huge distance to fall. But the modern playwright and his audience

---

[5] Ernst Kris, *Psychoanalytic Explorations in Art* (New York: International
Universities Press, 1952), pp. 45-46.
[6] See *The Modern Temper* (New York: Harcourt, Brace, 1927).
[7] *Poetics*, 1453a.

are disillusioned: they have no such natural heroes, no such cleavages between the tiny elite and common people. Krutch points to Ibsen's plays as the successors of tragedies; they are serious, pathetic, and much else, but they are not and cannot be tragic, for their heroes are ordinary men, the Oswalds and the Hjalmars, living in a world ruled not by the gods or fate, but by strict natural causality.

Krutch is undoubtedly right in asserting the difference between an authoritarian and a democratic attitude toward leaders. Perhaps a modern audience is not so ready to accept the prima facie nobility of a king or prince or general; but it is more likely to be able to accept the possibility that a person—man or woman—of less than princely status should in some sense be noble, and therefore should be a person whose fall may be greatly pitiful. It is not clear that modern man lacks heroes, or is incapable of admiration or reverence, however unwilling he may be to admit an elite by inheritance or by divine appointment. Perhaps in some ways there is in our day even greater opportunity for tragic art, even on a reasonably strict Aristotelian interpretation, since now men of humble origins may gain "great reputation and prosperity."

TRAGEDY AS THE CLASH OF IDEAS

Hegel found nowhere a more ingenious application of his "dialectical idealism" than in the subject matter of tragedy. A tragedy, he taught, consists in the fatal clash of fundamentally opposed forces, each of which is—though in too narrow a sense—right. Since all art is a concrete embodiment of what, philosophically considered, is abstract, these spiritual or ideational forces that tragically conflict must be represented through individualized characters and a distinctive plot. Hegel's favorite example was *Antigone:*

The completest species of this development is possible, when the persons in conflict appear, in respect of their concrete being, each as including the whole of the sphere concerned. They then, in their own nature, are in the power of that against which they do battle, and injure that, which by the law of their own existence they ought to honour. So, for example, Antigone lives within Kreon's civil authority; she herself is a king's daughter, and the betrothed of Haemon, so that she was bound to pay obedience to the sovereign's command. Yet Kreon, too, who on his side is father and husband, was bound to respect the sanctity of blood-relationship, and not to command what violated that piety. Thus each of them has imma- nent in him or herself that against which they respectively rebel, and they are seized and broken by that very principle which be- longs to the sphere of their own being.[8]

We who see or at least sense the "solution" of the clash are the more impressed by its inevitability and its futility. From the limited perspective of each of the contestants his own mission is clear and inviolable; and yet he is doomed to defeat precisely because his posi- tion is narrow and engenders its own antithesis. Get beyond both positions, reconcile them in a synthesis, and the tragedy is superseded.

Hegel makes out an excellent case for his theory by his very care- fully chosen example. If concrete dialectic is at the base of all other works we traditionally call "tragic," it is hard to recognize the fact. For all of Hegel's insistence upon the concreteness of art, he ex- aggerates the aesthetic importance of ideas. In some of what we are almost bound to call tragedy (unless we are going to be merely rid- den by a theory framed in splendid logical isolation) the individual- ity of the characters seems to take precedence over any principles or positions which they represent.

TRAGEDY AS LYRICAL MYSTICISM

The final theory which we will here briefly notice is that of William Butler Yeats. Yeats opposes two sorts of poetic drama, the drama of character and the drama of lyricism. Emphasis upon char- acter he takes to be typical of comedy or at least of the nontragic moments in works that may be ordinarily classified as tragedies:

Suddenly it strikes us that character is continuously present in comedy alone, and that there is much tragedy, that of Corneille, that of Racine, that of Greece and Rome, where its place is taken by passions and motives, one person being jealous, another full of love or remorse or pride or anger. In writers of tragi-comedy (and Shakespeare is always a writer of tragi-comedy) there is indeed

[8] Translated and quoted from Hegel's *Aesthetic*, in Bernard Bosanquet, *A His- tory of Aesthetic* (London: Swan Sonnenschein, 1892), pp. 358-59.

*character, but we notice that it is in the moments of comedy that
character is defined, in Hamlet's gaiety let us say; while amid the
great moments, when Timon orders his tomb, when Hamlet cries
to Horatio "absent thee from felicity awhile," when Antony names
"Of many thousand kisses the poor last," all is lyricism, unmixed
passion, "the integrity of fire."*[9]

Such tragic art is to be found not only in drama, not only in
literature, but in painting and presumably—though Yeats does not
specifically say so—in music, which surely is the lyrical, "character-
less," unrealistic art par excellence. This is what Yeats likes to call
"the art of the flood," in which individual distinctions are washed
away, leaving the pure swell and surge of the sea, "rhythm, balance,
pattern, images that remind us of vast passions, the vagueness of
past times, all the chimeras that haunt the edge of trance. . . ." It is
the art of pure passion, the antithesis alike of rationality and of
everyday practical reality:

*Tragic art, passionate art, the drowner of dykes, the confounder
of understanding, moves us by setting us to reverie, by alluring us
almost to the intensity of trance. The persons upon the stage, let us
say, greaten till they are humanity itself. We feel our minds expand convulsively or spread out slowly like some moon-brightened
image-crowded sea. That which is before our eyes perpetually
vanishes and returns again in the midst of the excitement it creates,
and the more enthralling it is, the more do we forget it.*[10]

One is grateful to Yeats for revealing here an exceedingly important moment in aesthetic life. One cannot read his account without recognizing the sort of thing he is describing, and remembering
instances. Yet, it is a serious question whether we want to agree with
him in calling this passionate lyricism "tragic."

Now, this is a problem about *any* theory of tragedy. It is of
course always possible to define tragedy as one wishes, stipulating
that the word shall mean, say, witty or pious or complicated or—
whatever.[11] Still, one feels some obligation—if only in the interest of

[9] "The Tragic Theatre," in *Essays* (New York: Macmillan, 1924); reprinted in
Criticism, ed. Mark Schorer, Josephine Miles, and Gordon McKenzie (New York:
Harcourt, Brace, 1948).
[10] *Ibid.*
[11] For a development of this point, see James L. Jarrett, "Tragedy: A Study in
Explication," *ETC.*, XII, No. 3 (Spring, 1955), 189-197.

making oneself intelligible—to take into account not only common (if vague) usage but also the most influential lines of criticism, and of the works which are commonly *called* tragedies. One may wish to develop a theory which differs sharply from Aristotle's or Hegel's in detail, but one will almost certainly want to cite the plays of, for instance, Sophocles. A theory that claims to define "tragedy" but seems to have no feasible explanatory value for *Prometheus* or *Othello* can scarcely interest us. Each of the theories here glanced at is doubtless tenable; perhaps no one of them is quite satisfactory for us who have in mind a longer history of tragedies than Aristotle could have known, a wider variety of tragic effects than Yeats' lyricism or Hegel's concrete dialectic, and who are less disillusioned than Krutch about the disappearance from the world of the very possibility of noble tragedy.

COMEDY

If we pass from tragedy to comedy, we pass from a topic on which there has been an abundance of relatively satisfactory theorizing to a topic which, though it has fascinated, has plainly baffled most critics and aestheticians. Some have tried to dodge the problem by calling all nontragedy "comedy." Some have indulged in such obvious oversimplifications as: Comedy is the type of play (or story) which ends happily; or, If tragedy concerns high and noble characters, comedy deals with lesser personages. But even when writers have explicitly dealt with "funny" comedy (which is what we will be here concerned with), their remarks have been typically fragmentary. Kant, for instance, taught that we laugh when an expectation suddenly ends in nothing. Hobbes is still much-quoted for his identification of the comic with "sudden glory." Others have noticed that there is always something ludicrous in comic. Still others have contented themselves with quoting Horace Walpole: "The world is a comedy to those that think, a tragedy to those who feel."

However, in our own time there have appeared at least two accounts of "the funny" which deserve a brief recounting here.

In his book *Le Rire*, Henri Bergson worked out a consistent and sustained explanation of the causes and results of laughter. With cryptic brevity the theory may be stated thus: In any laughable situation, the constant factor is something human giving signs of being subhuman; the intended result is correction of a moral fault. That is, a fully alive human being would be unique and infinitely sensitive to the uniqueness of every occasion. He would react in the same way only to the same stimuli—and no two stimuli are identical. The perfectly human is the fresh, the utterly creative, the unrepetitious; it is that which is constantly celebrated by the greatest artists. The painter shows us a scene which will never be that way again. The composer puts together his sounds in an utterly original way. The tragic dramatist shows us a protagonist who is above reality; that is, he is more nearly unique than any actual man. There is only one Hamlet, and one Lear. In affording us this glimpse of a hyper-real reality, the artist beckons to us to assume more fully our human condition, to be more truly alive. Now, the comic artist does much the same thing, but in a manner directly contrary to that of displaying freshness. The comic artist (in common with all who make us laugh) exposes for ridicule all of the multitudinous tendencies of the human being to settle for something less than human life. Every person fails to some extent; each of us is absent-minded, each is a bundle of habits, crotchets, mannerisms. Everyone is a victim of routine; everyone is a classifier of somewhat unlike things and a categorizer of that which does not altogether reduce to categories. The comic, Bergson teaches, is that which at once inhibits an emotional reaction and pitilessly illuminates these evidences of *rigidity*.

Going from the comic in general to more particularized matters, Bergson deals with the Comic in Situations, the Comic in Words, and the Comic in Character. The very type of the comic in situations is the action of the jack-in-the-box—the action, that is, of something half-human, half-mechanical. Two clowns rhythmically belaboring each other with bladders is an instance; or the irrepressible stage character, the one who is repeatedly driven away only to "pop up" again, now on this side, now on that, now from a window, now from a trap door, now perhaps from the audience itself. The comic character is the one who has become identified with a class or a type. He is Molière's physician who is a physician

in spite of himself—there being nothing to him except his physician-
ship. He is the man who is adequately summarized by "The Miser"
or "The Pedant" or "The Lawyer" or "The Jealous Husband."
He has no life outside his role, no flexibility. If he is a grammarian,
the whole world is construed by him in terms of subjects and predi-
cates, perfects and pluperfects, actives and passives. He is a man
with an *idée fixe:* a Don Juan monotonously bent on seduction, a
Falstaff whose budget allows for nothing but sack and capons. Such
a man demonstrates his abdication from manhood, the essence of
which is variety.

Words are used comically or wittily ("A word is said to be comic
when it makes us laugh at the person who utters it, and witty when
it makes us laugh either at a third person or at ourselves.")[12] when
they are used to condense laughable situations or present laughable
characters. We laugh at words when they have been manipulated
to reveal something mechanical in themselves or in the human
world. Take, for instance, puns or, more broadly, any play upon
words:

> *Whereas an illuminating comparison and a striking image always
> seem to reveal the close harmony that exists between language and
> nature, regarded as two parallel forms of life, the play upon words
> makes us think somehow of a negligence on the part of language,
> which, for the time being, seems to have forgotten its real function
> and now claims to accommodate things to itself instead of accom-
> modating itself to things. And so the play upon words always be-
> trays a momentary* lapse of attention *in language, and it is precisely
> on that account that it is amusing.*[13]

In short, language too, in being a human product and intimate tool,
ought somehow to participate in the flexibility of the human; when
it is revealed as in itself mechanical, or when it is employed to reveal
the mechanical, we laugh.

For Bergson, laughter is a moral corrective. The principal
immorality is to sink into nonhumanness, and when such sin is laugh-
ably exposed, we are somewhat shamed. Ridiculed for our absent-

---

[12] Henri Bergson, *Laughter*, trans. Cloudesley Brereton and Fred Rothwell
(London: Macmillan, 1911), p. 104.
[13] *Ibid.*, p. 121.

mindedness, we become more alert; shown to be a kind of jack-in-the-box, we try to make amends and become something better than creatures of cloth and springs.

It is even easier in the case of comedy than it is in that of tragedy to test a theory by confronting it with some instances, for however much "tragedy" may be what you define it to be, it is hard to deny the appellation "comic" to what actually makes us laugh. Let us take, then, three known instances of the comic. The first is from Chaucer's "The Miller's Tale." The humor is coarse, broad, earthy, obvious, and slapstick. The teller of the tale is trying to raise a laugh at the expense of a carpenter, so he makes a carpenter the goat of his story. A student has hoodwinked a silly carpenter by convincing him that there is going to be a recurrence of the Great Flood, so that he had better prepare as did Noah. The carpenter accordingly builds in his attic a boat, which he keeps supported from the ceiling by ropes; and it is in the boat that he sleeps.

> *The carpenter, startled from sleep above,*
> *And hearing shouts for water and a thud,*
> *Thought, 'Heaven help us! Here comes Nowel's Flood!'*
> *And up he sat and with no more ado*
> *He took his ax and smote the ropes in two*
> *And down went everything. He didn't stop*
> *To sell his bread and ale, but came down flop*
> *Upon the floor and fainted right away.*[14]

For our second example we turn to Sancho Panza's adventure as governor of an island. He is brought a series of difficult cases to decide, one of which tells of a certain bridge over a river, passage over the bridge being governed by a strict law:

> *Whoever intends to pass from one End of this Bridge to the other, must first upon his Oath declare whither he goes, and what his Business is. If he swear Truth, he may go on; but if he swear false, he shall be hang'd, and die without Remission upon the Gibbet at the End of the Bridge.*
> *After due promulgation of this Law, many People, notwithstanding its Severity, adventur'd to go over this Bridge, and as it appear'd they swore true, the Judges permitted 'em to pass unmo-*

[14] *Canterbury Tales,* trans. Nevill Coghill (Baltimore: Penguin Books, Inc., 1952), p. 127.

*lested. It happen'd one Day that a certain Passenger being sworn,
declar'd that by the Oath he had taken, he was come to die upon
that Gallows, and that was all his Business.*

*This put the Judges to a Nonplus; for, said they, If we let this
man pass freely, he is forsworn, and according to the Letter of the
Law he ought to die: If we hang him, he has sworn Truth,
seeing he swore he was to die on that Gibbet; and then by the same
Law we should let him pass.*

Sancho's first decision was that they ought to "let that Part of the
Man that swore true, freely pass; and hang the other Part of the
Man that swore false. . . ."[15]

The third sample of comedy is from Falstaff, found commenting
on the cold-blooded Prince John and on the many virtues of sherry
wine or sack:

*Good faith, this same young sober-blooded boy doth not love
me; nor a man cannot make him laugh; but that's no marvel, he
drinks no wine. There's never none of these demure boys comes
to any proof; for thin drink doth so over-cool their blood, and
making man fish-meals, that they fall into a kind of male green-
sickness; and then, when they marry, they get wenches: they are
generally fools and cowards; which some of us should be too, but
for inflammation. A good sherris-sack hath a two-fold operation in
it. It ascends me into the brain; dries me there all the foolish and
dull and curdy vapours which environ it; makes it apprehensive,
quick, forgetive, full of nimble, fiery and delectable shapes; which,
delivered o'er to the voice, the tongue, which is the birth, becomes
excellent wit. The second property of your excellent sherris is, the
warming of the blood; which is the badge of pusillanimity and cow-
ardice; but the sherris warms it and makes it course from the in-
wards to the parts extreme: it illumineth the face, which as a beacon
gives warning to all the rest of this little kingdom, man, to arm;
and then the vital commoners and inland petty spirits muster me
all to their captain, the heart, who, great and puffed up with his
retinue, doth any deed of courage; and this valour comes of sherris.
So that skill in the weapon is nothing without sack, for that sets
it a-work; and learning a mere hoard of gold kept by a deveil, till
sack commences in and sets it in act and use. Hereof comes it that
Prince Harry is valiant; for the cold blood he did naturally inherit*

[15] Miguel Cervantes, *Don Quixote*, trans. Peter Motteux, rev. by Ozell, Part II,
Bk. III, chap. li.

of his father, he hath, like lean sterile and bare land, manured, hus-
banded and tilled with excellent endeavour of drinking good and
good store of fertile sherris, that he is become very hot and valiant.
If I had a thousand sons, the first humane principle I would teach
them should be, to forswear thin potations, and to adict themselves
to sack.[16]

Only one who is eager to die in the last ditch for the Bergsonian
theory would maintain that Falstaff is not a unique, an absolutely
distinctive character, the one and only. If he is a wine-bibber, he is
infinitely more. He is just as little a type as Hamlet; just as much an
individual as Richard III. Nor is there anything especially mechanical about Sancho Panza trying to solve the insoluble problem. He is,
indeed, full of surprises, unlike predictable machines. And the
great burly, chaotic scenes that Chaucer paints, full of confusion
and mistaken identity and the bruises that are the reward for stupid
gullibility, seem hardly material for Bergson's analysis. In short,
Bergson's theory, though it is an exceedingly clever extension of
his metaphysics and an ingenious explanation of some aspects of
some comedy, is hardly broad enough to encompass the whole field.
It is revealing that he leans so heavily upon Molière for examples; it
might almost be said that his is a theory not of comedy but of social
satire, and as such, if not wholly satisfactory, is at least engaging
and challenging.

FREUD ON THE FUNNY

Among many debts we owe to Sigmund Freud, not the least—
though one of the least acknowledged—is for a rarely original and
brilliant theory of the comic, the humorous, and the witty. It may
be what no other theory had ever been: a reasonably adequate
explanation of the common elements in funny situations and expressions, and a classification of the major types, with their essential differences.

According to Freud, something is funny when it affords pleasure
by economizing our expenditure of psychic energy. This may or
may not involve a "sudden glory." It may or may not contrast
the rigid and the lively. It sometimes has to do with the ludicrous,

[16] Shakespeare, *Henry IV, Part II*, Act IV, scene iii.

but not always. It is neither always nor never a matter of morality.

The pre-condition of a "sense of humor" (in its broadest sense) is a childhood in which there was a considerable amount of pleasure gained from nonsense, for instance from the babbling and chanting and singing of meaningless vocables. The child's laughter at a new discovery in the world about him or at a new invention of his own is not, strictly speaking, a matter of something being funny to him. But in later life when he does laugh at something funny or when he says or does something amusing, he will be recapturing, to a degree, that childhood euphoria; his success will result from his escaping the pain of inhibition, of certain emotions, or of certain thoughts.

Wit, the kind of funniness that Freud most fully treats, is a way of circumventing the taboo on "nonsense." The child, who loves to make up new words and to say words with strange sounds and even to chant nonsense syllables, finds this delightful activity curbed by the adults who say, "Talk sense, don't be silly." So he learns to inhibit these impulses until he finds in witticisms a way to circumvent the restriction by combining sense and nonsense. A condensation such as "He seems to be enjoying his alcoholiday" uses a word not in the dictionary, or a pun uses a word in a grammatically unallowable way, without altogether failing to be meaningful. Wit may be purely harmless and merely for the sake of the fun, but very often it is tendentious, serving some additional need of its employer or of him who finds a release in somebody else's wit. Thus, it is no secret that wit is often barbed, and deliberately aimed at someone who may not be attacked in a grosser way. Jokes about "the Scotchman," "the Negro," "the Jew," or any other representative of a race, nationality, or religion, often betray some aggressive tendency on the part of those who tell and those who laugh at them.

In order for wit to exist, there must be someone who makes the witticism and someone to whom it is imparted. But where wit is made, the comic is *found;* and it may exist without there being anyone to whom the discovery is communicated. The essence of the comic, Freud maintains, lies in a discrepancy or an apparent discrepancy between the actual expenditure of psychic or physical energy and what is required by the situation. We laugh at exaggerated grimaces and gestures where the motion is more than is needed; we also laugh at naivete, where someone expends less psychic energy than would seem to be needed: he makes it too easy for himself.

Comic pleasure is perhaps somewhat more dependent than other forms of the funny upon certain conditions; for instance, a generally happy disposition in which almost anything may seem comic, or an eager expectation of comedy so that one is in the right mood. Given these favorable conditions, we are delighted by anything that does not require of us serious thinking, especially in things that might normally give us this kind of "pain."

The third kind of funniness, humor, is the most self-sufficient of all, requiring for its enjoyment no one else who is found to be funny nor anyone to whom to impart the discovery. We are struck by the humor of a situation when we are permitted to economize our expenditure of feeling or affect. That is, if we are told a sad story, one which gives every sign of requiring of us pity and sympathy, but then we are suddenly released from these feelings by an unserious turn in the story, we are in the presence of humor. It costs us something to "feel" for someone; we laugh at being saved the trouble and expense.

Here is Freud's own summary of his three-fold theory:

> It has seemed to us that the pleasure of wit originates from an economy of expenditure in inhibition, of the comic from an economy of expenditure in thought, and of humor from an economy of expenditure in feeling. All three modes of activity of our psychic apparatus derive pleasure from economy. All three present methods strive to bring back from the psychic activity a pleasure which has really been lost in the development of this activity. For the euphoria which we are thus striving to obtain is nothing but the state of a bygone time, in which we were wont to defray our psychic work with slight expenditure. It is the state of our childhood in which we did not know the comic, were incapable of wit, and did not need humor to make us happy.[17]

Freud's theory is probably not altogether satisfactory. In the first place it is much more fully developed on the side of wit than on

[17] "Wit and Its Relation to the Unconscious," taken from *The Basic Writings of Sigmund Freud*, transl. and ed. by Dr. A. A. Brill, Copyright, 1938, by Random House, Inc., p. 803. Reprinted by permission of the Trustees of the Brill Estate.

the sides of the comic and the humorous; indeed, humor comes in for only the briefest consideration. Furthermore, the treatment of the comic seems somewhat inconsistent, now emphasizing the economy of thought, now the disparity between optimum and actual expenditure of energy. And finally, it may very well be that Freud exaggerates the "return to childhood euphoria" theme in his account of the pleasures of laughing. Nevertheless, the theory probably goes further and certainly goes deeper than any rival theory known to the author, and has the great advantages of admitting a variety of funny things, sayings, persons and situations. For example, Freud seems entirely sound in maintaining that "The feeling of superiority bears no essential relations to comic pleasure,"[18] and in finding a place for "harmless" wit as well as the "tendentious."

Freud's account, it may be noticed, is not specifically about funny *art;* indeed his examples are mainly drawn from jokes, jests, and witticisms, rather than from dramas, prose fiction, painted caricatures, and other forms of fine art. Still, his theory can be *applied* without much elaboration to art, the positions of the after-dinner story-teller and the short story writer, for instance, being comparable on many points. The artist who employs comedy may impress us as Chaucer so often does: as mainly a good story-teller, one whose principal aim is to entertain and to delight. (The rejection by critics and aestheticians of any entertainment or amusement values in *real* art seems only snobbery.) Shakespeare is one who constantly impresses us with the possibilities of mixing wit and comedy with the utmost seriousness and even tragedy. Hamlet for instance is no less marvelous for his wit than for his depth of feeling, and Falstaff is not only, as he incomparably says, "witty in myself, but the cause that wit is in other men";[19] he is also at once a figure of fun and a severe commentator on the sober-minded and lofty virtues of the court. And Don Quixote is, of course, the most

---

[18] *Ibid.,* p. 773. James Sully, whose book *An Essay on Laughter* is a large-minded account of the subject, is particularly keen on the similarity between much of laughter and play, "good humor," and kindness. For instance: "While satire, sarcasm and their kind seem to be trying to push things away, or at least to alter them, humor, curiously enough, looks as if it were tenderly holding to the world which entertains it." *An Essay on Laughter* (London: Longmans, Green, 1902), p. 384.

[19] *Henry IV, Part II,* Act I, scene ii.

intricate mixture of madman, true knight, philosopher, and kind, lovable man; he is both satirizer and the object of satire. If, as is so often said, in order to laugh we must inhibit our pity, fear, hate, and other such "serious" feelings, and must become highly distanced in our attitude, an artist such as Cervantes at least demonstrates to us the possibilities for a most rapid alternation of various sorts of funniness and various sorts of seriousness—if indeed *this* distinction can be seriously made at all. There are works of art which are almost sheer fun—Mozart's *Musical Joke*[20] and Molière's *Physician in Spite of Himself*, for instances—but it is much commoner for the funny in art to be one of several ingredients that criticism can abstract for discussion. Little of great art is *just* funny; but a very great deal is funny among much else.

[20] In general, music is not rich in its resources for laughter, though intentional "mistakes," surprising runs on such an instrument as the bassoon, ludicrous combinations like the piccolo and the tuba, may make us laugh.

BIBLIOGRAPHY

Here is a highly selective list of books with which the serious student of aesthetics will want to acquaint himself. More complete bibliographies are to be found in Melvin Rader's *A Modern Book of Esthetics* and annually in the *Journal of Aesthetics and Art Criticism*.

ANTHOLOGIES

Carritt, E. F., *Philosophies of Beauty*, 1931. Short passages by eminent writers from the ancient Greeks to recent times. This is especially useful as a guide to aesthetics before Nietzsche, a long period not otherwise covered by this bibliography.

Elton, William, *Aesthetics and Language*, 1954. Essays by philosophers of the "analytic" persuasion. See especially "Feelings," by Gilbert Ryle; "Critical Communication," by Arnold Isenberg; and "The Expression Theory of Art," by O. K. Bouwsma.

Ghiselin, Brewster, *The Creative Process*, 1952.

Goldwater, Robert, and Marco Treves, *Artists on Art*, 1945.

Rader, Melvin, *A Modern Book of Esthetics*, rev. ed., 1952. A valuable source book for twentieth-century aesthetics. See especially the articles by Read, Fry, Freud, Morris, Bullough, Worringer, and Whitehead.

Vivas, Eliseo, and Murray Krieger, *The Problems of Aesthetics*, 1953. Another valuable collection of modern sources. See especially the articles by Henry James, Freud, Jung, Isenberg, Wellek and Warren, Blackmur, Boas, Wimsatt, and Walsh.

HISTORIES

Bosanquet, Bernard, *A History of Aesthetic*, 1892.
Gilbert, Katharine E., and Helmut Kuhn, *A History of Esthetics*, rev. ed., 1952.

GENERAL AESTHETICS

Collingwood, R. G., *The Principles of Art*, 1938.
Croce, Benedetto, *Aesthetic*, 1909.
Dewey, John, *Art as Experience*, 1934.
Ducasse, Curt J., *The Philosophy of Art*, 1929.
Edman, Irwin, *Arts and the Man*, 1939.
Gotshalk, D. W., *Art and the Social Order*, 1947.
Greene, Theodore M., *The Arts and the Art of Criticism*, 1947.
Langer, Susanne K., *Feeling and Form*, 1953.
Maritain, Jacques, *Art and Scholasticism*, 1930.
Munro, Thomas, *The Arts and Their Interrelations*, 1949.
Parker, DeWitt H., *The Principles of Aesthetics*, rev. ed., 1946.
Pepper, Stephen C., *Aesthetic Quality*, 1937.
Prall, David, *Aesthetic Judgment*, 1929.
Reid, Louis A., *A Study in Aesthetics*, 1931.
Santayana, George, *The Sense of Beauty*, 1896.
――――, *Reason in Art*, 1905.
Véron, Eugene, *Aesthetics*, 1879.

SPECIAL STUDIES

Alexander, Samuel, *Beauty and Other Forms of Value*, 1933.
Arnheim, Rudolph, *Art and Visual Perception*, 1954.
Barnes, Albert C., *The Art in Painting*, 3rd ed., 1937.
Bell, Clive, *Art*, 1913.
Berenson, Bernard, *Aesthetics and History*, 1948.
Bergson, Henri, *Laughter*, 1911.
Bosanquet, Bernard, *Three Lectures on Aesthetic*, 1915.
Bradley, A. C., *Oxford Lectures on Poetry*, 1909.
Eliot, T. S., *Selected Essays*, 1932.
Freud, Sigmund, *Wit and Its Relation to the Unconscious*, n.d.
Hanslick, Eduard, *The Beautiful in Music*, 1891.

Heyl, Bernard, *New Bearings in Esthetics and Art Criticism*, 1943.

Hospers, John, *Meaning and Truth in the Arts*, 1946.

Kallen, Horace, *Art and Freedom*, 1942.

Langer, Susanne K., *Philosophy in a New Key*, 1942.

Lewis, C. I., *An Analysis of Knowledge and Valuation*, 1946.

Maritain, Jacques, *Creative Intuition in Art and Poetry*, 1954.

Nietzsche, Friedrich, *The Birth of Tragedy from the Spirit of Music*, 1872.

Ortega y Gasset, José, *The Dehumanization of Art*, 1948.

Panofsky, Erwin, *Meaning in the Visual Arts*, 1955.

Parker, DeWitt H., *The Analysis of Art*, 1926.

Pepper, Stephen, *Principles of Art Appreciation*, 1949.

———, *The Work of Art*, 1955.

———, *The Basis of Criticism in the Arts*, 1946.

Prall, David, *Aesthetic Analysis*, 1936.

Rank, Otto, *Art and Artist*, 1932.

Read, Herbert, *The Meaning of Art*, 1931.

Richards, I. A., *Principles of Literary Criticism*, 1928.

———, *Science and Poetry*, 1926.

Spencer, Herbert, *Literary Style and Music*, 1857.

Tolstoi, Lyof N., *What Is Art?* 1899.

INDEX